Pathologies of Belief

Pathologies of Belief

Edited by
Max Coltheart
and
Martin Davies

BLACKWELL *Publishers*

Copyright © Blackwell Publishers 2000

ISBN: 0-631-221360 (pbk)

Blackwell Publishers Ltd
108 Cowley Road
Oxford OX4 1JF, UK

Blackwell Publishers Inc
350 Main Street
Malden, Massachusetts 02148, USA

British Library Cataloguing in Publication has been applied for

Library of Congress Cataloguing in Publication Data has been applied for

Typeset by Photographics
Printed and Bound in Great Britain
By MPG Books, Bodmin, Cornwall

This book is printed on acid-free paper

Contents

Acknowledgements

Between December 1997 and August 1999, a group of psychologists and philosophers from Australia and New Zealand met in a series of inter-disciplinary workshops on simulation theory and related topics. The workshops were supported by the Australian Research Council and hosted by Flinders University in Adelaide, Macquarie University in Sydney, the University of Tasmania in Hobart, and the Australian National University in Canberra. Each workshop focused on some particular aspect of mental simulation, theory of mind, and everyday psychological understanding. These specific themes were: tacit knowledge, psychopathology, modularity, and emotions and empathy. The overseas guest speakers were: Martin Davies (Oxford), Andy Young (York), Gary Marcus (New York University), and Keith Oatley (Toronto). We are grateful to the ARC and the host universities for financial support, to Greg Currie and Ian Ravenscroft for initiating and managing the project, to the local organizers, and to all the workshop participants.

The chapters in this volume are based on material that was presented at the workshop on theory of mind and psychopathology held at Macquarie University over the weekend of 31 July–2 August 1998. They first appeared in a special issue of *Mind and Language*, volume 15 number 1 (February 2000).

1

Introduction: Pathologies of Belief

MARTIN DAVIES AND MAX COLTHEART

Some people seem to believe quite extraordinary things. For example, people say:[1]

- My closest relatives have been replaced by impostors.
- I am dead.
- I am being followed around by people who are known to me but who are unrecognizable because they are in disguise.
- The person I see in the mirror is not really me.
- A person I knew who died is nevertheless in the hospital ward today.
- This arm [the speaker's left arm] is not mine it is yours; you have three arms.
- Someone else is able to control my actions.
- Someone else's thoughts are being inserted into my mind.

These apparent claims are so bizarrely false that we might have some doubt whether the utterances can really be expressions of beliefs. But alternative interpretations of the utterances are not easy to sustain (see below, section 1.1). These people seem to understand what they are saying, they seem to be sincere, and they sometimes act in ways that make sense in the light of the beliefs that they seem to be expressing. So there is a strong case for taking their utterances at face value. But if we do accept that these people are expressing genuine

---

We are grateful to all the participants in the workshop at Macquarie University at which the chapters in this volume were first presented. Early versions of material in this Introduction were presented in talks at the Australian National University, at the Novartis Foundation in London and at the Institute of Psychiatry also in London; we learned much from discussions on those occasions. Special thanks to Mark Greenberg, Robyn Langdon, Christopher Peacocke, Ian Ravenscroft, Tony Stone and Andy Young for comments and conversations.

[1] These eight examples are, respectively: the Capgras delusion (Capgras and Reboul-Lachaux, 1923; Young, this volume); the Cotard delusion (Cotard, 1882; Berrios and Luque, 1995; Young, this volume); the Fregoli delusion (Courbon and Fail, 1927; de Pauw, Szulecka and Poltock, 1987; Ellis, Whitley and Luauté, 1994); the delusion of mirrored-self misidentification (Foley and Breslau, 1982; Breen et al., this volume); a delusion of reduplicative paramnesia (Benson, Gardner and Meadows, 1976; Breen et al., this volume); a delusion sometimes found in patients suffering from unilateral neglect (Bisiach, 1988); and the delusions of alien control and of thought insertion, which are characteristic of schizophrenia (Frith, 1992).

beliefs then, in each case, we are bound to ask how such a bizarrely false hypothesis could come to be believed.

The difficulty in taking these utterances as expressions of beliefs can be seen to flow from the fairly widely accepted idea that the attribution to people of beliefs is governed by a constraint of rationality or reasonableness.[2] It is not easy to say just what this constraint comes to and it would clearly not be right to insist that a proper interpretation of a person's mental life must make him or her out to be perfectly logical and rational at every point. But we normally expect that a person's beliefs, desires and intentions will exhibit a certain kind of intelligibility that is distinctive of the folk psychological domain of experiencing, thinking, reasoning and planning.

Christopher Cherniak (1986) argues against accounts of belief that impose an 'ideal general rationality condition'. Such a condition, he says, is too strong because it ignores the fact that 'human beings are in the *finitary predicament* of having fixed limits on their cognitive capacities and the time available to them' (p. 8). But he also maintains that the rationality requirements on belief attribution should not be too weak (1986, p. 6):

> A cognitive theory with no rationality restrictions is without predictive content; using it, we can have virtually no expectations regarding a believer's behavior. There is also a further metaphysical, as opposed to epistemological, point concerning rationality as part of what it is to be a *person*: the elements of a mind . . . must *fit together* or cohere.

If we cannot make any sense at all of how a certain person could reasonably have arrived at a particular belief on the basis of experience and inference then this counts, provisionally even if not decisively, against the attribution of that belief to that person. One way that we can apply this test of intelligibility is to imagine ourselves in the other person's situation, or even imagine being the other person, and then to consider what, from that person's point of view, would be a reasonable thing to believe. We *simulate* the other person in imagination and seek to understand him or her 'from the inside'. This simulation methodology has its limitations. It seems possible in principle that someone might rationally arrive at a belief on the basis of an experience that is so strange, or so terrifying even to imagine, that it is not possible for us to bring ourselves fully to identify with that person in imagination. But, whether or not simulation is a good way of applying the intelligibility test, the first question to ask about the apparent beliefs with which we began is whether we can under-

---

[2]   This idea is familiar from the work of Davidson, 1984, on radical interpretation and Dennett, 1987, on the intentional stance. But even someone who thought that the connection between beliefs and rationality was just contingent should allow that we have to address the question how such a strange hypothesis could come to be believed. For the distinction between rationality and reasonableness, see e.g. Church, 1987.

stand them as at least prima facie reasonable responses to experienced situations.[3]

The requirement of an intelligible link between belief and experience is one aspect of an overarching constraint of rationality or reasonableness. But we also expect to find a person's beliefs fitting together with each other tolerably well, particularly in the person's deductive and probabilistic reasoning. This is a second aspect of the constraint.

Given our finitary predicament, it is important not to overstate this expectation of overall consistency.[4] If a person believes some proposition A, and B is a proposition that follows logically from A, we do not always expect him to believe B as well. Indeed, a person might believe A, recognize that A entails B, and yet believe not-B rather than B. Suppose, for example, that a thinker antecedently believes A and has also reached the view that B is false on the basis of what seem to be quite strong considerations. He now sees that there is a logical relation between A and B, so that he cannot be right both in his belief that A is true and in his view that B is false. Something needs to give. But the task of deciding which belief should be changed might be a difficult and complex one, and he might lack the time and resources to carry it out immediately. He might take the strategic decision to tolerate the unresolved inconsistency until time and resources become available. We should also note that our thinker might find the prospect of changing either of the incompatible beliefs deeply uncomfortable and so, quite apart from issues of time and resources, might be motivated to tolerate a cognitive dissonance (Festinger, 1957).

Our thinker might live, for the time being or even permanently, with an acknowledged tension in his system of beliefs. And if this is the case when the tension arises from a deductive relation then it is all the more so for tensions arising from probabilistic relations. In short, an overarching constraint of rationality or reasonableness must allow that there are many ways to explain or excuse departures from the ideal of overall consistency in a system of beliefs.

We have said that we should not pitch too high the standard of overall consistency that is required for the attribution of beliefs. But there is still a

---

[3]   We might be able to understand these apparent beliefs as *prima facie* reasonable responses to experienced situations even though, because of their implausibility, they are not really reasonable all things considered. This leads on to the second question in the text.

[4]   Dennett, 1981, p. 44, says, 'The belief store must be – in the main – consistent', and goes on to cast doubt on the idea that a 'neurocryptographer' could insert into someone's (Tom's) brain the single belief, 'I have an older brother living in Cleveland', where this is not only false but also inconsistent with much that Tom already believes. According to Dennett, the outcome of the neurocryptographer's efforts will be either that the candidate belief will be rejected by Tom on the grounds of its incompatibility with his other beliefs or else that Tom will end up endorsing contradictions, such as 'I am an only child and have an older brother living in Cleveland'. In the latter case, we are to conclude that Tom's basic rationality is impaired so that 'in neither case has our neurocryptographer succeeded in wiring in a new belief' (ibid.). Dennett's vivid example is clearly relevant to the topic of delusional beliefs.

second question to be faced if we are to regard those bizarrely false apparent beliefs as genuine. In addition to the question whether the hypothesis in question can be understood as a prima facie reasonable response to the subject's experience, we have to ask why the hypothesis is adopted and maintained as a belief despite its utter implausibility and the uniform scepticism with which other people greet it. We can establish that this question may have an answer by pointing out that departures from overall consistency do occur and can be excused. But an answer still needs to be given.

1. Understanding Delusions

If the examples with which we began are regarded as genuine beliefs then they would seem to be delusions according to the definition offered by the American Psychiatric Association's *Diagnostic and Statistical Manual of Mental Disorders* (*DSM-IV*, 1994, p. 765):

> **Delusion** A false belief based on incorrect inference about external reality that is firmly sustained despite what almost everyone else believes and despite what constitutes incontrovertible and obvious proof or evidence to the contrary.

The eight examples of apparent beliefs are all, we assume, false and they are all, at least to some extent, about the external world rather than being exhaustively about the subject's own experience. They are adopted and maintained despite the best efforts of relatives, friends and medical staff to assure the subject that they are not true and despite the fact that they are massively implausible in the light of other things that the subject knows. The aspect of the *DSM-IV* definition about which we might be cautious at this stage is the idea that a delusion must be 'based on incorrect inference'. It is plausible that many delusional beliefs are arrived at by a route that involves a flawed inference, either deductive or inductive, from true premises about experience to a false conclusion about external reality. But we should also allow that some delusional beliefs might be arrived at just by taking an illusory experience to be veridical (see below, section 4.3). That need not, strictly speaking, involve a step of inference on the part of the subject since the subject might make a judgement about the external world without going via any premises about his or her own experience.[5]

Theorists – whether philosophers, psychologists, psychopathologists, or psychiatrists – have taken differing views of the extent to which delusions can be understood, or rendered intelligible, in folk psychological terms. It is often remarked, for example, that Karl Jaspers (1963) held that the primary delusions

---

[5]   For a helpful survey of definitions of delusion, see Garety and Hemsley, 1994, ch. 1.

of schizophrenic patients are not understandable, by which he seems to have meant that they are not folk psychologically intelligible and cannot be understood empathetically 'from the inside'. One gloss on Jaspers's view would be that the onset of a delusion does not have a rational explanation but just a causal explanation in terms of some organic disease process. For these purposes, a rational explanation of a subject's belief is an explanation that reveals the belief to be the right thing for the subject to think, or at least a reasonable thing for the subject to think, given the subject's experiences and other beliefs. But the issues here are quite complex because the notions of a belief that is folk psychologically intelligible, a belief that can be understood empathetically, and a belief that has a rational explanation do not coincide perfectly.

We have already noted, in effect, that a belief might have a rational explanation in terms of a subject's experience although the strange or terrifying nature of that experience might stand in the way of our identifying properly with the subject in imagination. It may also be that a belief is folk psychologically intelligible even though it does not have an explanation that is cast wholly in terms of right thinking. Our everyday psychological understanding includes some understanding of excusable departures from right thinking and some understanding of the not-ideally-rational strategies that we employ in the face of the finitary predicament.

In addition, a belief might be folk psychologically intelligible even though it cannot be wholly understood 'from the inside' just by imagining being in the subject's situation. We understand, for example, that a person's dispositions to form beliefs on the basis of evidence might be perturbed in the direction of excessive caution or excessive boldness by factors such as mood or by the operation of a drug. If we imagine ourselves in the situation of a subject whose thinking is being perturbed in one way or another then we may sometimes be able to simulate the subject's thinking just by bringing to bear our own knowledge 'from the inside' of what it is like to be in that kind of situation. But there may be perturbing influences that we understand quite well even though we have never experienced them ourselves, and this understanding may fall within the scope of folk psychology. In these cases of folk psychological intelligibility, simply imagining ourselves in the subject's situation is not enough; we have to rely on a body of third-personal knowledge 'from the outside' about the way in which the particular perturbing influence works.[6]

Given these distinctions, it is possible to develop Jaspers's view in more than

---

6   These two paragraphs show (i) that a belief may have a rational explanation but not be understandable by simulation; (ii) that a belief may be folk psychologically intelligible but not have a purely rational explanation; and (iii) that a belief may be folk psychologically intelligible but not be understandable purely by simulation. It is plausible that simulation of flawed thinking by someone susceptible to the same error illustrates the converse of (i) and that the thinking of savants may illustrate the converse of (ii). Perhaps it is not obvious that the converse of (iii) is a possible combination. In any case, it is clear enough that the three notions are distinct.

one way. Each possible development is potentially problematic in the light of a corresponding way of taking the initial idea that the attribution of beliefs is governed by a constraint of rationality or reasonableness. Thus, for example, if Jaspers's view is that delusions are not folk psychologically intelligible then a problem arises when this is combined with the idea that the attribution of beliefs is governed by an overarching constraint of intelligibility. The problem in this case is that, given the constraint on attribution, if the so-called delusions really defy folk psychological understanding then patients should not, after all, be credited with beliefs with those bizarrely false contents. In the same way, a problem arises if we combine the view that delusions do not have purely rational explanations with the idea that attributions of belief are governed by an overarching constraint of rationality, or if we combine the view that delusions cannot be understood 'from the inside' with the idea that an over-arching constraint on belief attribution can be cast in terms of simulation. In each case, the upshot would be that we should not attribute delusional beliefs.[7]

In fact, given the distinctions that we have drawn, we have considerable room for manoeuvre to avoid this problem; and, in any case, we are not bound to accept Jaspers's view. So the option of attributing bizarrely false beliefs to patients surely remains open. But we shall briefly consider the alternatives to such attributions.

1.1 Reinterpreting Patients' Utterances

If we were not to attribute bizarrely false beliefs then the utterances that are apparent expressions of delusions would have to be given some other interpretation.

One possibility is that those utterances should not be regarded as expressions of the subject's thoughts at all but should be regarded, from a psychological point of view, as nothing more than noise.[8] Another possibility is that they should be treated as metaphorical, or in some other way non-literal, expressions of beliefs that are not bizarrely false. But the 'mere noise' and 'non-literal' options do not seem to offer satisfying accounts of examples such as those with which we began. On the one hand, it does not seem right to take the extreme course of giving up on psychological interpretation as the 'mere noise' option suggests. On the other hand, it is inadequate to offer interpretations of patients' utterances as innocuous remarks to the effect that it is, in certain respects, *as if* their closest relatives had been replaced by impostors or *as if* they were dead.

There is a third possible way of avoiding the attribution to patients of bizarrely false beliefs, an alternative to both the 'mere noise' and the 'non-literal' options. The patients' utterances might be interpreted as expressions of mental

---

7   See Eilan, 2000, for a discussion of the apparent paradox implicit in Jaspers's approach.
8   This is one way of taking the suggestion by Berrios, 1991, that the utterances of deluded patients should be regarded as 'empty speech acts'.

states with those false contents, but not as expressions of beliefs. They might be expressions of imaginative mental states or (if this is different) of states of the kind involved in supposing that something is the case or in entertaining a hypothesis.[9] As it stands, this third possibility, like the 'non-literal' option, seems to involve underdescribing the strangeness of the patients' psychological state. There is nothing at all pathological in merely imagining that one is being followed around by people who are known to one but who are unrecognizable because they are in disguise nor in toying with the supposition that the person one sees in the mirror is not really oneself. But the third possibility might be elaborated. It might lead to the idea that so-called delusional states belong to a category that is somehow intermediate between imagination and belief or to the proposal that subjects suffering from delusions may confuse what is imagined with what is believed.

The proposal that some delusions have their origin in a 'misidentification of imagination' (Currie, this volume) is an important one. There is considerable plausibility in the idea that some schizophrenic patients fail properly to distinguish between imagining something to be the case and believing it to be the case. A subject who imagines something to be so and then mistakes what is imagined for a belief may end up in a state that is intermediate between imagination and belief. Perhaps some so-called delusions in schizophrenia are states of this intermediate kind rather than bizarrely false beliefs. So the 'misidentification of imagination' approach can provide an alternative interpretation of some utterances that are apparent expressions of delusions. But there are other cases in which it seems plausible that a subject who starts by imagining that P and misidentifies this as a belief that P comes, in the end, genuinely to believe that P (Currie, this volume). So the 'misidentification of imagination' approach still allows that some schizophrenic patients have delusional beliefs.

We have been considering the idea that utterances that are apparent expressions of delusions should be given some other interpretation. The 'mere noise' and 'non-literal' options are not adequate. A third option is inadequate as it stands but can be elaborated into an approach that does suggest alternative interpretations for some apparent expressions of delusions in schizophrenia. However, even this 'misidentification of imagination' approach allows that some schizophrenic patients genuinely have delusional beliefs and, of course, it does not suggest any alternative interpretation in cases that are unrelated to schizophrenia.

In most cases, then, it seems that patients should be interpreted as having the bizarrely false beliefs that their utterances seem to express. So we return to the two questions that have to be asked about each of the eight examples

---

[9]   Gendler, 2000, argues that supposing for the sake of argument is different from, and does not involve, the kind of imagining that figures in make-believe.

with which we began. Can the delusional hypothesis be understood as a prima facie reasonable response to the subject's experience and how does the hypothesis come to be adopted and maintained as a belief despite its implausibility?

1.2 Delusions as Responses to Unusual Experiences

Everyday psychological understanding does not rule out the possibility of a belief that has a causal explanation but not a purely rational explanation. We ordinarily allow that beliefs may be produced by wishful thinking, subliminal advertising or hypnosis, for example. But intuitive notions of folk psychological intelligibility do struggle somewhat with the idea of a belief that is brutely caused by disease or injury. We can stay close to the intuitive conception of beliefs as being adopted on the basis of experience and inference if the element of brute causation enters one step earlier and disease or injury causes abnormal experiences. We can also avoid a struggle with intuitive notions of folk psychological intelligibility if disease or injury perturbs reasoning processes in ways that are not too far removed from the familiar effects of mood, tiredness or alcohol, for example.

Other theorists working at about the same time as Jaspers allowed that delusions might have their origins in perceptual disorders or in faulty reasoning.[10] Indeed, Jaspers himself allowed that there are delusion-like ideas that can be seen as intelligible responses to aspects of experience such as affect, mood or hallucination. More recently Brendan Maher (1974, 1988, 1992) has defended the proposal that delusions are false beliefs that arise as rational responses to unusual experiences. Maher's proposal certainly addresses our first question about the way in which the delusional hypothesis arises. But it has little to offer in response to our second question about how the delusional hypothesis is actually adopted and maintained as a belief despite its implausibility and despite the scepticism of others.[11]

For an account of delusions that treats them as folk psychologically intelligible responses to unusual experiences and offers answers to both our questions we turn to Tony Stone and Andrew Young's chapter, 'Delusions and brain injury: The philosophy and psychology of belief' (1997). According to Stone and Young, many delusions arise from anomalous experiences that result from brain damage. Since the way that brain damage leads to anomalies in experi-

---

[10]   See Garety and Hemsley, 1994, ch. 6.

[11]   It is natural to say that in accepting a delusional hypothesis despite its implausibility patients depart from norms of rationality. But it is not straightforward to say just which norms are being infringed. Gold and Hohwy, this volume, follow Lewis, 1986, in distinguishing between procedural rationality and content rationality and then argue that the irrationality of delusional beliefs in schizophrenia cannot be understood as a failure of either of these aspects of rationality. For a different distinction, between norms that relate to logical consistency and norms that govern the use and management of evidence, see Bermúdez, forthcoming.

ence is not itself a matter for folk psychology, Stone and Young's account of delusions is not purely folk psychological. But they do regard the link between the unusual experience and the delusional belief as being folk psychologically intelligible.

Stone and Young offer their account as applying specifically to delusions that result from brain damage. Also, they are concerned with delusions that have two properties: they are *monothematic* – specific to a particular topic – and *circumscribed* – relatively unelaborated. (We can note that, in principle, these two properties are independent of each other. A subject might have a bizarrely false belief about just one specific topic but might follow out many of the consequences of this belief: monothematic but not circumscribed. Or a subject might have bizarrely false beliefs about many unrelated topics but not follow out the consequences of any of them: circumscribed but not monothematic.) Stone and Young contrast circumscribed monothematic delusions resulting from brain damage with some kinds of schizophrenic delusions which 'can be florid and wide-ranging, with patients seeming to produce a new delusion in answer to almost every question, and effectively living in a solipsistic delusional world' (1997, p. 329). Some schizophrenic patients exhibit circumscribed monothematic delusions that may well fall within the scope of Stone and Young's account, but that account is not intended to apply to the extreme cases of florid schizophrenic delusions.[12]

2. The Capgras Delusion

The key idea in Stone and Young's account of monothematic and circumscribed delusions that result from brain injury is that (1997, p. 330):

> these delusions can be best explained in terms of the person suffering from the delusion trying to make sense of or explain a disturbing perceptual experience that is brought about by the brain injury. On this view, the brain injury does not alter beliefs directly, but only indirectly by affecting the person's perceptual experiences.

The account is illustrated in terms of the explanation of the Capgras delusion that Young and his colleagues have developed.[13]

Patients who suffer from the Capgras delusion believe that someone close

---

[12]   Stone and Young's (1997) account begins from the idea that patients have anomalous experiences as a result of brain damage. See Breen et al., this volume, for discussion of the comparison between delusions that occur as part of a primary psychiatric disorder, such as schizophrenia, and delusions that occur as the result of an identifiable neurological correlate.

[13]   See Ellis and Young, 1990; Ellis and de Pauw, 1994; Ellis et al., 1997; Young, this volume. As we shall see at the end of this section, Stone and Young hold that this key idea about the patient trying to make sense of an unusual experience needs to be augmented by an appeal to reasoning biases.

to them, often a close relative, usually their spouse in the first instance, has been replaced by an impostor who looks just like the replaced person. This is not an especially rare condition. The first major report of the delusion was in 1923 and a recent review surveys 174 published cases.[14] The Capgras delusion is monothematic and it is also relatively circumscribed. If the person in front of you is not your spouse of many years then a remarkable switch must have taken place; but how was the trick turned? Your spouse must be somewhere else, but where? And is your spouse alive or dead? The case is of evident interest to the police; have they been informed? Capgras patients sometimes elaborate their delusion to the extent of invoking some piece of technology, perhaps robots or, in a biotechnological age, clones. Sometimes they express an attitude of antagonism or of friendliness towards the impostor and act in a way that is intelligible in the light of that attitude (sometimes with tragic results). But they are remarkably uninterested in the location or fate of their spouse and do not initiate a search or report the disappearance to the police. Capgras patients do not seem to incorporate the consequences of their belief into their general account of how the world works.

Until recently, the Capgras delusion was often explained in psychodynamic terms. On one hypothesis, the delusion serves to resolve conflicting feelings of love and hate towards a close relative; an impostor can be hated without guilt. Alternatively, Oedipal guilt can be alleviated if the attractive person who looks just like your mother is not in fact a relative of yours at all.[15] But wholly psychodynamic accounts are cast into doubt by the fact that neuropsychological investigations of patients with the Capgras delusion have shown evidence of right hemisphere damage in many cases.[16] It would be highly surprising that so many Capgras patients should show brain damage, and that a vast majority of those showing brain damage should have damage to the right hemisphere, if the explanation of their delusion were to be wholly psychodynamic.

The explanation of the Capgras delusion developed by Young and his colleagues postulates that the delusion arises from a deficit in face processing that is a kind of mirror image of prosopagnosia. Prosopagnosic patients are unable to recognize familiar faces but they still show autonomic affective responses, as indicated by increased skin conductance, to familiar faces. So it is proposed that Capgras patients have an intact face recognition system but a loss of affective responses to familiar faces. As a result (Stone and Young, 1997, p. 337):

> [They] are subject to an anomalous perceptual experience – an experience of seeing a face that looks just like their relative, but without experiencing the affective response that would normally be part and parcel of that experience.

---

[14]   Capgras and Reboul-Lachaux, 1923; Förstl et al., 1991.
[15]   For psychodynamic accounts, see Capgras and Carrette, 1924; Enoch and Trethowan, 1991.
[16]   See Breen et al., this volume, for a review of findings about right hemisphere abnormalities.

The delusion itself arises, according to this proposal, from an attempt on the part of the patient to explain this peculiar experience.

Some recent empirical evidence provides support for the proposal that the Capgras delusion arises from an affective deficit in face processing. Skin conductance responses were measured in Capgras patients who were shown familiar and unfamiliar faces. As predicted by the proposal, the increased response to familiar faces that is found in normal subjects was absent or greatly reduced in these patients (Ellis et al., 1997; Hirstein and Ramachandran, 1997).

But this affective deficit is not sufficient, by itself, to generate the delusion. There are patients in whom brain damage has led to a failure to discriminate autonomically between familiar and unfamiliar faces, but who are despite this not delusional (Tranel, Damasio and Damasio, 1995). Presumably, these nondelusional patients experience just the same absence of affective response to the faces of loved ones that is experienced by patients suffering from the Capgras delusion. More generally, it seems clear that someone could suffer from the affective deficit in face processing, and have anomalous experiences when seeing the faces of loved ones, without adopting the implausible hypothesis that spouse and relatives have been replaced by impostors. Such a subject might say that his experience of the faces of loved ones is strange, flat, not quite right, and even that it is *as if* these were not really his loved ones. He might agree that one possible explanation of what is going on that would be adequate to the nature of this particular experience would be that the perceived faces are not, in fact, the faces of his loved ones. In an imaginative spirit, he might entertain and explore that hypothesis. But he could still stop short of actually adopting and maintaining the explanatory hypothesis as a belief. It seems, then, that a perceptual or affective deficit resulting from brain injury is a factor in the aetiology of the Capgras delusion but that this deficit is not sufficient, by itself, to account for the delusion.

We find this pattern in the case of other delusions as well. A patient with right hemisphere brain damage may suffer from paralysis of his left limbs, may neglect objects and events in the left side of his world, and may have the delusional belief that his left arm is not his own (the sixth of the eight examples at the beginning). It seems plausible that the patient's paralysis is a factor in the aetiology of this delusion. But many patients with left-sided paralysis resulting from right hemisphere damage are not delusional (and do not show unilateral neglect). So the paralysis is not sufficient, by itself, to account for the delusion.[17] A schizophrenic patient may suffer from the delusion of alien control, believing that someone else can control his actions (the seventh of the eight examples at the beginning). It seems that an experience of alien control is a factor in the aetiology of this delusion. But patients with depersonalization disorder describe their experiences as being *as if* an alien is con-

---

[17] See below, section 6.6, for further discussion.

trolling their actions, yet these patients are not delusional. So an experience in which it feels as if one is not controlling the movement of one's arm, for example, is not enough to produce the delusional belief that one's arm is being controlled by someone else. The anomalous experience of alien control is not sufficient, by itself, to account for the delusion of alien control.[18]

In these cases, as in the case of the Capgras delusion, there must be other factors at work. Stone and Young themselves make a proposal about the nature of these further factors (1997, p. 341):

> We ... think that the perceptual deficit account [of the Capgras delusion] needs to be augmented by a theory of the reasoning biases that lead to the delusional interpretation of the perceptual anomalies produced by the perceptual deficit.

3. Reasoning Biases and Attributional Biases

In a discussion of the formation and maintenance of delusional beliefs, Richard Bentall (1994; see also Bentall and Kinderman, 1998) begins with a contrast between accounts that follow Maher in saying that delusions are rational interpretations of anomalous experiences and accounts that focus on the role of cognitive biases. He acknowledges that some delusions arise from anomalous experiences, including experiences that result from perceptual or affective deficits, as proposed, for example, by Young and his colleagues. But Bentall maintains that, nevertheless, persecutory delusions often occur without any perceptual or other experiential anomaly. For such delusions, Maher's approach is not appropriate and an account in terms of cognitive biases is obligatory.[19]

At the end of the previous section we reached the view (following Stone and Young) that, even where perceptual anomalies do occur, Maher's kind of approach is not adequate by itself. It is true that the hypothesis that loved ones have been replaced by impostors provides one possible explanation of the Capgras patient's experience of familiar faces, and to that extent the delusional hypothesis offers a rational interpretation of that experience. But this does not explain why Capgras patients adopt and maintain the hypothesis as a belief, since many subjects share the experience but not the delusion and the hypoth-

---

[18]   See below, section 7.1, and Langdon and Coltheart, this volume, for further discussion.

[19]   Bentall and Kinderman, 1998, p. 121: '[Maher's] account consists of two logically unrelated elements: first Maher proposes the positive hypothesis that delusions are always a reaction to some kind of unusual perception and, second, he proposes the negative hypothesis that delusions are *never* the product of abnormal (nonperceptual) cognitive processes.' Bentall and Kinderman's assessment is that Maher's positive hypothesis is not generally correct, but does offer a correct account of some cases such as the Capgras delusion. Their main point (as in Bentall, 1994) is to show that Maher's negative hypothesis is not well supported.

esis is intrinsically implausible. So we could hope that the biases to which Bentall appeals in his account of persecutory delusions where there is no experiential anomaly might also be of some help in augmenting the perceptual-affective deficit account of the Capgras delusion.

It is no part of Bentall's position that deluded subjects suffer from a gross and pervasive deficit in logical reasoning. But, he does draw attention to a body of experimental work that indicates that deluded patients perform differently from normal subjects on probabilistic reasoning tasks.[20] The basic finding from this research is that deluded subjects seek less information than normal controls do before reaching a judgement. In short, deluded subjects show a tendency to jump to conclusions. This is clearly a suggestive finding. Someone who jumps to conclusions might move too readily from the thought that the hypothesis that loved ones have been replaced by impostors provides one possible explanation of his experience to the judgement that this hypothesis is indeed true.

On the other hand, it may seem that this bias in probabilistic reasoning cannot be enough, by itself, to explain delusional beliefs. The performance of deluded subjects is, on average, closer to the Bayesian norms than the performance of normal subjects, who tend to be overly cautious. So it could appear unlikely that just this difference from the reasoning of normal subjects would lead into such bizarre falsehood. But there is, amongst deluded subjects, a substantial subgroup (between one third and a half) who are prepared to reach a conclusion when presented with just one item of evidence.[21] Patients who show this pattern of performance with completely neutral material may, as Bentall and Kinderman say, be 'vulnerable to accepting ideas that seem nonsensical to others' (1998, pp. 122–3).

A bias in probabilistic reasoning does not, however, explain the particular theme or content of the hypothesis that a deluded patient adopts. So Bentall's account of persecutory delusions appeals, in addition, to biases in the kinds of explanations that subjects give for their own behaviour and the behaviour of other people: attributional biases. Empirical results in this area indicate that, by comparison with normal subjects, patients with persecutory delusions tend to blame other people when something goes wrong and tend to take the credit themselves when something goes right.[22] Patients with persecutory delusions thus show an exaggerated 'self-serving bias' of a kind that has sometimes been

---

[20]   Huq, Garety and Hemsley, 1988; Garety, Hemsley and Wessely, 1991. The work is reviewed in Garety and Hemsley, 1994, ch. 7.

[21]   In the experiments in question, the prior probability of the hypothesis is 50 per cent and the probability of the hypothesis given the one item of evidence is 85 per cent.

[22]   See e.g. Kaney and Bentall, 1989, 1992.

regarded as a mechanism for maintaining self-esteem.[23] There is also some evidence that patients with persecutory delusions show a bias in the deployment of attentional and memory resources in favour of stimuli that are related to threats. These patients are unable to avoid attending to the meanings of threat-related words. In a similar way, negative trait words are particularly salient for depressed patients. It is of particular interest that patients with persecutory delusions show this same effect with respect to negative trait words (Kinderman, 1994), a result that supports the idea that 'deluded patients have an implicit, but explicitly denied, negative self-concept' (Bentall and Kinderman, 1998, p. 130; see also Lyon, Kaney and Bentall, 1994).

On the basis of a wide-ranging review, Bentall assembles the following account of persecutory delusions (1994, p. 353):

> [P]aranoid patients show a tendency to 'jump to conclusions' in situations requiring probabilistic reasoning, attend selectively to threatening events, and exhibit a characteristic pattern of attributions, most marked when they make external attributions for negative events. . . .
> The biases observed indicate that persecutory delusions may have the function of protecting the individual against chronic feelings of low self-esteem.

Let us now turn back from Bentall's account of persecutory delusions that occur without any experiential anomaly to Stone and Young's account of the Capgras delusion. Stone and Young note that 'outside the topic of the [monothematic and circumscribed] delusion itself, patients may appear quite rational' (1997, p. 329). These patients do not have major problems with logical reasoning. But it is open to Stone and Young to augment the perceptual-affective deficit account of the Capgras delusion by appealing to probabilistic reasoning, attentional and attributional biases. Indeed, because Capgras patients often exhibit suspiciousness and persecutory delusions, Stone and Young might appeal to some of the very same biases as those that figure in Bentall's account. The attributional bias ('external attributions for negative events') would help to explain why the hypothesis that loved ones have been replaced by impostors is treated as a particularly salient candidate explanation of the Capgras patient's experience. The probabilistic reasoning bias, which is exhibited even on tasks in which there is no connection with threat or persecution, would help to explain why that hypothesis, once considered, is actually adopted as a belief.

---

[23]   We are not committing ourselves to this claim about self-esteem – or even to the idea that the unrefined concept of self-esteem is a useful one. For different kinds of 'self-representation', see Higgins, 1987; and for a review of discrepancies between these self-representations in deluded patients, see Bentall and Kinderman, 1998.

Then, if Bentall is right about the function of persecutory delusions, the maintenance of the Capgras delusion might be explained in motivational terms.[24]

So, on Stone and Young's account, augmented by appeal to various biases, the Capgras delusion depends on contributions from two sets of factors. In the first set are perceptual or experiential abnormalities resulting from brain damage. The second set is a heterogeneous collection of factors that lead to a misinterpretation of an anomalous experience (1997, p. 344):

> The unusual perceptual experiences are considered to follow directly from brain malfunction, but their misinterpretation may reflect a further consequence of brain disease, an exacerbation of pre-morbid dispositions, or an indirect result of other changes.

This leaves it open that, in Capgras patients, the misinterpretation of anomalous experience might result from a cognitive deficit; that is, from impairment to, or even abolition of, a particular component or module within the normal cognitive processing machinery.

In contrast, Bentall is explicit that he is proposing cognitive biases rather than deficits (1994, p. 353):

> It is worth repeating that these are cognitive biases rather than deficits. There is no evidence that deluded patients are incapable of reasoning; rather, they tend to weigh evidence relevant to their beliefs in a different way than normal individuals.

It may not be clear just what the bias–versus–deficit distinction is supposed to amount to here.[25] But we can note that in the quoted passage Bentall does not provide a compelling general argument to rule out the possibility that deluded patients have a reasoning deficit. For it is not right to suppose that the only cognitive deficit that could be proposed would be the total abolition of the reasoning system. If the reasoning system were to be made up of many components, then it might be that impairment to, or abolition of, one component would have the result that subjects would become less cautious and would jump to conclusions. An analogy may be useful. Surface dyslexic patients are more likely to produce a regular pronunciation of irregular or exception words (reading 'pint' to rhyme with 'mint') than are normal subjects. But it would not be right to insist on an explanation of this disorder in terms of a cognitive

---

[24] The empirical results on probabilistic reasoning by deluded patients do not indicate tenacious maintenance of hypotheses. On the contrary, some of the deluded subjects were ready to abandon a hitherto well confirmed hypothesis on the basis of just one item of disconfirmatory evidence (Garety, Hemsley and Wessely, 1991).

[25] See below, section 5.1, for further discussion of biases and deficits.

bias rather than a cognitive deficit on the grounds that 'there is no evidence that surface dyslexic patients are incapable of reading'.

The point that we have now reached, following Stone and Young, is that the Capgras delusion arises from an affective deficit in face processing together with other factors including attributional biases, motivational factors, and abnormalities of probabilistic reasoning. But Stone and Young also provide another way of thinking about biases in the system of belief formation and maintenance and this is the topic of our next section.

4. Observational Adequacy and Conservatism

Beliefs, once formed, have a kind of inertia. As we revise our beliefs, we prefer changes that require less rather than more disruption in our system of beliefs as a whole. We tend to reject hypotheses that are inconsistent with many things that we already believe, especially if the hypotheses clash with propositions that play a pivotal organizing role in the web of our beliefs. Stone and Young call this a principle of *conservatism*.

The most conservative strategy would be to avoid all change in our system of beliefs. Suppose that I antecedently believe that there are no mice in the Coombs Building and then have a perceptual experience that would be well explained by the hypothesis that there is a mouse in my office.[26] Adopting the ultra-conservative strategy, I could decline to believe that there is a mouse in my office and instead could try to generate an alternative explanation of my experience in a way that was consistent with my antecedently held beliefs. It is not really clear that any alternative explanation could consistently preserve all of my antecedent beliefs, but for present purposes the more important point is that, in general, it is unwise to refuse to alter one's beliefs about the world in the light of one's experiences. So there is another principle governing belief revision which Stone and Young call a principle of *observational adequacy*.

The idea of this second principle is that beliefs should be revised so as to be consistent with the observed data. Sitting in my office, sober and in good light, I seem to see a mouse in the corner. In general, I accept the deliverances of perceptual experience as veridical and the principle of observational adequacy dictates that my system of beliefs should be updated in the light of the observed datum that there is a mouse in the corner of my office. I should revise my belief that there are no mice in the Coombs Building.

But suppose that, sitting in my office, I seem to see in the corner several little green men playing blackjack with a pink elephant dealing the cards. It might be that I antecedently have an explicitly articulated and compelling set of reasons for believing that there are no blackjack-dealing pink elephants in

---

[26]   The Philosophy Program, Research School of Social Sciences, Australian National University is located in the Coombs Building.

the Coombs Building. Or it might be that, although I have never set out to construct an explicit justification, the proposition that my office is not populated by green men and pink elephants figures as an implicit background assumption in my assessments of the way in which evidence confirms or disconfirms hypotheses. Either way, if I accept my experience as veridical and try to incorporate the 'little green men and a pink elephant' hypothesis into my system of beliefs then very substantial disruption will result. Here, the principle of conservatism outweighs the principle of observational adequacy and dictates that I should not take my experience at face value. I should deny the apparent data.

Conservatism and observational adequacy tend to pull in opposite directions. There is no general formula for balancing the two principles against each other. We shall not always do well to reject the deliverances of perceptual experience just because they clash with our antecedent beliefs and expectations; we have to learn from our experience. But we also understand that experience can sometimes be misleading.

4.1 Two Ways of Understanding Observational Adequacy

Usually, our attention is on the world that we perceive rather than on our experience of it. I used to believe that there were no mice in the Coombs Building; now I have to take account of the fact that there is one right here in my office. This is what the principle of observational adequacy requires.

But when, in the light of the principle of conservatism, we reject the deliverances of perceptual experience as misleading, our experience itself may become an object of enquiry. I still believe that there are no pink elephants in the Coombs Building; but I want to understand why it perceptually seemed to me that there was a pink elephant in the corner of my office. Now the data to be accounted for, according to the principle of observational adequacy, concern the character of my experience. The principle of conservatism dictates that the facts about my experience should be explained with the minimum of disruption to my system of beliefs; and we can suppose that this will turn out to be a relatively simple matter.[27]

Experience itself may become the object of enquiry because it has been classified as illusory rather than accepted as veridical. But this is not the only

---

[27] It is easier to update my system of beliefs to accommodate the proposition that it misleadingly seemed to me that there was a pink elephant dealing blackjack than to accommodate the proposition that there really was a pink elephant there. But we must allow for the possibility that accounting for an illusion might turn out to be difficult. It is possible that an experience might first be classified as illusory, that updating the system of beliefs to account for the illusion might turn out to be massively disruptive, and that, in the end, the experience might be accepted as veridical after all. In such a case, a conclusion about the external world would be reached on the basis of detailed consideration of the character of my experience. This is quite different from the way in which, usually, I unreflectively take perceptual experiences at face value without directing attention on the experiences themselves.

way in which our explanatory interest can come to be fixed on the nature of our experience rather than on events in the external world. In the case of some experiences, there is no question of a correct or incorrect presentation of how things are in the external world. Itches and tickles, for example, are not classified as either veridical or illusory, but they can certainly claim the attention of the person undergoing them. The occurrence of such an experience may itself constitute data. Its occurrence may be quite unexpected; it may conflict with many things that I believe. In that case, the principle of observational adequacy dictates that the web of beliefs should be updated to take into account the data concerning the occurrence and nature of this experience. The principle of conservatism, as usual, requires that the updating should be done in such a way as to minimize overall doxastic disruption.

We can thus distinguish two slightly different ways of understanding the principle of observational adequacy. On the first construal, the observational data to which belief revision should be adequate concern the external world (e.g. there is a mouse in the corner of my office) rather than my experiences. On the second construal, the data to which belief revision should be adequate are data about my experiences (e.g. I have an itch; it seems to me that there is a pink elephant dealing blackjack). It will be helpful to keep this distinction in mind as we consider the proposal that Stone and Young make about biases in the system of belief formation and maintenance.

4.2 Two Ways of Interpreting Stone and Young's Suggestion

Stone and Young suggest (1997, p. 349) that, in cases of delusion, the balance between the principle of observational adequacy and the principle of conservativeness is tipped too far in favour of observational adequacy. There are two ways of interpreting this suggestion corresponding to the two ways of understanding observational adequacy.

According to Stone and Young, Capgras patients undergo an unusual kind of experience (1997, p. 337): 'an experience of seeing a face that looks just like their relative, but without experiencing the affective response that would normally be part and parcel of that experience'. This focus on the nature of the patients' experience makes it seem natural to interpret Stone and Young's suggestion in line with the second of the two construals that we just distinguished. But on further reflection it is not so clear that this interpretation makes best sense of Stone and Young's account of the Capgras delusion. It is not clear that Capgras patients attach too much weight to data that concern the nature of their experience.

A Capgras patient undergoes an anomalous experience and the hypothesis that a relative has been replaced by an impostor provides one possible explanation of the occurrence of an experience of this kind ('seeing a face that looks just like their relative, but without experiencing the affective response'). With respect to the occurrence and nature of the experience, a revision of the subject's beliefs to incorporate that hypothesis would be observationally adequate.

On the other hand, adopting that hypothesis and then following out all of its consequences would require a major upheaval in the subject's system of beliefs. Adopting the hypothesis as a belief would be very far from conservative and the judgement of a normal subject would be that the hypothesis should be rejected. But, the Capgras patient gives too little weight to conservatism and so adopts and maintains the hypothesis. It does not seem right, however, to say that the Capgras patient goes wrong by attaching too much weight to data about the nature of his experience. That anomalous experience does demand explanation. The Capgras patient's mistake is to be too ready to adopt a particular explanation of his experience, an explanation involving the delusional hypothesis rather than a more conservative alternative.

We suggest, therefore, that it is worth considering an interpretation of Stone and Young's suggestion in line with the first construal of the principle of observational adequacy so that the relevant data concern, not the subject's experience, but the external world. On this second interpretation,[28] a Capgras patient is too ready to accept a putative datum about the external world, a datum that is furnished by, but does not directly concern, the patient's anomalous experience. This interpretation would have to start from the idea that, when the patient sees a close relative, it seems to the patient that there is someone present who is not the relative but looks just like the relative.[29] The patient accepts this experience as veridical and so takes himself to be in possession of a piece of observational data; namely, that this person who looks just like the relative (and claims to be the relative) is not really the relative. Observational adequacy then requires a revision of the subject's system of beliefs to incorporate the hypothesis that this person who looks just like the relative is really an impostor. On the other hand, that would amount to a quite drastic breach of the principle of conservatism and the judgement of a normal subject would be that the hypothesis should be rejected. According to this interpretation of Stone and Young's suggestion, the Capgras patient attaches too much weight to the putative observational datum and not enough weight to conservatism and so adopts and maintains the delusional hypothesis.

A critic might say that there is something artificial about our distinction between two ways of construing observational adequacy and so also about our distinction between two interpretations of Stone and Young's suggestion. It might be said that our first construal of observational adequacy can be assimilated to the second. According to the first construal, the observational data

---

[28] Note that the *second* interpretation of Stone and Young's suggestion goes with the *first* construal of observational adequacy.

[29] This idea goes naturally with the thought that, in normal subjects, the affective response really is 'part and parcel' of the experience of recognizing a particular close relative or loved one. If the affective response normally contributes to the experience of visual recognition then the absence of the affective response would make a difference to a subject's experience of the world. The subject might say that, so far as the visual experience goes, the person no longer seems to be that particular close relative.

concern the external world; according to the second construal the data concern experience. For the second construal, we considered experiences, such as itches, for which the question of correct or incorrect presentation of events in the external world does not arise, and we considered experiences that have already been classified as illusory. But, it might be said, we could also consider experiences that are accepted as veridical. Instead of talking about the worldly datum that there is a mouse in the corner of my office, we could talk about the experiential datum that it seems to me that there is a mouse in the corner of my office. When this experience is accepted as veridical, the system of beliefs is updated in the light of acceptance of a particular explanation of the experience; namely, that things are as they appear to be and there really is a mouse in the corner of my office. Thus, it might be said, what we aim at, quite generally, is to update our system of beliefs so as to afford explanations of the occurrence and nature of our experiences (observational adequacy) and to do so in a way that minimizes doxastic disruption (conservatism). We do not need to separate out the first construal of observational adequacy on which the observational data concern the external world.

Similarly, our critic might continue, the second interpretation of Stone and Young's suggestion can be assimilated to the first.[30] On the second interpretation, we say that the Capgras patient gives too much weight to the putative worldly datum that this is not a relative but an impostor. But we can say, instead, that the Capgras patient gives too much weight to the experiential datum that it seems to him that this is not a relative but an impostor. However we have, in effect, already rejected this assimilation. It does not give an adequate account of the Capgras patient's error. There is, after all, nothing wrong with giving weight to that experiential datum. The patient's anomalous experience does demand explanation. But the correct explanation is that, as a result of brain injury, the patient is suffering from an affective deficit.

The critic who thinks that our distinctions are artificial may respond by saying that Stone and Young should be interpreted as suggesting that delusions arise from a bias in favour of accepting experiences as veridical. But now we no longer have any substantive disagreement with the critic. A bias in favour of accepting experiences as veridical can be described as going 'too far towards observational adequacy and against conservatism' (Stone and Young, 1997, p. 349). But this is only because the principle of observational adequacy dictates that belief revision should take account of the putative worldly data that a subject arrives at by accepting experiences as veridical. Our aim has been to highlight this construal of observational adequacy and to contrast it with the thinner idea that all that is required is that our system of beliefs should afford some explanation of the occurrence and nature of our experiences.

---

[30]   Recall that the *second* interpretation of Stone and Young's suggestion goes with the *first* construal of observational adequacy.

4.3 Prioritizing the Delusional Hypothesis

Our reason for dwelling on the notion of observational adequacy is that the different interpretations of Stone and Young's suggestion involve different accounts of how the delusional hypothesis comes to be prioritized in the thinking of the Capgras patient.

When Stone and Young suggest that delusions arise from a bias in favour of observational adequacy and against conservatism it is natural to suppose that, on their view, the hypothesis that loved ones have been replaced by impostors scores higher than alternative hypotheses on observational adequacy. But, as we have seen, that hypothesis is no more observationally adequate to the nature of the Capgras patient's experience ('seeing a face that looks just like their relative, but without experiencing the affective response') than any of a host of alternative hypotheses. The observationally adequate alternatives include the correct hypothesis that the patient's experience is anomalous because of a brain injury. So, if we adopt the first interpretation of Stone and Young's suggestion (in line with the second construal of observational adequacy), then tipping the balance in favour of observational adequacy does not favour the delusional hypothesis over all others. It just leaves the delusional hypothesis as one candidate amongst many.

If we interpret Stone and Young's suggestion in this first way then the overall account of the formation of delusional beliefs needs to appeal to something like attributional biases to prioritize the delusional hypothesis over the other equally observationally adequate candidates (as suggested in section 3). The delusion could not be explained in terms of just two factors, a perceptual-affective deficit plus a bias towards observational adequacy at the expense of conservatism.

The situation is rather different if we adopt the second interpretation of Stone and Young's suggestion so that the observational data concern, not the subject's experience, but the external world. Recall that this interpretation starts from the assumption that the experience of a Capgras patient looking at the face of a close relative is not just anomalous but has a particular representational character. It seems to the patient that this person who looks just like the relative is not really the relative. It is then immediate that observational adequacy requires the adoption of beliefs that are consistent with the proposition that the person who is seen is not the relative despite looking just like (and claiming to be) the relative. So there is no evident need to appeal to attributional biases in order to prioritize the hypothesis that this person who looks just like the relative is really an impostor. The delusional hypothesis is prioritized by the default readiness to accept perceptual experiences as veridical and, to that extent, it is not ruled out that the delusion might be explained in terms of just the two factors that we mentioned.

If, however, the representational content of the patient's experience is less definite than we have assumed then accepting the experience as veridical will not, by itself, prioritize the delusional hypothesis. If, for example, it seems to the patient merely that this is a person who looks just like the relative but leaves him feeling emotionally flat then some other factor will have to enter the account of how the specific delusional hypothesis comes to be prioritized.

We should also allow that, even when the delusional hypothesis is prioritized by the default readiness to accept perceptual experiences as veridical, attributional biases may enter the picture as factors in determining the representational character of the patient's experience itself. It may be only in the presence of some attributional bias in addition to the affective deficit that it would determinately seem to the patient that this person who looks just like the relative is *not* the relative.

5. Outline of an Account of Delusions

Stone and Young suggest that deluded patients show an abnormality in belief revision that can be described as a bias in favour of observational adequacy at the expense of conservatism. In this section, we consider more closely the nature and scope of the suggested abnormality in belief revision and then turn to the circumscription of delusions. We end the section with a summary of the various factors that might figure in the aetiology of a monothematic and circumscribed delusion following brain injury.

5.1 Belief Revision: Biases and Deficits
The most fundamental question about the abnormality in belief revision that is exhibited by deluded patients is, of course, what exactly it consists in. A secondary question that can help to organize the discussion is whether the abnormality is best conceived as a bias or as a deficit. We mentioned the bias-versus-deficit issue near the end of section 3. Bentall argues that the reasoning or belief revision abnormality in patients with persecutory delusions is a bias rather than a deficit on the grounds that the patients are not totally deficient in reasoning. But we noted that this does not, by itself, rule out the possibility that deluded patients have a reasoning deficit because impairment to, or abolition of, just one component of a complex cognitive system would normally be regarded as a cognitive deficit. We can clarify the issues here by distinguishing between two notions of deficit.

The notion of a deficit as an impairment to, or as the abolition of, a component of information-processing machinery is a familiar one, particularly in discussions of the cognitive psychological consequences of brain injury. But we can also allow that there is a notion of a deficit which, like the notion of a bias, figures in descriptions of particular patterns of behaviour. If a subject did not engage in any probabilistic reasoning at all then we might classify this as a total probabilistic reasoning deficit. If a subject's probabilistic reasoning was merely skewed in some way then this would be a probabilistic reasoning bias. Given these behavioural notions of both bias and deficit, it would be correct to say (with Bentall) that deluded patients show a reasoning bias rather than a total reasoning deficit. But it would also be correct to point out that a bias in behaviour can sometimes be explained in terms of a deficit in the cognitive machinery underpinning that behaviour. (Surface dyslexia is evidenced as a bias towards over-regularization in the pronunciation of exception words. But that is quite consistent with its explanation being a deficit in the reading system consisting in impairment to, or abolition of, one component of that system.)

In investigations of patients following brain injury, a cognitive deficit is usually taken to be an information-processing impairment that is the result of brain damage. In that same context, the term 'bias' usually indicates something that was premorbidly present and is not related to the injury. So if, following brain injury, a patient shows a behavioural bias in reasoning, then this might be explained in terms of a cognitive deficit resulting from the injury or in terms of a condition that was already present before the injury.

According to Young and his colleagues, one factor in the Capgras delusion is an anomalous experience that results from brain injury but there are other factors at work as well. Bentall offers an account of persecutory delusions in patients without any brain injury and appeals to various reasoning and attributional biases. So the simplest extrapolation from Bentall's account of persecutory delusions would say that the additional factors at work in producing the Capgras delusion are premorbidly existing biases that are unrelated to the brain injury. What Stone and Young allow, however, is that the additional factors may include premorbid dispositions but may also include further consequences of brain damage (1997, p. 344). They allow, that is, that the explanation of the Capgras delusion may involve a second cognitive deficit.

We have seen that deluded patients do seem to show what might be called behavioural biases in their probabilistic reasoning. They tend to jump to conclusions. But what concerns us here is not just the initial adoption of the delusional hypothesis but also the robustness of the maintenance of that hypothesis in the face of conflicting considerations. It may be that for a period of weeks, months or even years, no amount of disconfirmatory evidence will persuade the patient to abandon the delusional belief. This is not, of course, a total deficit in reasoning or in belief revision. But nor is it a mere tendency to hold onto the hypothesis, or to require more disconfirmatory evidence than normal subjects do. Abandoning the delusional hypothesis is something that many patients simply do not do and so we are inclined to say that the abnormality in belief revision can be described in behavioural terms as a deficit, rather than just as a bias.[31] It is, of course, a further question whether this

---

[31]   The notions of bias and deficit that are used in the description of patterns of behaviour are to some extent interchangeable. A pattern that is described as a bias, rather than as a total deficit in some domain such as reasoning or reading, may nevertheless be redescribed as a more specific deficit – as the absence of some particular aspect of normal reasoning or reading, for example.

We note here that the Capgras delusion is not always maintained over an extended period.

particular deficit in belief revision behaviour is to be explained in terms of an underlying deficit in some component of belief revision machinery.

Before we can pursue that further question, we need a fuller account of what it is that the deluded patient does not do. As we have already noted, it would not be correct to say that patients fail to manifest any understanding of inferential liaisons. Understanding of those liaisons is surely manifested in patients' anticipation that other people will find their beliefs massively implausible. Nor would it be correct to say that patients do not actually engage in any inferences involving their delusional hypothesis. Even where delusions are relatively circumscribed rather than florid, patients engage in some degree of elaboration. What patients do not do is to allow antecedent beliefs or stored knowledge to undermine their commitment to the delusional hypothesis.

It would not be right to describe this by saying that patients attach no weight at all to their antecedent beliefs or stored knowledge. Their life would be impossible unless they were sometimes prepared to reject a hypothesis on the grounds of conflict with something that they already knew. We might describe the situation by saying that patients attach no weight to their antecedent beliefs or stored knowledge *by comparison with* their delusional hypothesis. Equally, and more straightforwardly, we can say that they attach to their delusional hypothesis a weight greater than any other. But now we must ask what property of their delusional hypothesis it is that results in its being given this greatest weight.

5.2 Belief Revision: The Nature and Scope of the Abnormality

We have suggested that patients attach greatest weight to hypotheses in some class that includes the delusional hypothesis. In order to pursue the question what the defining characteristic of this class of hypotheses is, it will be helpful to recall the two ways of interpreting Stone and Young's suggestion about a bias in favour of observational adequacy at the expense of conservatism (section 4.2). Each interpretation of their suggestion leads to a possible answer to our question.

We said that on the first way of taking Stone and Young's suggestion, the overall account would need to appeal to something like attributional biases to prioritize the delusional hypothesis. So it might be that the hypotheses to which greatest weight is attached are those that are favoured by the attributional bias that prioritizes the delusional hypothesis. If this were the right answer to our question then it is not obvious that there would be any good

---

Mackie, Ebmeier and O'Carroll, 1994, p. 212, describe a case as follows: '[The patient] stated that over the past year people had "changed", particularly his parents and close relatives. They would often leave a room and an almost identical impostor would return. He could identify impostors, because they were marginally shorter and wider than real individuals. Such changes would occur repeatedly, often many times within the same day. The process angered him considerably, and he felt it was carried out in an attempt to "get" him.'

reason to postulate an underlying deficit in belief revision machinery in order to account for the maintenance of the delusional hypothesis in the face of conflicting considerations. As Bentall (1994) notes, there is some support for a link between attributional biases and motivation via the idea that attributional biases have the function of protecting self-esteem. So it would be natural to suppose that the maintenance of hypotheses that are favoured by an attributional bias would have a motivational explanation.

If anything like this were right then the overall account of the Capgras delusion would have two components. There would be the perceptual-affective deficit in face processing and there would be the motivated maintenance of a hypothesis favoured by an attributional bias. The apparent behavioural deficit in belief revision would simply be a consequence of this second attributional-motivational component rather than a manifestation of impairment to, or abolition of, some component of the cognitive machinery that underpins belief revision.

On the second way of interpreting Stone and Young's suggestion, making use of the idea of a default readiness to regard perceptual experiences as veridical, we can propose that the hypotheses to which greatest weight is attached are those that are the immediate deliverances of perceptual experience. If this were correct then we might reasonably postulate an underlying cognitive deficit in some component that is implicated in bringing antecedent beliefs or stored knowledge to bear on perceptually generated hypotheses (Langdon and Coltheart, this volume).

But this proposed answer to our question yields some very strong empirical predictions. A patient who is genuinely unable to allow antecedent beliefs or stored knowledge to trump the deliverances of perceptual experience will be irremediably taken in by every visual illusion.[32] Suppose, for example, that a Capgras patient views an Ames room in which an adult is positioned at the taller corner and a child at the shorter corner. The proposed answer to our question seems to yield the prediction that the patient will maintain, in the face of all conflicting considerations, that the child is really taller than the adult.

This is just a hypothetical case and we do not have data to report. But we are very doubtful that a Capgras patient would inevitably be taken in by every illusion. So there is a serious problem for this second answer to our question. In order to account for the Capgras delusion, it must be that greatest weight is attached to the hypothesis that this person who looks just like the relative is not really the relative. But greatest weight must not be attached to the hypothesis that the child in the Ames room is taller than the adult. Yet both hypotheses result from accepting illusory experiences as veridical.

In response to this problem it may be said that there is an important differ-

---

[32]   Similar worries could be raised against the proposal that it is always the hypothesis that first comes to mind that has greatest weight attached to it.

ence between an experience of the Ames room illusion and the Capgras patient's anomalous experience of a close relative. When a subject views an Ames room, he or she has an illusory experience for a short time. But the Capgras patient's experience of a close relative remains anomalous over days, months or even years. If we say that the hypotheses to which greatest weight is attached are those that are the immediate deliverances of consistently repeated perceptual experiences then this seems to promise an account of the Capgras delusion without yielding any prediction about the patient inevitably being taken in by brief exposure to the Ames room illusion.

However, this revised version of the proposed answer to our question still yields quite strong empirical predictions. It is possible for a deluded patient to have repeated exposure to an illusion. Perhaps a Capgras patient has a picture of the Müller-Lyer illusion in a prominent position on his or her bedroom wall. In such a case, the prediction is that the patient will maintain that one line is longer than the other in the face of all conflicting considerations including assurances from friends and relatives that this is just an illusion and detailed accounts of the illusion from psychology textbooks. Once again we have no data to report. But we suggest that this prediction raises a doubt about even the revised version of the second answer to our question.

We have been trying to answer the fundamental question what the deluded patients' belief revision abnormality consists in. It is intuitively correct that deluded patients show a particular behavioural deficit in their belief revision and it is tempting to suppose that this is to be explained in terms of a deficit in some component of the cognitive machinery underpinning belief revision. But we have seen that it is not at all easy to describe the abnormality in a way that meets two criteria.

The first criterion is, of course, that the description of the abnormality should collect together just the cases in which a hypothesis is maintained in the face of all conflicting considerations. The suggestion that the abnormality consists in always attaching greatest weight to the immediate deliverances of (consistently repeated) perceptual experiences seems likely to fail on this criterion. The second criterion is that it should be plausible that the behavioural deficit is underpinned by a deficit in the cognitive machinery that is distinctively implicated in belief revision. The suggestion that the abnormality consists in attaching greatest weight to hypotheses that are favoured by a certain attributional bias seems to fail on this criterion. Unless the fundamental question can be answered in a way that meets the two criteria, doubt is cast on the idea that the particular deficit in belief revision behaviour is to be explained in terms of an underlying deficit in some component of belief revision machinery.

On the other hand, the association between delusions and damage to the right cerebral hemisphere offers some support to the conjecture that the failure to reject delusional hypotheses depends on a deficit in some right hemisphere cognitive function. If that conjecture were correct then the aetiology of many delusions would involve two cognitive deficits: one that causes an anomaly in perceptual or affective experience and another that causes an abnormality in belief revision (see Langdon and Coltheart, this volume). What we have just seen, however, is that difficult questions remain about the prospects for such a two-deficit account.[33]

5.3 Conservatism and Circumscription

Stone and Young suggest that deluded patients show a bias in favour of observational adequacy at the expense of conservatism. We have considered the notion of observational adequacy in some detail; now we turn to conservatism. Stone and Young take the principle of conservatism from Fodor, who says (1987, p. 63):

> [B]elief fixation appears to be a *conservative* process: the goal of the game is to accomplish the maximum in accommodating data at the minimum cost in overall disturbance to previous cognitive commitments.

Their suggestion is that deluded patients adopt hypotheses as beliefs even though doing so goes against the principle of conservatism. So it might be thought that, when a delusional hypothesis is adopted as a belief, there is substantial disturbance to the patient's previous cognitive commitments. But, at least in the case of circumscribed delusions, this kind of doxastic disruption is not what happens. A Capgras patient, for example, typically does not follow through and adopt all or even many of the consequences of the delusional belief that loved ones have been replaced by impostors. To a considerable extent, the patient's previous cognitive commitments remain in place.

We need to clarify how it can be that a deluded patient gives insufficient weight to the principle of conservatism and yet does not suffer from substantial doxastic disruption. Ideally, when we adopt a new belief we also update our web of beliefs to maintain overall consistency. There will be more than one way of doing this, and the principle of conservatism says that updating should involve minimum overall disturbance. Sometimes, however, it may turn out that there is no way to adopt a new belief and maintain overall consistency without substantial disturbance to previous cognitive commitments. If the cost

---

[33]   In this discussion we are supposing that, in normal subjects, there are domain-general processes of belief revision. We have not considered the alternative view according to which the adoption, maintenance and revision of beliefs is a function of domain-specific heuristics. On this view, overall consistency would normally be maintained to the extent that the various domain-specific heuristics do a good job of tracking the truth. There would be no holistic processes for evaluating hypotheses or for updating the web of beliefs. If this alternative view were correct, then the adoption and maintenance of a delusional hypothesis might simply result from the operation of a domain-specific heuristic on the input provided by an anomalous experience.

in terms of disturbance is too high, then this counts against adoption of the belief. This is how conservatism and observational adequacy can come into conflict.

When Stone and Young say that a delusional hypothesis scores low on conservatism they mean that adopting the hypothesis as a belief, and then making adjustments elsewhere in the light of logical and probabilistic relations, would involve considerable disturbance to the subject's antecedent system of beliefs. A normal subject who strikes the right balance between observational adequacy and conservatism would abandon the observationally adequate hypothesis rather than depart from conservatism to the extent of making all those adjustments. But it does not follow that a subject who adopts a delusional hypothesis will actually disturb his antecedent system of beliefs by making all the adjustments that would be required for overall consistency. For we noted at the outset that even a normal subject may very well live with an acknowledged tension in his system of beliefs. A normal subject might believe A and believe not-B while recognizing that A entails B. So too, a patient might adopt a delusional hypothesis but fail to make the revisions in his system of belief that would be needed to maintain overall consistency.

The principle of conservatism says that we should minimize doxastic disruption as we update the web of beliefs to maintain overall consistency; it brings together the ideals of minimal disruption and overall consistency. We give too little weight to conservatism if we adopt a belief that requires substantial disruption if consistency is to be maintained. But by moving away from the ideal of overall consistency, a deluded patient can avoid substantial doxastic disruption even while adopting a hypothesis that scores low on conservatism.[34]

In the case of normal subjects, we said that a departure from the ideal of overall consistency might be the result of a strategic decision in the light of a shortage of the resources needed for a considered revision. Alternatively, it might be motivated by the prospect of the discomfort that would accompany either of the revisions that would improve consistency. In the case of deluded patients, the latter, motivational, style of explanation may seem more plausible than the former, strategic, one. For a Capgras patient, the belief revisions that would be required to maintain overall consistency given the hypothesis that loved ones have been replaced by impostors would surely be disruptive and uncomfortable. In the case of some other delusions, aiming for overall consistency and embracing the resulting doxastic disruption might even lead to madness.

To suggest a motivational explanation for the circumscription, rather than elaboration, of a delusion is to commit ourselves to the idea that the deluded subject has some understanding of the consequences that follow logically from

---

[34]   In effect, there are three constraints on belief revision: observational adequacy, overall consistency, and minimal doxastic disruption. A circumscribed delusion involves preserving observational adequacy and minimal disruption at the expense of overall consistency.

his delusional belief. This is suggested, in any case, by the fact that deluded patients recognize that their beliefs will be found implausible by other people. So we assume that deluded patients appreciate that their beliefs are inconsistent with many deeply entrenched beliefs of other people and, indeed, with many beliefs to which they themselves are strongly committed as well. We might put this by saying that the circumscription of a delusion is a matter of a motivated limitation of inferential *performance* rather than of a lack of knowledge or *competence* concerning inferential relations.[35]

5.4 Multiple Factors in the Aetiology of Delusions

We can now summarize the various factors that might figure in the aetiology of a monothematic and circumscribed delusion following brain injury. First, there is a cognitive deficit resulting from the brain injury and this gives rise to a perceptual, affective or other experiential anomaly.

Second, a hypothesis about the cause of this anomaly is generated. Some factor privileges a false but observationally adequate hypothesis that would normally be rejected on the grounds that it does not measure up to the principle of conservatism. This factor might be an attributional bias. Alternatively, it might simply be a default readiness to accept perceptual experiences as veridical. In addition, attentional factors or even psychodynamic factors could enter the story at this point.

Third, the hypothesis is adopted and maintained as a belief despite the fact that it is inconsistent with many other things that the subject believes including propositions that play a pivotal organizing role in the subject's web of beliefs. This total resistance against conflicting considerations is appropriately described, at a behavioural level, as a deficit in belief revision though it is not easy to characterize the deficit precisely. It is provisionally suggested that this deficit is to be explained in terms of impairment to, or even abolition of, some component of the cognitive system responsible for belief revision and that this damage is also the result of brain injury. However, there are some serious open questions about this suggestion. Alternative accounts would appeal again to attributional and motivational factors.

Fourth, adoption and maintenance of the delusional hypothesis is achieved without a major upheaval in the subject's belief system. This is not a result of total failure to appreciate the inferential liaisons of the delusional belief; nor is there a total failure to deploy the delusional hypothesis in reasoning. But elaboration of the delusion does not extend to the point where substantial

---

[35]   On some 'functional role' accounts of the necessary conditions for possessing particular concepts or having thoughts with particular contents, what is required is (tacit) knowledge of (some of) the inferential liaisons in which thought contents stand. We intend our remarks about delusions to be consistent with such accounts.

doxastic disruption would result. It is suggested that this circumscription of the delusion is supported by motivational factors.[36]

In even briefer form, the four steps in this schematic account are an anomalous Experience, a prioritized Hypothesis, the adoption of this hypothesis as a Belief, and then finally the Circumscription of the delusion within the subject's web of beliefs. We turn now to the application of this EHBC account.

6. Applying the Account

Throughout our discussion up to this point we have followed Stone and Young (1997) in using the Capgras delusion as our central example. In this section, we briefly review that case and then attempt to apply the four-step (EHBC) schematic account of the aetiology of delusions to five more examples from the list of eight with which we began.

6.1 The Capgras Delusion

A Capgras patient usually believes that his spouse or another close relative has been replaced by an impostor. In terms of the four steps in our schematic account, we can propose, first (E), that as a result of brain injury the patient has a disorder of face processing that produces anomalous experiences when he sees a familiar face. Second (H), a hypothesis is generated: This person that the patient is looking at is not his spouse despite looking very much like his spouse and claiming to be his spouse. This person is claiming to be someone that she is not and so is an impostor. This might be an explanatory hypothesis prioritized by an attributional bias or it might simply be the result of the patient accepting an anomalous experience as veridical. Third (B), this hypothesis is adopted and maintained as a belief as the result of a deficit in belief revision that Stone and Young characterize as a bias in favour of observational adequacy. Fourth (C), on the basis of motivational factors, the delusion remains relatively unelaborated or circumscribed.

6.2 The Cotard Delusion

Stone and Young show how their style of account can be extended to the Cotard delusion in which a patient believes that she is emotionally dead, or

---

[36]   It might be objected that this suggestion about the role of motivational factors like those that operate in more familiar cases of cognitive dissonance makes the psychological state of the delusional patient seem altogether too normal. On our view, the circumscription of the delusion may be intelligibly motivated to the extent that following through the consequences of the delusion would lead to substantial doxastic disruption and perhaps, in the limit, to the fracturing of the patient's conception of the world and his place in it. But this account of the fourth step does not involve us in underdescribing the strangeness of the patient's psychological state. Rather, it highlights the pathology of the third step. What is strange is the adoption and maintenance of the delusional hypothesis in the first place.

that she is not a real person, or simply that she is dead. It is proposed, first (E), that as a result of brain injury the patient either has a similar disorder of face processing to the one that figures in the Capgras delusion or else suffers from a more general flattening of affective responses to stimuli (Ramachandran and Blakeslee, 1998, p. 167; Gerrans, this volume; Young, this volume). Second (H), a hypothesis is generated. In its simplest and most dramatic form, the hypothesis is that the patient is dead. Corresponding to the two accounts of the anomalous experience in the first step, there are different possible accounts of how this delusional hypothesis comes to be prioritized as a candidate for belief.

On one account (given by Stone and Young), the Cotard patient's experience of other people's faces is the same as a Capgras patient's but because of a different attributional bias (associated with depression rather than persecution) a different hypothesis is generated to explain the nature of this experience. The patient locates the cause of the anomaly in herself ('I am dead') rather than in the external world ('My loved ones have been replaced by impostors').

On the other account, the experience of the Cotard patient when she sees the face of a loved one is different from that of a Capgras patient. This may seem to open up the option of saying that the two patients generate different hypotheses just because they accept different experiences of faces as veridical. We have already allowed that perhaps it seems to the Capgras patient that this person who looks just like the loved one is not really the loved one. But it is not plausible that we would give a correct account of the representational character of the Cotard patient's experience when looking at the face of a loved one by saying that it seems to the patient that she herself is emotionally dead. Nevertheless, it may be that the Cotard patient's hypothesis arises as an attempt to accept as veridical experiences of globally flattened affect, in which it seems to the patient that nothing has any significance for her and even that she is disembodied (Gerrans, this volume). From an initial delusional hypothesis, the patient might take one or two steps of non-conservative elaboration to arrive at the claim that she is not a real person or that she is dead.

The account, third (B), of how the hypothesis is adopted and maintained as a belief and, fourth (C), of why the delusion remains relatively circumscribed is as before.

6.3 The Fregoli Delusion

Patients suffering from the Fregoli delusion believe that they keep seeing someone close to them, perhaps their mother or brother, wherever they go or that they are being followed around by people who are known to them but who are unrecognizable because they are in disguise. In such a case, it is quite plausible to propose, first (E), that the patient has a heightened affective response even to unfamiliar faces (Ramachandran and Blakeslee, 1998, p. 171). When he sees someone whom he does not know and therefore cannot recognize he nevertheless experiences a sense of familiarity. Second (H), a hypothesis is generated: 'These are people whom I know but they are in disguise.' There are two possible accounts of how this happens.

On one account, the hypothesis is generated to explain the patient's unusual experience. The hypothesis that they are people known to the patient explains the affective response; the hypothesis that they are in disguise explains the fact that the patient does not recognize them. This candidate is then prioritized over other explanatory hypotheses by an attributional bias. On the other account, the representational character of the patient's experience when seeing someone unfamiliar is correctly described by saying that it seems to the patient that this is someone whom he knows but does not recognize. He accepts these experiences as veridical and then slightly elaborates the delusion into the claim that he does not recognize these people because they are in disguise.

The account (B and C) of how the hypothesis is adopted and maintained as a belief and of why the delusion is not further elaborated is as before.

6.4 Mirrored-Self Misidentification and Mirror Agnosia

Some patients believe that the person they see in the mirror is not really them. But there seem to be rather different ways in which the same delusional belief may arise. In principle, mirrored-self misidentification might perhaps be explained along similar lines to the Capgras delusion. However, mirrored-self misidentification can occur without the suspiciousness that is characteristic of Capgras patients. One case reported in detail by Nora Breen and her colleagues (Breen et al., this volume) involves a patient (FE) with apparent right hemisphere damage and a problem with face recognition, prosopagnosia. FE believes that the person he sees in the mirror is not him but someone else who looks very much like him. A possible account of FE's case would be along the following lines. First (E), as a result of his brain damage, FE has anomalous experiences of familiar faces. When he looks in the mirror, the face that he sees looks quite like his but not exactly like his as he remembers it. Second (H), an obvious hypothesis is generated: The person in the mirror is someone else, not him. Then the third (B) and fourth (C) steps in the account – how the hypothesis is adopted and maintained as a belief and why the delusion is not further elaborated – would be as in the first three examples.

Breen and her colleagues also report a second case of mirrored-self misidentification, but in this case the patient (TH) has intact face processing. TH's problem is, rather, a loss of his understanding of mirrors (mirror agnosia). A possible account of TH's case would be along the following lines. First, when TH witnesses events in a mirror it seems to him that those events are happening in a separate location from the location of the events that are going on in front of the mirror. So when he sees himself in the mirror, it seems to him that this is someone who looks just like him but is in a different location from him. Second, accepting his perceptual experience as veridical he supposes that the person that he is seeing is in a different location from him and concludes that the person cannot be him. The account would then continue along familiar lines.

6.5 Reduplicative Paramnesia

Patients suffering from reduplicative paramnesia believe that there are doubles of known people or places. For example, patient FE came to believe that his wife, Alison, was (so to speak) two people. One Alison was indeed his wife while 'the other Alison' was the mother of his children.[37]

In another case that is described by Breen and her colleagues (this volume), a patient (DB) who knew that her husband had been dead for several years came to believe, following a stroke in the right parietal lobe, that her husband was nevertheless in the same hospital where she was being treated.[38] The medical condition of this patient was complex and she had a further delusional belief to the effect that she was able to use her left arm although in reality it was paralysed following the stroke. But in a speculative spirit we suggest that the reduplicative paramnesia for her husband might be explained as being the result, in part, of an anomalous experience of unfamiliar faces similar to that of a Fregoli patient. We suggest that, because of a deficit in DB's belief revision system, the delusional hypothesis that her husband was present in the hospital was not rejected. It was adopted and maintained as a belief even though DB also believed (correctly) that her husband was dead and despite the fact that she could recount the events surrounding his death and their consequences. We suggest, finally, that as a result of motivational factors DB's delusion about her husband remained relatively unelaborated.

6.6 Unilateral Neglect

Patients who suffer from left unilateral neglect, often following a stroke to the right parietal lobe, are indifferent to objects and events in the left side of their world, including sometimes the left side of their own bodies. A unilateral neglect patient may believe that his left limbs are not his own. If his left arm

---

[37] This is not, however, a straightforward case of duplication as FE believed that 'the other Alison' was not his wife Alison but could be mistaken for her. This is something like the idea that 'the other Alison' was an impostor.

[38] Someone might query whether this should really be classified as a case of reduplicative paramnesia; it might be said that believing that a husband who is long dead is also present and alive is not quite the same as believing in duplicates. In fact, the classification of cases is not crucial for our purposes. But we accept the classification of this case as reduplicative paramnesia by analogy with an imagined case in which the patient knows that her husband migrated to Canada long ago and is currently living there but also believes that her husband is present in the hospital in Sydney. It is worth noting that DB did have just such a pair of beliefs about her daughter. She knew that her daughter lived a considerable distance away but also believed that her daughter worked each day in the hospital kitchen, even while acknowledging that this combination of employment and domestic arrangements would be impossible for any one person.

is pricked with a pin, for example, then he may believe that it is actually his right arm that has been pricked. A neglect patient may even believe that his left limbs belong to someone else. In a memorable example reported by Eduardo Bisiach (1988, p. 469), a patient who insisted that his hand was the examiner's responded to the question, 'Ever see a man with *three* hands?' with: 'A hand is the extremity of an arm. Since you have three arms it follows that you must have three hands.' This belief is a case of monothematic and circumscribed delusion following brain injury.

It seems plausible that part of the basis of a patient's belief that his left arm is not really his is the paralysis, and loss of kinaesthetic and proprioceptive experience of the arm, immediately following his stroke. But (as we noted in section 2) many patients suffer from paralysis of the left arm after a stroke without becoming deluded. So there must be some additional factor at work. Unilateral neglect is not well understood and we shall not be offering any account of the relationship between neglect and the delusion. But it does seem that our four-step schematic account can be applied. We might assume, first (E), that as a result of damage to the right side of the brain the patient has anomalous experiences of the paralysed left side of his body. Second (H), a hypothesis is generated: His left limbs do not exist or are not really his. The hypothesis might be a prioritized attempt at explaining this strange experience or it might just be the result of accepting anomalous bodily experiences as veridical. Third (B), because of a deficit in the belief revision system the hypothesis is retained rather than being rejected, despite the fact that it conflicts with many of the patient's other beliefs, such as the belief that people do not usually go around with other people's arms attached to them. Fourth (C), for reasons given already, the delusion remains relatively unelaborated.

7. Extending the Account: Schizophrenic Delusions

Delusions are one of the characteristic symptoms of schizophrenia.[39] Some of the delusions suffered by schizophrenic patients are extreme cases of florid delusions; some are delusions that we have already considered such as the Capgras and Cotard delusions. But two delusions that are particularly associated with schizophrenia and to which our account might apply are the alien control delusion and the thought insertion delusion (the last two on the list of eight at the beginning). In the delusion of alien control, a patient believes that someone else is able to control his actions. In the delusion of thought insertion, a patient believes that someone else's thoughts are being inserted into her mind.

These delusions are among the so-called positive symptoms of schizo-

---

[39]   *DSM-IV* (APA, 1994, pp. 285–6) requires two or more characteristic (Criterion A) symptoms for a diagnosis of schizophrenia, but allows that 'Only one Criterion A symptom is required if delusions are bizarre'. There are other criteria having to do with social or occupational dysfunction, with duration, and with exclusion of other possible diagnoses.

phrenia, along with other delusions, such as persecutory delusions, and hallucinations, particularly auditory hallucinations. The delusions of alien control and of thought insertion are sometimes called 'passivity phenomena' because they involve the denial of one's own agency (alien control) or initiation (thought insertion). If these delusions are to be brought within the scope of our schematic account then the key step is the first. We need to identify an anomalous experience that might prompt the generation of the delusional hypothesis. For the most part, the anomalous experiences that we have considered up to this point have been experiences resulting from perceptual or affective deficits. Now we need to allow for anomalies in our experience of intentional action and thought itself.

One of the most important ideas in recent research on schizophrenia has been that aspects of our experience of thought and agency may be underpinned by mechanisms of self-monitoring and particularly by comparisons that involve efference copies (Feinberg, 1978; Frith, 1992, ch. 5). We are all familiar with the idea that the brain makes use of a copy of the motor instruction sent to the muscles of the eye in order to make a prediction about the way in which the retinal array will change. Information about the actual change in the retinal array is then compared with this prediction. Where the actual change in the retinal array is as predicted it is 'cancelled' and the visual image remains stable. But, where there is a mismatch between the actual change and the change predicted on the basis of the motor instruction, this is interpreted visually as a shift in the world. This kind of shift is experienced if an eye movement is produced in a way that does not involve motor instructions to the muscles of the eye or if a motor instruction is issued but the eye does not move because of paralysis. In the absence of external manipulation of the eye or of paralysis, these comparisons based on efference copies permit discrimination between changes in us (an eye movement to the right) and changes in the world (a shift to the left).[40]

Copies of motor instructions, efference copies, play other roles as well. For example, comparison between the position of a limb as predicted on the basis of an efference copy and the actual position of the limb according to visual or proprioceptive feedback can be used in the development of motor skills. Information about the difference between predicted position and actual position can be used to update the mapping on which the prediction rests, namely, the mapping between target limb positions and motor instructions.[41] Once

---

[40]   For a great deal more detail about eye position signals, see e.g. Jeannerod, 1988, ch. 4. For the notion of efference copy, see von Holst and Mittelstaedt, 1950; for the virtually identical notion of corollary discharge, see Sperry, 1950; for an authoritative review, see Jeannerod. 1997, ch. 6.

[41]   The motor instructions are determined, not just by the target limb positions, but by the target positions together with the current positions. Also, it is useful, here, to distinguish between the generation of motor instructions conceived as codes and the actual initiation of muscle movements achieved by sending the instructions from primary motor cortex to

that mapping has been learned, comparison between predicted limb position and target limb position allows revision of motor instructions in the light of changes in the position of a target object, without any need to wait for feedback information. Also, comparison between predicted limb position (according to the efference copy) and actual limb position (according to feedback information) can again serve as the basis for discrimination between changes that result from us and changes that result from the world.

Nielsen (1963) describes some experiments in which subjects are provided with misleading visual feedback about the movement of their hand. Normal subjects reach through a hole in a box and, using a pencil held in a gloved hand, try to follow a straight line that is printed on a sheet of paper. Subjects do not know that on some trials the hand that they see is not their own hand but the similarly gloved hand of the experimenter's assistant reflected in a mirror. The crucial trials are those in which the assistant traces about half way along the line and then starts deviating towards the right (as seen by the subject). On such trials, subjects typically produce a line (which they do not see, of course) deviating to the left. Of particular interest for our present purposes are subjects' reports of their own experiences under these experimental conditions. While the assistant's hand traced along the line, making the same movement as the subject's hand, the subject had a normal experience of controlling his or her hand movement. But, as the assistant's hand deviated from the straight line, this experience changed (1963, pp. 228–9):

> On several occasions five [out of twenty] subjects spontaneously described that they directly felt that something outside themselves was pushing their hand towards the right or was resisting the free mobility of their hand. Ten other subjects declared on some occasions that they felt that their hand was sliding towards the right in a passive way.

Nielsen goes on to report how these subjects tried to explain their anomalous experience (1963, p. 229): '[The five subjects] suggested that "magnets", "unidentified forces", "invisible traces under the paper", or the like could be the cause.' Most subjects offered explanations in terms of environmental factors though '[some subjects] experienced right away that something was wrong with themselves and this alarmed them' (ibid.).

It seems that, in most of these subjects, a mismatch between hand position according to the prediction based on an efference copy and hand position according to visual feedback gave rise to an experience of something in the

---

the spinal cord and thence to the muscles. When we engage in motor imagery without actual muscle movement, motor instructions are apparently generated in pre-motor cortex and mapped to changes in limb position, even though no instructions are actually sent out to initiate movement. See Jeannerod, 1997, ch. 4. and Currie and Ravenscroft, 1997, for discussions of motor imagery.

environment robbing them of control of the movement of their hand. They reported that 'they did not cause the bend to the right on purpose' (ibid.).

7.1 Alien Control

In order to apply our four-step (EHBC) account of the aetiology of delusions to the delusion of alien control, we need to identify an anomalous experience that might prompt the generation of the delusional hypothesis. Comparisons involving efference copies could, of course, occur in an information-processing system from which consciousness was quite absent. But it does not seem absurd to suppose that our experience of our actions as initiated by ourselves depends in some way on information processing that involves efference copies.

The experimental results from Nielsen (1963) suggest that a cognitive abnormality, either in the generation of the efference copy or in the comparison between the efference copy and feedback information, might give rise to anomalous experiences of actions. The subject would be aware of trying to move his arm, say, in a particular way, but it would seem to the subject that the arm was being moved in a different way by some external force. We can also speculate that a more dramatic abnormality, in which no efference copy is even available for comparison, could give rise to anomalous experiences of a different kind. In this case, it might seem to the subject that his arm is moving, not of his own volition (since no efference copy is detected), but not exactly as the result of an external force either (since there is no definite mismatch between an efference copy and feedback information). It might seem to the subject that his arm is moving as the result of an agency that is not his own. It is fairly plausible that accepting experiences of one or other of these kinds as veridical would be a step on the way to the delusion of alien control.[42]

In terms of our four-step schematic account, first (E), a cognitive abnormality related to efference copies gives rise to an anomalous experience, perhaps of an external force or an unknown agency, or perhaps simply of lack of the subject's own volition. Second (H), a hypothesis is generated. The subject accepts the anomalous experience as veridical, and then elaborates the hypothesis that is thus prioritized by offering some more determinate account of the nature of the agency that is at work. Third (B), as the result of a deficit in

---

[42]   Spence et al., 1997, used neural imaging (PET) to investigate the neural basis of the experiences that give rise to the delusion of alien control. Seven schizophrenic patients who experienced passivity phenomena were scanned while they made voluntary movements using a joystick. Patients' descriptions of their phenomenology during PET scanning included (p. 2001): 'I felt like an automaton, guided by a female spirit who had entered me'; 'I thought you [the experimenter] were varying the movements with your thoughts'; and 'The spirits were moving my shoulder'. The brains of patients experiencing passivity phenomena showed hyperactivity in regions including the right inferior parietal lobule and the cingulate gyrus. Spence et al. note that other authors, including e.g. Cutting, 1989, have suggested the right parietal lobe as the possible origin of 'alienation' where this condition is characterized by qualities of detachment, 'non-belongingness' or spatial dislocation.

belief revision, the hypothesis is adopted and maintained as a belief despite its implausibility in the light of other things that the subject believes. Fourth (C), adoption and maintenance of the delusional hypothesis might be achieved without a major upheaval in the subject's belief system.

This fourth step figures in our account because we began from Stone and Young's suggestion about the aetiology of monothematic and circumscribed delusions. Stone and Young quite explicitly do not propose to apply their suggestion to more florid schizophrenic delusions. But it is consistent with the four-step account to allow that sometimes the motivational factors that support circumscription may fail. In such a case a subject may move in the direction of substantial and even disastrous doxastic disruption.

7.2 Some Other Symptoms of Schizophrenia

Before moving on to the delusion of thought insertion, we pause briefly to speculate on the possibility that abnormalities in the cognitive mechanisms implicated in comparisons involving efference copies may play a role in the aetiology of other schizophrenic symptoms.

Suppose, for example, that shifting the direction of one's attention can be regarded as analogous to moving one's arm. Then there would be room for two kinds of anomalous experiences involving attention. One would be an experience in which the subject's attention seems to be dragged somewhere by something external. The other would be an experience in which it seems to the subject that his attention shifts not of his own volition but not exactly as the result of an external attraction either. Perhaps it seems to shift under the control of a will other than his own. The first of these anomalous experiences might give rise, through a process of explanatory elaboration, to the hypothesis that there is something attention-claiming, such as people talking about the subject, going on at a particular location. It is possible that this kind of experience might play a role in the aetiology of delusions of reference in which the patient believes that other people are referring to him (Frith, 1987; Gold and Hohwy, this volume).

Suppose too that somewhat the same structure of comparisons is present in the mental activity of imagining hearing speech in one's own natural language. Someone might imagine, for example, hearing the critical voice of a parent. If an analogy between the activity of imagining hearing speech and the activity of moving one's arm can be made out at all then it might be that a cognitive abnormality could give rise to an impression of alien control of the words heard in one's mind. So it is conceivable that there may be the resources here to provide an outline account of certain anomalous experiences that are characteristic of schizophrenia, namely, auditory hallucinations (hearing voices) and of delusions that arise from those hallucinations.[43]

---

[43]   One complication here is that there is not literally any auditory feedback information to be compared with a prediction based on an efference copy. For a detailed account of auditory

7.3 Thought Insertion

Imagining hearing speech is different from imagining speaking, and inner speech can itself be of various kinds. Inner verbalized idle speculation is different from inner verbalized story telling and from inner verbalized serious thinking in pursuit of the truth, for example. Perhaps a cognitive abnormality related to efference copies could give rise to impressions of loss of control over one's inner speech. So it might seem to a subject that an external force, or an unknown agency, is causing him to experience inner speech. It might also be that a subject's impression of verbalized serious thinking that is directed by a will other than his own is different from an impression of verbalized story telling or verbalized idle speculation that is under alien control. An anomalous experience of the first kind might play a role in the aetiology of the delusion that verbalized thoughts are being inserted into the subject's mind.

Thinking itself is carried out, at least sometimes, as part of some specific intellectual project. I might set out to think through the consequences of some proposition P that I am inclined to believe, checking those consequences for plausibility in the light of a further battery of knowledge. As I carry out this project, information about the course of my actual thinking is, presumably, checked against my original intention. But then there is the possibility that my actual thinking might fail to measure up to my intention or indeed that there might be no record of that intention available for comparison. Given what has already been said about the experience of alien control, it is at least conceivable that this kind of mismatch or comparison failure would be experienced as serious thought about P and its consequences taking place in my mind yet without being intended or initiated by me.[44] An anomalous experience of that kind could play a role as the first step in the aetiology of the delusion of thought insertion; and this could be so quite independently of any equation of thought with inner speech.

8. Conclusion: Delusions and Theory of Mind

At the end of section 5, we outlined a four-step account of the aetiology of monothematic and circumscribed delusions following brain injury: Experience,

---

hallucinations that sets the operation of the 'mind's ear' and the 'mind's voice' against the background of a box-and-arrow model of normal speech perception and production, see David, 1994.

[44] This is intended to be in the spirit of the proposal by Frith, 1992, ch. 5, that the experience of thought insertion arises from a failure of central monitoring. In fact, Frith's account involves two kinds of central monitoring. There is the monitoring of actions, which enables us to distinguish 'changes due to our own actions and changes due to external events' (1992, p. 81); and there is also the monitoring of intentions, which enables us to distinguish 'between actions caused by our own goals and plans (willed actions) and actions that are in response to external events (stimulus-driven actions)' (ibid.). For discussion of Frith's application of these ideas about central monitoring to the case of thought, see Currie, this volume; Gold and Hohwy, this volume; and Campbell, 1999.

Hypothesis, Belief, Circumscription. In that account, the third step is that a hypothesis is adopted and maintained as a belief despite the fact that it is inconsistent with many other things that the subject believes. We suggested, cautiously and provisionally, that this resistance against conflicting considerations might be explained in terms of impairment to, or even abolition of, some component of the cognitive system responsible for belief revision and that this might be a further result of brain injury.[45] In section 6, we applied the EHBC account to examples of frankly neuropsychological delusions and, in section 7, we showed how it might plausibly be extended to certain delusions that occur in schizophrenic patients. The extension of the account to schizophrenic delusions, if it is taken to include the cautious suggestion, involves the claim that at least some patients with schizophrenia have a deficit in the cognitive mechanisms that underpin belief revision.

We have already noted that there is an association between delusions and right hemisphere damage. Furthermore, delusions occur in some patients with unilateral neglect and these patients may have intact left hemispheres. So it seems quite likely that, if there is indeed a belief revision deficit that figures in the aetiology of delusions, then this deficit normally results from damage to the right hemisphere. If the extension of the account to schizophrenic delusions is correct, then in at least some cases of schizophrenia there must be impairment to cognitive functions that are, in normal subjects, subserved by right hemisphere neural mechanisms.

Robyn Langdon and her colleagues (1997) used a picture-sequencing task to assess theory of mind abilities in twenty schizophrenic patients.[46] A subgroup of six patients was found to have a specific problem with the task in those cases where the story involved a character acting on a false belief.[47] Also, in a study of non-clinical adults, Langdon and Coltheart (1999) found that high schizotypal subjects showed specific theory of mind problems that could not be accounted for in terms of either executive planning deficits or failure to inhibit cognitively salient but inappropriate information.[48] Because delusions

---

[45]   See Langdon and Coltheart, this volume, for a more forthright commitment to this proposal.

[46]   We speak of 'theory of mind' abilities without prejudging the question whether the basis of those abilities is a matter of knowing a psychological theory, or being able to engage in mental simulation, or something else.

[47]   These patients were able to put the pictures in the correct order when the stories involved causal relations or social scripts, for example. The remaining fourteen patients either succeeded for all categories of story or else had a general sequencing difficulty and no additional difficulty with false belief stories.

[48]   Experimental work with schizophrenic patients is complicated by the fact that the subjects are typically receiving medication and these antipsychotic drugs themselves have cognitive effects. See Williams et al., 1998, for discussion. However, when the same pattern of task performance is found in patients who are receiving medication and in non-clinical high schizotypal subjects (who are not receiving medication) this supports the hypothesis that the patients' performance is not just a result of their medication.

are one of the characteristic symptoms of schizophrenia,[49] these findings are at least suggestive of an association between delusions and theory of mind problems in schizophrenic patients.

Langdon and her colleagues (1997) did not, in fact, find any correlation between reality distortion symptoms such as delusions and hallucinations, on the one hand, and membership of the subgroup of schizophrenic patients with specific theory of mind problems, on the other.[50] But that lack of correlation is consistent with the speculation that there is a common factor in the aetiologies of both delusions and theory of mind problems. Perhaps there is some cognitive function that is implicated in normal belief revision and also in the understanding of false belief stories.

If there is a cognitive function whose impairment is a factor in the aetiology of delusions then, we have already said, it is plausible that it is normally subserved by right hemisphere neural mechanisms. So it is of some interest that Francesca Happé and her colleagues (1999) report theory of mind problems in patients who have suffered right hemisphere strokes.

In this study, fourteen right hemisphere stroke patients (average age 64 years) and a group of healthy elderly control subjects were given short passages to read, with a question after each passage. When the passage was a theory of mind story, giving a correct answer to the question involved making an inference about the thoughts, intentions or feelings of a character in the story. When the passage was a non-mental story, answering the question correctly involved making an inference about, for example, physical causation. The right hemisphere stroke patients scored less well than controls on the theory of mind stories but not on the non-mental stories. Also, the right hemisphere patients scored less well on theory of mind stories than on non-mental stories, whereas this was not so for control subjects. In addition, five left hemisphere stroke patients were tested on modified versions of the tasks and had no greater difficulty with the theory of mind stories than with the non-mental stories.[51]

These results are consistent with the idea that some cognitive function that is required for success on theory of mind tasks is normally subserved by right hemisphere neural mechanisms. It is also consistent, therefore, with the speculation that there is some cognitive function, normally subserved by right hemi-

---

[49] The presence of delusions is virtually sufficient for a diagnosis of schizophrenia if the delusions are of the bizarre variety (see again note 39).

[50] However, Doody et al., 1998, found significant correlations between performance on (relatively difficult) theory of mind tasks and ratings of positive symptoms such as delusions and hallucinations. Also, Drury, Robinson and Birchwood, 1998, found poor theory of mind performance when schizophrenic patients were in acute episodes (characterized by delusions, hallucinations and bizarre speech or behaviour) but not when the patients had recovered from acute episodes.

[51] The tasks had to be modified because left hemisphere patients typically have impaired language.

sphere structures, that is crucial both for normal belief revision and for theory of mind abilities.[52]

This is just a speculation and the reality may be much less interesting. It may be, for example, that there are mechanisms that are implicated in belief revision and functionally quite distinct mechanisms that are involved in theory of mind abilities. Perhaps these mechanisms are neuroanatomically close to each other in the right hemisphere so that right hemisphere damage or dysfunction sometimes leads to co-occurrence of delusions and theory of mind problems. Even if there is a cognitive common factor in some cases of these co-occurring symptoms, the line of thought that we have been exploring is complicated by the fact that we cannot assume that theory of mind problems have the same basis across different groups of subjects.

In this context, it is a striking fact that deaf children of hearing parents show performance on theory of mind tasks much like that of autistic children. Peterson and Siegal (this volume) propose that this is because deaf children of hearing parents have very limited opportunities for conversation with their parents. Because of the absence of a shared language between child and parents, topics of conversation are restricted to things that are perceptibly present and there is little discussion of more abstract matters such as beliefs, emotions and reasons for action. This means that deaf children of hearing parents are deprived of the cognitive input that would normally play a role in the development of everyday psychological understanding and theory of mind abilities.[53]

Despite these complications, it may be that there is a cognitive common factor involved in both some cases of delusions and some cases of theory of mind problems. So it is important to consider how alternative theories of everyday psychological understanding (including understanding of false beliefs) might account for the co-occurrence of those symptoms. Frith (1992) suggests that both delusions and theory of mind problems flow from impairments to the mechanisms of meta-representation (Leslie, 1987, 1994). Currie (this volume) criticizes this suggestion and proposes that delusions may arise from a disorder of imagination in which what is imagined is mistaken for what is believed. According to the simulation theory of everyday psychological understanding,

---

[52]   The stroke patients investigated by Happé and her colleagues were not delusional. So if there is some right hemisphere cognitive function that is implicated in normal belief revision and also in the understanding of false belief stories then impairment of that function is not sufficient, by itself, for the production of delusions.

[53]   Peterson and Siegal, this volume, also observe that the situation is quite different in the case of deaf children who grow up with signing deaf parents. These children, who are 'native signers', develop theory of mind abilities at the same age as children with normal hearing. Paul Harris proposes, 1996, p. 211, 'that children learn about thoughts and beliefs in the context of conversation' and notes the prediction that 'children with limited or delayed exposure to conversation (e.g. deaf children) should show difficulties on tests of belief understanding' (1996, p. 220).

of course, imagination would also be a vital factor in successful performance on false belief tasks.

The occurrence of theory of mind problems in patients with a psychiatric diagnosis characterized by delusions may turn out to pose an important challenge for theories of everyday psychological understanding. But in order to judge the success of competing theories in measuring up to the challenge we first need to investigate the nature of delusions themselves. Our aim has been to offer a framework for that investigation.

References

American Psychiatric Association 1994: *Diagnostic and Statistical Manual of Mental Disorders*, Fourth Edition (*DSM-IV*). Washington, DC: American Psychiatric Association.

Benson, D.F., Gardner, H. and Meadows, J.C. 1976: Reduplicative paramnesia. *Neurology*, 26, 147–51.

Bentall, R.P. 1994: Cognitive biases and abnormal beliefs: Towards a model of persecutory delusions. In A.S. David and J.C. Cutting (eds), *The Neuropsychology of Schizophrenia*. Hove, E. Sussex: Psychology Press, 337–60.

Bentall, R.P. and Kinderman, P. 1998: Psychological processes and delusional beliefs: Implications for the treatment of paranoid states. In T. Wykes, N. Tarrier and S. Lewis, *Outcome and Innovation in the Psychological Treatment of Schizophrenia*. Chichester: John Wiley and Sons, 119–44.

Bermúdez, J.L. Forthcoming: Normativity and rationality in psychiatric disorders.

Berrios, G.E. 1991: Delusions as 'wrong beliefs': A conceptual history. *British Journal of Psychiatry*, 159, 6–13.

Berrios, G.E. and Luque, R. 1995: Cotard's syndrome: Analysis of 100 cases. *Acta Psychiatrica Scandinavica*, 91, 185–8.

Bisiach, E. 1988: Language without thought. In L. Weiskrantz (ed.), *Thought Without Language*. Oxford University Press, 464–84.

Campbell, J. 1999: Schizophrenia, the space of reasons, and thinking as a motor process. *The Monist*, 82, 609–25.

Capgras, J. and Carrette, P. 1924: Illusion des sosies et complexe d'Oedipe. *Annales Médico-Psychologiques*, 12, 48–68.

Capgras, J. and Reboul-Lachaux, J. 1923: L'illusion des 'sosies' dans un délire systématisé chronique. *Bulletin de la Société Clinique de Médecine Mentale*, 11, 6–16.

Cherniak, C. 1986: *Minimal Rationality*. Cambridge, MA: MIT Press.

Church, J. 1987: Reasonable irrationality. *Mind*, 96, 354–66.

Cotard, J. 1882: Du délire des négations. *Archives de Neurologie*, 4, 152–70, 282–95.

Courbon, P. and Fail, G. 1927: Syndrome d'"illusion de Fregoli' et schizophrenie. *Bulletin de la Société Clinique de Médecine Mentale*, 20, 121–5

Currie, G. and Ravenscroft, I. 1997: Mental simulation and motor imagery. *Philosophy of Science*, 64, 161–80.

Cutting, J. 1989: Body image disorders: Comparison between unilateral hemisphere damage and schizophrenia. *Behavioural Neurology*, 2, 210–10.

David, A.S. 1994: The neuropsychological origin of auditory hallucinations. In A.S. David and J.C. Cutting (eds), *The Neuropsychology of Schizophrenia*. Hove, E. Sussex: Psychology Press, 269–313.

Davidson, D. 1984: *Inquiries into Truth and Interpretation*. Oxford University Press.

de Pauw, K.W., Szulecka, T.K. and Poltock, T.L. 1987: Fregoli syndrome after cerebral infarction. *Journal of Nervous and Mental Diseases*, 175, 433–8.

Dennett, D.C. 1981: Brain writing and mind reading. In *Brainstorms: Philosophical Essays on Mind and Psychology*. Brighton: Harvester Press, 39–50.

Dennett, D.C. 1987: *The Intentional Stance*. Cambridge, MA: MIT Press.

Doody, G.A., Gotz, E.C., Johnstone, E.C., Frith, C.D. and Cunningham Owens, D.G. 1998: Theory of mind and psychosis. *Psychological Medicine*, 28, 397–405.

Drury, V.M., Robinson, E.J. and Birchwood, M. 1998: 'Theory of mind' skills during an acute episode of psychosis and following recovery. *Psychological Medicine*, 28, 1101–12.

Eilan, N. 2000: On understanding schizophrenia. In D. Zahavi and J. Parnas (eds), *Exploring the Self: Philosophical and Psychopathological Perspectives on Self Experience*. Amsterdam: John Benjamins.

Ellis, H.D. and de Pauw, K.W. 1994: The cognitive neuropsychiatric origins of the Capgras delusion. In A.S. David and J.C. Cutting (eds), *The Neuropsychology of Schizophrenia*. Hove, E. Sussex: Psychology Press, 317–35.

Ellis, H.D., Whitley, J. and Luauté, J.P. 1994: Delusional misidentification: The three original papers on the Capgras, Fregoli and intermetamorphosis delusions. *History of Psychiatry*, 5, 117–46.

Ellis, H.D. and Young, A.W. 1990: Accounting for delusional misidentifications. *British Journal of Psychiatry*, 157, 239–48.

Ellis, H.D., Young, A.W., Quayle, A.H. and de Pauw, K.W. 1997: Reduced autonomic responses to faces in Capgras delusion. *Proceedings of the Royal Society: Biological Sciences*, B264, 1085–92.

Enoch, M.D. and Trethowan, W.H. 1991: *Uncommon Psychiatric Syndromes*, 3rd edn. Oxford: Butterworth-Heinemann.

Feinberg, I. 1978: Efference copy and corollary discharge: Implications for thinking and its disorders. *Schizophrenia Bulletin*, 4, 636–40.

Festinger, L. 1957: *A Theory of Cognitive Dissonance*. Stanford, CA: Stanford University Press.

Fodor, J. 1987: *Psychosemantics: The Problem of Meaning in the Philosophy of Mind*. Cambridge, MA: MIT Press.

Foley, J.M. and Breslau, L. 1982: A new syndrome of delusional misidentification. *Annals of Neurology*, 12, 76.

Förstl, H., Almeida, O.P., Owen, A.M., Burns, A. and Howard, R. 1991: Psychiatric, neurological and medical aspects of misidentification syndromes: A review of 260 cases. *Psychological Medicine*, 21, 905–10.

Frith, C.D. 1987: The positive and negative symptoms of schizophrenia reflect impairments in the perception and initiation of action. *Psychological Medicine*, 17, 631–48.

Frith, C.D. 1992: *The Cognitive Neuropsychology of Schizophrenia*. Hove, E. Sussex: Lawrence Erlbaum Associates.

Garety, P.A. and Hemsley, D.R. 1994: *Delusions: Investigations into the Psychology of Delusional Reasoning*. Oxford University Press. (Reprinted, Hove, E. Sussex: Psychology Press, 1997.)

Garety, P.A., Hemsley, D.R. and Wessely, S. 1991: Reasoning in deluded schizophrenic and paranoid patients: Biases in performance on a probabilistic inference task. *Journal of Nervous and Mental Disease*, 179, 194–201.

Gendler, T.S. 2000: The puzzle of imaginative resistance. *Journal of Philosophy*, 97, 55–81.

Happé, F., Brownell, H. and Winner, E. 1999: Acquired 'theory of mind' impairments following stroke. *Cognition*, 70, 211–40

Harris, P.L. 1996: Desires, beliefs, and language. In P. Carruthers and P.K. Smith (eds), *Theories of Theories of Mind*. Cambridge University Press, 200–20.

Higgins, E.T. 1987: Self-discrepancy: A theory relating self and affect. *Psychological Review*, 94, 319–40.

Hirstein, W. and Ramachandran, V.S. 1997: Capgras syndrome: A novel probe for understanding the neural representation of the identity and familiarity of persons. *Proceedings of the Royal Society: Biological Sciences*, B264, 437–44.

Huq, S.F., Garety, P.A. and Hemsley, D.R. 1988: Probabilistic judgements in deluded and non-deluded subjects. *Quarterly Journal of Experimental Psychology*, 40A, 801–12.

Jaspers, K. 1963: *General Psychopathology*, trans. J. Hoenig and M.W. Hamilton. Manchester: Manchester University Press.

Jeannerod, M. 1988: *The Neural and Behavioural Organization of Goal-Directed Movements*. Oxford University Press.

Jeannerod, M. 1997: *The Cognitive Neuroscience of Action*. Oxford: Blackwell Publishers.

Kaney, S. and Bentall, R.P. 1989: Persecutory delusions and attributional style. *British Journal of Medical Psychology*, 62, 191–8.

Kaney, S. and Bentall, R.P. 1992: Persecutory delusions and the self-serving bias. *Journal of Nervous and Mental Disease*, 180, 773–80

Kinderman, P. 1994: Attentional bias, persecutory delusions and the self concept. *British Journal of Medical Psychology*, 67, 53–66.

Langdon, R. and Coltheart, M. 1999: Mentalising, schizotypy, and schizophrenia. *Cognition*, 71, 43–71.

Langdon, R., Michie, P.T., Ward, P.B., McConaghy, N., Catts, S. and Coltheart, M. 1997: Defective self and/or other mentalizing in schizophrenia: A cognitive neuropsychological approach. *Cognitive Neuropsychiatry*, 2, 167–93.

Leslie, A.M. 1987: Pretense and representation: The origins of 'theory of mind'. *Psychological Review*, 94, 412–26.

Leslie, A.M. 1994: Pretending and believing: Issues in the theory of ToMM. *Cognition*, 50, 211–38.

Lewis, D. 1986: *On the Plurality of Worlds*. Oxford University Press.

Lyon, H.M., Kaney, S. and Bentall, R.P. 1994: The defensive function of persecutory delusions: Evidence from attribution tasks. *British Journal of Psychiatry*, 164, 637–46.

Mackie, J., Ebmeier, K.P. and O'Carroll, R.E. 1994: An MRI, SPECT and neuropsychological study of a patient presenting with Capgras syndrome. *Behavioural Neurology*, 7, 211–15.

Maher, B.A. 1974: Delusional thinking and perceptual disorder. *Journal of Individual Psychology*, 30, 98–113.

Maher, B.A. 1988: Anomalous experience and delusional thinking: The logic of explanations. In T.F. Oltmanns and B.A. Maher (eds), *Delusional Beliefs*. Chichester: John Wiley and Sons, 15–33.

Maher, B.A. 1992: Delusions: Contemporary etiological hypotheses. *Psychiatric Annals*, 22, 260–8.

Nielsen, T.I. 1963: Volition: A new experimental approach. *Scandinavian Journal of Psychology*, 4, 225–30.

Ramachandran, V.S. and Blakeslee, S. 1998: *Phantoms in the Brain: Human Nature and the Architecture of the Mind*. London: Fourth Estate.

Spence, S.A., Brooks, D.J., Hirsch, S.R., Liddle, P.F., Meehan, J. and Grasby, P.M. 1997: A PET study of voluntary movement in schizophrenic patients experiencing passivity phenomena (delusions of alien control). *Brain*, 120, 1997–2011.

Sperry, R.W. 1950: Neural basis of the spontaneous optokinetic response produced by visual inversion. *Journal of Comparative and Physiological Psychology*, 43, 482–9.

Stone, T. and Young, A.W. 1997: Delusions and brain injury: The philosophy and psychology of belief. *Mind and Language*, 12, 327–64.

Tranel, D., Damasio, H. and Damasio, A.R. 1995: Double dissociation between overt and covert recognition. *Journal of Cognitive Neuroscience*, 7, 425–32.

von Holst, E. and Mittelstaedt, H. 1950: Das Reafferenzprinzip: Wechselwirkungen zwischen Zentralnervensystem und Peripherie. *Naturwissenschaften*, 37, 464–76.

Williams, J.H., Wellman, N.A., Geaney, D.P., Cowen, P.J., Feldon, J. and Rawlins, J.N.P. 1998: Reduced latent inhibition in people with schizophrenia: An effect of psychosis or of its treatment. *British Journal of Psychiatry*, 172, 243–9.

2

Wondrous Strange: The Neuropsychology of Abnormal Beliefs

ANDREW W. YOUNG

1. Preview

Psychiatric diagnostic manuals usually define delusions in terms of a combination of their implausibility to other people with a similar cultural background and their resistance to counter-suggestion or obvious evidence to the contrary (see Langdon and Coltheart, this volume). Although this may seem straightforward in principle, many of the beliefs considered to be delusions do not meet these criteria (or are not tested against them) in practice (Maher, 1988). For example, persecutory delusions often involve claims about people spying, conspiring, stealing things, or similar events which could indeed be occurring. Despite this, there is often no attempt to check whether such things actually are happening to people who say they are being persecuted. Instead, it is usual for the intuitive implausibility of a belief to medical staff to form the primary yardstick, and it is often regarded immediately as a delusion because this possibility fits with other presenting symptoms.

Some of the delusions that can follow brain injury come close to the psychiatric ideal of false beliefs held despite what others take as incontrovertible counter-evidence. Using the Capgras delusion (the delusion that certain other people, who are usually close relatives, have been replaced by impostors) as the most thoroughly researched example, I will point out similarities between the subjective accounts, brain injuries, and cognitive test performances of people who experience this delusion. These common features can be developed into a simple account of critical components in the pathogenesis of the Capgras delusion which treats this delusion as resulting from the patient's attempt to make sense of abnormal perceptual experiences in which things seem strange and devoid of affective significance (Ellis and Young, 1990; Ellis, Young, Quayle and de Pauw, 1997). This approach puts the patients' accounts of their experiences back into a prominent position among the facts needing explanation (cf. Breen et al., this volume). It also brings together a number

I am very grateful to participants in the workshop held at Macquarie University in July/August 1998 for helpful discussion of many issues, and especially to Max Coltheart, Greg Currie, Martin Davies and Robyn Langdon.

of clinical features and incorporates otherwise puzzling anomalies, such as the curious clinical overlap between the Capgras delusion and the seemingly unrelated Cotard delusion (the delusional belief that you are dead) noted in several reports (Young, 1998; Young and Leafhead, 1996).

This general approach forms part of what has been characterized as 'cognitive neuropsychiatry' (David, 1993)—the application of the methods and models of cognitive neuropsychology to psychiatric disorders. Its most enthusiastic proponents see cognitive neuropsychiatry as an extension of the logic of cognitive neuropsychology into a new area. In cognitive neuropsychology, cognitive deficits are used to test and refine models of normal cognitive abilities, and in cognitive neuropsychiatry the same process is applied to more 'psychiatric' symptoms. Whilst this position may have merit as an overarching remit, it will need care in working out the details because the ground rules of cognitive neuropsychiatry are not going to be the same as those we have come to know and love from cognitive neuropsychology.

A more reckless project involves using neuropsychiatric phenomena as tests of philosophical positions concerning the nature of beliefs and how these relate to our perception of the world—in some ways, they are like natural analogues of philosophers' 'thought experiments' (Stone and Young, 1997). The claim here is not that neuropsychological or neuropsychiatric findings should *determine* the philosophy of belief and perception—rather, it is simply proposed that there might be some useful symbiosis in which neuropsychiatric phenomena constrain plausible accounts of belief and philosophical theories clarify what we need to explore. A similar general interest in bringing together philosophical and neuropsychiatric studies is shown in other chapters in this volume (Currie; Gerrans; Gold and Hohwy).

To see how neuropsychiatric studies might impact on debates in philosophy, consider the implications of the fact that some of the delusions investigated can be monothematic—as if a single belief has been altered. This does not sit easily with holistic theories that emphasize the importance of an integrated 'web of belief'. For example, Stone and Young (1997) used Dennett's (1981) example of how, if we could ever learn to read and write in brain language, we might insert the false belief that 'I have an older brother living in Cleveland' into someone's brain. He argued that this is a more difficult task than might be thought. If this belief is to be successfully inserted, we would also have to insert answers to questions about the putative brother—'What's your brother's name?', 'How old is he?', 'Is he married?', and so on. Then we would also have to alter other existing true beliefs, for example the belief 'I am an only child'. Dennett (1981, p. 44) concludes that this does not show that wiring in false beliefs is impossible, but that 'one could only wire in one belief by wiring in many (indefinitely many?) other cohering beliefs so that neither biographical nor logical coherence would be lost'.

Delusions do not seem to respect the idea that the belief system forms a coherent whole and that adjustments to one belief will require adjustment to many others. From the standpoint of the web of belief, one might expect that experiencing the Capgras delusion would result in the formation of numerous other false beliefs. A person who thinks their spouse is an impostor should have beliefs about where the original spouse has gone, whether they are alive or dead, how the transformation was effected, and so on. In practice, though, what one finds is that people who experience this delusion may generate answers to some of these questions, but remain detached from or unperturbed by others. Although they have something which can seem in certain respects like a false belief, it need not be integrated into anything like a coherent web.

But to turn the point round and see that philosophy is important too, we need only consider why we ascribe the status of a false *belief* to something as bizarre as the Capgras delusion. The idea of delusions as false beliefs has been challenged, and these challenges can work well for some of the delusions found in schizophrenia. For example, a person who receives a diagnosis of schizophrenia may claim to be Napoleon, yet never issue any orders to his troops. In such cases, one may reasonably question whether this delusion reflects a false belief about the external world, or is better considered to refer only to a privately experienced world (Sass, 1994) or as an empty speech act (Berrios, 1991). I will show why such analyses apply less well to phenomena such as the Capgras delusion, largely because some of these patients do act in ways which can be seen as consistent with their delusion. However, even when patients do seem to act on their delusions, there are often inconsistencies in accompanying affect and a curiously circumscribed quality to the delusion itself. All of these features merit careful consideration and investigation.

2. The Range of Delusions that Can Follow Brain Injury

Throughout this century, delusions have been seen as one of the hallmarks of psychotic disorders, in which a person is said to be out of touch with reality. Yet there has also been abundant evidence that delusions can follow brain injury in a variety of aetiological settings, including strokes, tumours and dementing illnesses. These delusions of neurological patients are as patently absurd, and can be as resistant to counter-evidence, as the delusions found in cases with a less clearly 'organic' aetiology which usually fall within the province of psychiatry.

The classic observations were made by Von Monakow (1885), Anton (1899), and Pick (1903). Von Monakow's and Anton's patients denied having severe sensory or motor deficits, including blindness, deafness and paralysis. Unawareness of disability after brain injury is now known as anosognosia, and the specific problem of denial of blindness is called Anton's syndrome (Förstl, Owen and David, 1993). Patients with Anton's syndrome may behave as if they can see, and even confabulate visual experiences (McGlynn and Schacter, 1989). In cases of anosognosia and Anton's syndrome, the existence of major neurological disabilities is readily apparent to everyone except the patient, and causes them severe daily difficulties. To deny having such incapacitating physical problems clearly meets the psychiatric criteria for a delusion.

Pick (1903) described a different type of delusion after brain injury. His two patients insisted on the existence of duplicate places with nearly identical attributes. Patient 1 'asserted that there were two clinics exactly alike in which he had been, two professors of the same name were at the head of these clinics', and so on. Patient 2, who was in a clinic in Prague, 'imagined she was in K., and in reply to the assistant's question how it was that he was in K. also, she said that she was very pleased to see him *here too*'. Both of Pick's cases were similar in that they thought there were duplicate hospitals; they differed in that for patient 1 the hospital staff and patients had been duplicated as well, whilst when patient 2 was asked how the same staff and patients could be in both clinics she replied that 'They come from one place to the other'.

Since these pioneering reports, there have been many further descriptions of delusional beliefs following brain injury. Here are some recent examples:

A woman who had suffered a right temporo-parietal infarct was convinced that for several months she was pursued by a cunningly-disguised cousin and his female accomplice. She was committed to a mental hospital for her own safety after she started haranguing passers by, who she accused of being her cousin or his accomplice (de Pauw, Szulecka and Poltock, 1987).

A man who had suffered a right hemisphere stroke, with left hemiplegia and left unilateral neglect, mistook a postgraduate student who came to test him for his daughter, and kept her at his house for several hours. When she got home from school he accused his real daughter of lying, stealing someone else's identification, playing truant, and driving a car before she had passed her test (Young, Flude and Ellis, 1991).

A man with bilateral frontal damage and contusions affecting temporo-parietal areas of the right cerebral hemisphere was convinced that he was dead, even though he was able to walk and talk (Young, Robertson, Hellawell, de Pauw and Pentland, 1992).

Following a haematoma in the right basal ganglia, a man thought he had acquired an extra arm, protruding forward from the middle of his body (Halligan and Marshall, 1995).

A man with a pituitary tumour thought that his wife and nephew had been stealing his belongings (Anderson, 1988). He kept a record of over 300 items he believed they had stolen, and claimed that some of these items had been replaced by almost identical but inferior versions.

A man thought that his house and family had been replaced by duplicates after he sustained right temporal and bilateral frontal brain damage in a traffic accident (Alexander, Stuss and Benson, 1979).

A woman who suffered a right hemisphere stroke developed the delusion that she was in a second-floor hospital ward, even though she knew she was in a single-storey building (Halligan and Marshall, 1994).

Even from this brief list, it is apparent that the content of such delusions may involve anything that can form a focus of concern for a human being: the person's body (thinking that you have an extra arm), the environment (thinking that you are somewhere other than where everyone around you claims to be), the self (thinking that you are dead), personal possessions (being stolen or replaced), or other people (thinking that people are not who they say they are).

A particularly intriguing feature of the delusions is that they can be circumscribed and specific. It thus seems unlikely that they can be attributed to any global impairment of mental function, and in fact patients can have insight into the absurdity of their delusions, even though they are subjectively convincing. For example, Alexander's patient (Alexander et al., 1979) recognized that his claim that his house and family had been duplicated must seem unbelievable to others, but this did not stop *him* believing it. Similarly, Anderson's (1988) patient recognized that others would find his claim that members of his family were stealing and replacing his belongings difficult to believe, yet he made his wife sleep on the kitchen floor because of his delusions. Joseph (1986a) described the case of Mr A, a 30-year-old man with bilateral frontal and temporal lobe atrophy who claimed that on five separate occasions since he was aged 17 he had actually been dead—yet he realized that others who saw him at these times thought he was alive.

The view that the delusions that can follow brain injury do not result from global changes in mental function is strengthened by important observations in cases of anosognosia which demonstrate that patients with more than one neurological deficit may be unaware of one impairment yet perfectly well aware of others. For example, Bisiach, Vallar, Perani, Papagno and Berti (1986) found dissociations between anosognosia for hemiplegia and anosognosia for hemianopia. Paralysis to one side of the body (hemiplegia) and blindness for half the field of vision (hemianopia) are relatively common consequences of brain injury. The fact that patients can show awareness of their hemiplegias but not their hemianopias, and vice versa, shows that anosognosia can be specific to particular disabilities. As Bisiach (1988) put it:

Outside the decayed branch, cognitive processes may remain unaltered, but totally unable to influence pathological ideation (p. 468).

This curiously encapsulated quality of delusional beliefs is elaborated in the chapters by Breen et al. (this volume) and Langdon and Coltheart (this volume).

3. Sincerely Held, But Not Always Acted On

The examples discussed so far show that brain injury can lead to what certainly appear to be false beliefs. However, there are some curious features of these beliefs, which can be explored using the Capgras delusion. The Capgras delusion involves a particularly striking form of reduplication, in which patients are convinced that close relatives have been replaced by 'dummies' or 'impostors' (Capgras and Reboul-Lachaux, 1923). This has clear parallels with Pick's (1903) reduplicative paramnesia, but primarily involves other people as its focus, rather than the patient's environment (Alexander et al., 1979).

Usually, the Capgras delusion starts with the claim that one particular relative (often the patient's spouse) has been replaced by an impostor, but if it persists then the number of people who have allegedly been duplicated can increase. The patient's attempt to account for the substitution may involve the secret services, Martians, robots, clones, or a frank admission of its inexplicability, but a commonly recurring feature is that the impostors are considered in some way ill-intentioned. Although people who experience the Capgras delusion claim to be able to tell the real person from the impostor, they are unable to explain convincingly how they do this. For example, ML, a 60-year-old woman with Capgras delusion following a probable cerebral infarction, thought that her son was an impostor who was out to kill her:

> There's been someone like my son's double which isn't my son at all ... I can tell my son because my son's different ... but you've got to be very quick to notice it you see (Young, Reid, Wright and Hellawell, 1993).

One has to ask whether patients really believe their claims, or whether they are meant as some form of metaphor, or even constitute what Berrios (1991) calls 'empty speech acts that disguise themselves as beliefs'. This raises difficult issues concerning the nature of beliefs, and the criteria for judging sincerity and conviction. One simple criterion would be to ask what patients *do* about their expressed delusional beliefs. This has been carefully examined in Capgras cases.

The Capgras delusion can lead to verbal and physical aggression. One of Christodoulou's (1977) patients reported to the police that her husband had died and been replaced by an identical-looking man; she put on black mourning clothes, refused to sleep with the double and angrily ordered him out of the house, shouting 'go to your own wife'. In other reported incidents, a man who believed that his family had been replaced by clones used a toy gun to force a television newscaster to read out a statement about the substitution, and a man who believed wicked people had moved into the bodies of his family shot his father and his nephew, killing one and seriously wounding the other (Silva, Leong, Weinstock and Boyer, 1989). De Pauw and Szulecka (1988) noted a particularly chilling incident in which a patient accused his stepfather of being a robot and decapitated him to look for batteries and microfilm in his head.

If actions reflect the strength of one's convictions, there can be no doubting the sincerity of these patients. A review of 260 cases of delusional misidentification by Förstl et al. (1991a) found that physical violence had been noted in 46 cases (18%).

However, whilst extreme violence can be found in conjunction with the Capgras delusion, it is not the norm. Many people who experience the Capgras delusion accept the substitutes with a kind of compliant equanimity. Others are actively friendly; this was certainly true for Alexander et al.'s (1979) patient, who 'described positive feelings toward "both wives", showed no anger or distress about his first wife's desertion, and specifically expressed thankfulness that she had located a substitute' (Alexander, Stuss and Benson, 1979, p. 335). In Christodoulou's (1977) study, four out of eleven patients had a strongly positive relationship with the misidentified person, and Wallis (1986) also noted in a review of cases that around 30% were friendly toward the duplicates.

Closer examination of the behaviour of people who experience the Capgras delusion shows other anomalies. For example, many patients don't show much concern about what has happened to the real relatives; they do not grieve, search for them, or report their disappearance to the police.

So, although in some cases of Capgras delusion patients act in accordance with their bizarre beliefs, in many other cases there is a curious asynchrony between the firmly stated delusional belief and actions one might reasonably expect to have followed from it. Notice that this is not just a motor versus verbal dissociation; telephoning the police station to inform them that your real husband is missing would be just as much a verbal action as stating that he is an impostor.

Failure to maintain a close coordination of beliefs and actions may be typical of the delusions that can follow brain injury. Anton recognized this, noting that patients with what he described as unilateral loss of proprioception 'try to walk in spite of their paresis, and they fall, only to repeat the same attempt after a short time' (Förstl et al., 1993).

Further examples of the same point come from studies of anosognosia reviewed by Marcel (1993). As has been noted by Bisiach and Geminiani (1991), there can be inconsistencies between denial as evidenced in actions and verbal reports. For example, a patient with left-sided paralysis following a right hemisphere stroke may act in the way Anton noted, bemoaning her or his paralysis yet constantly trying to get out of bed and walk, whilst another patient denies having any deficit on verbal interrogation yet makes no attempt to get out of bed. In the one case, a verbally acknowledged deficit does not seem to constrain behaviour, whereas in the other behaviour is constrained even though there is no verbal acknowledgement. Which are we to take as reflecting the patient's 'real' insight, when words and actions are inconsistent with each other?

The delusional claim that one is dead, now known as the Cotard delusion, can show similar inconsistencies. One of the first reports was made in the eighteenth century, when Bonnet described the case of an elderly lady who probably suffered a stroke (Förstl and Beats, 1992). When she recovered the ability to speak, she demanded to be dressed in a shroud and placed in a coffin, saying that she was already dead. Yet when they began to dress her in her shroud and lay her out, the old lady supervised carefully, checking the arrangement of the shroud and the whiteness of the linen. It was thus noted that 'even in death she cannot abstain from her female habit of beautifying herself, etc.' (Förstl and Beats, p. 417).

Of course, the notion of the living dead has had a powerful appeal down the centuries, and still exercises the imaginations of people drawn to horror movies and science fiction. But the claim that they are dead made by someone who insists on being buried when everyone else thinks they are still alive is again clearly intended as more than a metaphor, even if all its implications do not seem to the outside observer to be completely carried through.

A second type of dissociation noted by Marcel (1993) reflects the use of a first-person or third-person perspective. It is standard practice in investigations of anosognosia to ask the person directly about his or her disabilities: 'can you walk?', 'can you tie your shoes?', and so forth. But Marcel (1993) reports that when he and Tegnér asked anosognosic patients with paralysis affecting one side of the body to rate how well the examiner could perform each activity 'if I (the questioner) were in your (the patient's) current condition' much better insight into the implications of the paralysis could be obtained.

Marcel (1993) has pointed out that such phenomena are reminiscent of hypnosis and other dissociative states; part of the patient's mind seems to know the relevant facts, but another part doesn't. Again, Anton had noted the same point: 'These disturbances of perception (*Gefühlsstörungen*) show a great similarity to other forms that develop *in the course of hysteria*' (Förstl et al., 1993).

4. Symptoms, Syndromes, and the Urge to Classify

Much of the work that has been done on delusions involves attempts to classify them into different types. Neurologists have developed a complex nomenclature which distinguishes anosognosias (unawareness of impairment, leading to denial of disability), reduplications (in which things are claimed to be copies or duplicates of the real object), and so on. This classificatory enterprise has pros and cons. The advantage of such schemes is that they allow certain delusions to be seen as related to each other, since they vary in content but not underlying form; for example, the Capgras delusion and reduplicative paramnesia seem to take a similar reduplicative form, but the reduplication is applied to different content (persons or places). The danger is that such classifications depend on concealed theoretical assumptions about which are the *important* similarities in form, and that the descriptions of different types of delusion become tailored to this theoretical straitjacket.

For example, although neurologists usually consider Capgras delusion as a reduplicative phenomenon (Alexander et al., 1979), in what sense does it involve reduplication? Isn't there a difference between believing that there are two of your wives (i.e. the wife has been *duplicated*) and believing that your wife has been *replaced* by an impostor, which isn't really your wife? In the second case, the wife has not been duplicated—just replaced. Similarly, a person might have the delusion that they are not in the York District Hospital but in another building which is very similar to it, looks just the same, but isn't the District Hospital—which would be like an exact geographical analogue of the Capgras delusion.

The point is not that the logical distinction between duplication and replacement *is* important, but that it could be. Seeing Capgras delusion as a form of reduplication simply elides this distinction. It is an empirical question whether this elision provides an appropriate or inappropriate way to proceed, but once made it is harder to disentangle.

Even so, the classificatory schemes of neurologists are timid in comparison to those of psychiatrists (Sims, 1988). For example, the Capgras delusion is considered to be just one among several different delusional misidentification syndromes which have been identified by clinicians—a review by Joseph (1986b) gives a list of 11 specific variants.

The idea of psychiatric syndromes derives its power from the fact that a basic requirement is an agreed and reliable way of classifying the phenomena encountered. Psychiatrists therefore tend to look for syndromes which are defined by clusters of co-occurring symptoms. Their hope is, of course, that such syndromes will often prove diagnostic of underlying mental illnesses, by analogy with the value of symptom clusters in diagnosing physical illnesses.

However, despite its widespread use in diagnosis, the usefulness of the syndrome concept in psychopathological *research* has been the subject of much debate in recent years (Costello, 1992). For research purposes, there are many different possible classification systems one might adopt, and these exist at different levels of generality. Rather than starting by trying to relate observations to a wide-ranging but necessarily abstract overall theory, a useful strategy may instead be to try to understand in detail a particular, relatively tightly defined phenomenon, and then see whether one's explanation can be broadened to encompass other observations. This is what is done here, by examining in detail specific delusional beliefs.

Similar lines of reasoning have led some authors to propose that research into symptoms is in general likely to prove more informative than is research into syndromes (Costello, 1992). Whilst sympathetic to this position, my own view is that what is best depends largely on what one wants to achieve. Syndromes can often have diagnostic usefulness, and broadly based groupings of cases are appropriate to support certain types of inference. However, I think that research into the value of explanations involving psychological factors needs to be directed at deficits defined at the same level of generality as the psychological theory employed. Since my colleagues and I have been interested in developing and applying specific, detailed psychological models, we have preferred to concentrate on understanding particular symptoms. Our interest has been in understanding psychological factors that can underlie delusions, and we have used terms like 'Capgras delusion' or 'Cotard delusion' simply as convenient shorthands for some of the varieties of delusions.

In fact, whilst variants of delusional misidentification are usually considered as distinct syndromes in the psychiatric literature (Enoch and Trethowan, 1991), we can question this. Each type of delusional misidentification is really only defined by a single symptom (the delusion itself) and the different types can quite often occur in combination with each other (Cutting, 1991; Förstl et al., 1991a). Whilst the syndrome concept may still provide a useful clinical shorthand under such circumstances, it does not seem to have much logical impact.

5. Types of Account, and What We Need to Explain

We have seen that brain injury can affect beliefs in highly selective ways. These new and often strange beliefs do not always translate into consistent actions, and there is some useful conceptual work to be done in evaluating the best way to think about these inconsistencies. Even so, if considered as false beliefs, in some cases they can have all the appearance of being sincerely held.

Although their content can be bizarre, we still need to account for these delusions. However, there are actually a number of different phenomena which need to be explained, and these exist at levels of discourse requiring different types of explanation. Consider again the Capgras delusion. One might ask any or all of the following questions:

(1) What types of brain injury are involved in this delusion?
(2) Is brain injury a sufficient cause of the delusion, or just one contributory factor?
(3) What causes the person suffering the delusion to say that a relative is an impostor?
(4) What makes this delusion subjectively convincing to the person experiencing it?

(5) Why is the delusion usually restricted to close relatives?

These all seem valid questions, but they can have different kinds of answer; a rough classification might be between neurological or psychological answers. Neurological answers could be something like 'because right parietal cortex is damaged', or 'because serotonergic pathways are affected'. Psychological answers might be more like 'because of poor memory', or 'because of inappropriate sensations'. Although there is a region of overlap, some types of answer are more appropriate to some types of question. Moving from the top to the bottom of the list requires shifting from neurological to psychological explanations. Although questions from the middle of the list might well receive either type of answer, a full account will need to give due respect to neurological *and* psychological factors (see also Breen et al., and Coltheart and Langdon, this volume).

The main neurological finding has been that, diverse though they may be, delusional beliefs tend to follow brain injury affecting the right cerebral hemisphere. When found in a setting of localized brain injury, *every* delusion discussed so far has been shown to be more frequent after right- than after left-sided brain damage.

The underlying cause of the finding that delusions tend to follow right-sided brain injury has not been established. At the simplest level, one could reason that because many people with left-sided brain injuries show significant language impairments, they may find it more difficult to express any delusions they may experience. Although this requires careful investigation, it seems unlikely given the wide range of delusions that have been studied. More complicated speculations include the idea that the right hemisphere is intimately involved in self awareness, reality testing, and so on. At present, we just do not know.

Whatever its origin, the remarkable link to right hemisphere disease shows that delusions are not merely random effects of brain injury, and sets definite constraints on what can be an appropriate corresponding account at the psychological level. In particular, it makes clear the inadequacy of accounts which suggest that delusions are directly explicable as emotional reactions to the various disabilities suffered. For example, denial of paralysis is more common after brain injury affecting the right cerebral hemisphere, which creates paralysis of the left side of the body, than after brain injury affecting the left cerebral hemisphere and consequent right-sided paralysis (Bisiach and Geminiani, 1991). So it is unlikely that denial of paralysis only reflects an emotional reaction, since for a right-handed person paralysis of the right hand is potentially much more upsetting, yet it is left-sided paralysis which is usually denied. Even more strikingly, it is known that failure to acknowledge left-sided paralysis (anosognosia for hemiplegia) is often associated with a more general failure to respond to the left side of space (known as unilateral neglect), and that temporary remission of both problems can be obtained after stimulation of the vestibular system through irrigation of the canals of the left outer ear with cold water (Cappa, Sterzi, Vallar and Bisiach, 1987). This procedure generates a reflex response which involves eye and head turning in the direction of the stimulated ear, but the exact mechanism by which it leads to remission of unilateral neglect and anosognosia is not understood in detail. However, such findings again point one away from psychodynamic interpretations.

More subtle psychodynamic hypotheses can also be ruled out. Delusional misidentification is a problem which used to be considered to be purely psychodynamic, but modern neuro-imaging techniques have revealed evidence of brain injury in many cases. Recent reviews have therefore emphasized the importance of organic factors in delusional misidentification (Cutting, 1991; Förstl et al., 1991a), and modern psychiatric opinion is that a thorough search for organic factors should always be made when such delusions are present (Collins, Hawthorne, Gribbin and Jacobson, 1990).

This is important because accounts of the Capgras delusion were for many years dominated by psychodynamic theories (Berson, 1983; Capgras and Carrette, 1924; Vogel, 1974). The most common version proposed that conflicting or ambivalent feelings of love and hate create a profound unease that is resolved by the delusion, so that the double can be hated without guilt (Enoch and Trethowan, 1991). However, psychodynamic hypotheses do not imply a direct role for brain disease, and hence have difficulty in accommodating the now frequent finding of an organic contribution. Advances in brain imaging have resulted in many of the case reports of Capgras delusion published in the last 20 years showing clear neurological damage (Förstl et al., 1991a); these show that, at the very least, psychodynamic accounts do not offer a full explanation. Again, in such cases, the underlying brain injuries often involve the right cerebral hemisphere; for patients with focal lesions the injuries were right sided in 19/20 cases of delusional misidentification reviewed by Förstl et al. (1991a).

In drawing attention to these neurological factors, I am not trying to deny that psychological factors play a role in some or all cases of delusional beliefs after brain injury; the point is only that it is clear that the particular psychological hypotheses used in psychodynamic accounts are insufficient as a sole explanation. We need a way of bringing together neurological and psychological factors.

So how do we construct an adequate account? In Capgras cases with clear neurological damage, there are usually occipitotemporal or temporoparietal lesions, often of the right hemisphere only, and frontal lesions which can be bilateral (Alexander et al., 1979; Feinberg and Shapiro, 1989; Förstl et al., 1991a; Förstl, Burns, Jacoby and Levy, 1991b; Joseph, 1986b; Lewis, 1987). However, although such observations of brain injury in patients who experience the Capgras delusion are obviously important, they do not in themselves explain the peculiar content of the delusion. The observed prevalence of brain injury involving the right cerebral hemisphere provides a useful pointer, but it is not an explanation in itself. Instead, we need to know what abilities the right hemisphere supports, and to understand how damaging these can create delusions. We thus need a theory that can link the observed brain disease to the disturbed psychological functions (cognitive and emotional) that create the delusion.

To do this, a number of researchers have sought to extend the logic used in cognitive neuropsychology where a very influential strategy has been to relate the effects of brain injury to models of normal function (Ellis and Young, 1988). In this approach, a model of normal performance is tested by its ability to account for the effects of brain injury. Where the model of normal performance also provides a convincing account of brain injury it is retained; when it fails to account for effects of brain injury it is revised or abandoned. The key theoretical move has been to argue that an adequate model of normal performance should be able to account for *any* disordered pattern, including neuropsychiatric phenomena (Ellis and Young, 1990). As has been mentioned, this approach is now called cognitive neuropsychiatry (David, 1993; Ellis and de Pauw, 1994).

6. Towards an Explanation

The Capgras delusion has been claimed as one of the early successes for cognitive neuropsychiatry (Ellis, 1998). From detailed studies of people who have experienced the Capgras delusion, there have been some advances in four areas:

(1) constructing an account which can deal with the basic symptomatology;
(2) testing alternative possibilities;
(3) generating and testing non-trivial predictions;
(4) broadening the scope of the basic account to encompass other delusions.

During the last 12 years, my colleagues and I have had the opportunity to meet and carry out tests with people who have experienced the Capgras delusion (Ellis et al., 1997; Young, 1998; Young, Leafhead and Szulecka, 1994; Young et al., 1993). From this work, a constellation of features has stood out, and these are also evident in other published case reports. People who experience the Capgras delusion usually claim that they can see that their relative is an impostor, though they have great difficulty explaining just what this visible difference entails. On tests of face perception, they tend to perform less well than normal controls, but seldom at chance level. When questioned carefully, they report a more widespread feeling that things have changed in a way that makes them seem not quite right—strange, somehow unfamiliar, almost unreal. Their mood is often one of some suspiciousness.

This pattern fits the idea that the Capgras delusion is caused by the misinterpretation of unusual perceptual experiences. But what kind of unusual experiences?

One suggestion has been that the Capgras delusion is related to the neurological condition of prosopagnosia—an inability to recognize familiar faces after brain injury (Shraberg and Weitzel, 1979). The presence of right occipitotemporal lesions in Capgras cases is reminiscent of the brain lesions that cause prosopagnosia, and the possibility of a link between prosopagnosia and the Capgras delusion is strengthened by observations that Capgras patients perform poorly on face processing tests (Morrison and Tarter, 1984; Shraberg and Weitzel, 1979; Tzavaras, Luauté and Bidault, 1986; Wilcox and Waziri, 1983; Young et al., 1993). However, we have found it necessary to treat this possible link carefully (Ellis and Young, 1990; Lewis, 1987), as the pattern of face processing impairment found in Capgras delusion does not form a close parallel to what is found in cases of prosopagnosia.

For people with prosopagnosia the impairment of familiar face recognition can be very severe (affecting the recognition of faces as familiar as their spouse's face or their own face when seen in the mirror), but other aspects of face perception (such as recognition of emotion from facial expression), may remain relatively spared. In Capgras delusion, recognition of familiar faces is much less severely compromised in absolute terms (sufferers can recognize their spouse's face, even if they maintain it is not the real person), and it does not seem to be any more affected than other aspects of face perception, most of which are somewhat abnormal.

A promising approach seemed to us to think of Capgras delusion as something akin to a mirror-image of prosopagnosia (Ellis and Young, 1990). In prosopagnosia, overt recognition of familiar faces is severely affected but, remarkably, some non-conscious forms of response to familiar faces can still be demonstrated (Bruyer, 1991; Young, 1998; Young and Burton, 1999). In particular, autonomic nervous system responses to familiar faces can be shown (Bauer, 1984; Tranel and Damasio, 1985) by measuring changes in skin conductance (the skin conductance response, or SCR). These autonomic responses are usually interpreted as reflecting some form of emotional orienting to stimuli which have personal significance. If one lost these autonomic responses, it seemed to us conceivable that familiar faces would seem strange, unusual, not quite right.

Note that these emotional orienting responses to faces with personal significance are different from the recognition of another person's emotions from their facial expression (is this a sad face or an angry face). That is, detecting affect in a face is not the same as experiencing affect in response to a face—the distinction is between (a) recognizing what emotion another person is feeling and (b) having an emotional response oneself. It is the emotional response to faces that is thought to be impaired in people who experience the Capgras delusion.

To account for his findings of preserved autonomic responses to familiar faces in prosopagnosia, Bauer (1984, 1986) suggested that overt recognition of a familiar face depends on the intactness of a 'ventral' visual system–limbic system pathway involving ventromedial occipitotemporal cortex, whereas a more 'dorsal' visual–limbic pathway through the superior temporal sulcus and the inferior parietal lobule subserves processes of emotional arousal. In prosopagnosia, Bauer argued that the ventral pathway is impaired but the dorsal pathway may remain intact, leading to covert recognition of familiar faces that cannot be recognized overtly.

It is worth spending a little more time on the properties Bauer attributed to the dorsal pathway. He suggested that it 'subserves processes of selective attention and tonic emotional arousal, and is implicated in the process whereby 'relevance' is attached to an attended object' (Bauer, 1984, p. 466). Thus it has multiple functions encompassing automatic emotional responses to stimuli which have personal relevance; these have been widely implicated as putative specialized functions of the right cerebral hemisphere (Bear, 1983; Van Lancker, 1991).

In discussing Bauer's model, however, it is important to keep separate his general conception that autonomic and conscious recognition involve dissociable pathways and his specific proposals concerning the underlying neurology. The neurology of Bauer's (1984) proposals has been questioned by other experts (Hirstein and Ramachandran, 1997; Tranel and Damasio, 1988; Tranel, Damasio and Damasio, 1995) who have none the less accepted what I think is the more important proposition that autonomic and overt indices of recognition tap different neural systems.

In prosopagnosia, then, overt recognition of familiar faces is profoundly impaired, whereas autonomic responses to the same faces can be relatively spared. We hypothesized that in Capgras delusion the opposite pattern applies—autonomic responses to familiar faces are lost, whereas overt recognition is relatively preserved (Ellis and Young, 1990). The delusion that relatives have been replaced by impostors is then an attempt to make sense of the fact that they no longer generate appropriate emotional responses.

This account explains why the Capgras delusion is mainly found for close relatives, since these are the people who would normally produce the greatest autonomic response, and hence for whom the absence of this response is the most noticeable and disconcerting. It also explains why the delusion occurs in a background of more pervasive feelings that things are not as they should be. More importantly, it made the prediction that people who experience the Capgras delusion will not show differential skin conductance responses to familiar compared to unfamiliar faces. Since this prediction did not follow from any other theory as to what might cause the Capgras delusion, it was nontrivial. Two recent studies have demonstrated the predicted loss of differential skin conductance response (Ellis et al., 1997; Hirstein and Ramachandran, 1997) in people who suffered Capgras delusion due to organic or to 'functional' psychiatric causes. In total, these studies report skin conductance data for six people who experienced the Capgras delusion, and every one showed no differential response to familiar faces. In addition, Hirstein and Ramachandran (1997) also noted that their patient claimed his parents were impostors when he was looking at them, but treated them as his real parents when talking to them on the telephone—as might be expected if the cause of the delusion is a discrepant response to visual information.

These studies show a clear association between Capgras delusion and loss of emotional responses to familiar faces, as would be predicted by Ellis and Young's (1990) account. An important topic for further research is therefore to understand better what such emotional responses entail. Is the emotional orienting system specific to faces, or do the same mechanisms apply to any visual stimulus with personal significance? Can we use the same idea to account for Capgras-like delusions involving the substitution of pets (Wright, Mindham and Burn, 1994) or inanimate objects (Anderson, 1988)? Are there parallel deficits affecting auditory or tactile modalities (Reid, Young and Hellawell, 1993)? Such questions can now be explored.

7. Interacting Contributory Factors

We have seen that a plausible hypothesis which has received empirical support is that the basis of the Capgras delusion lies in a loss of appropriate emotional orienting responses to familiar visual stimuli. However, there seems to be something missing.

A minor discrepancy is that people who suffer the Capgras delusion also tend to be poor on a range of face perception tasks—it is not just their autonomic responses to faces that are impaired. However, it is the loss of autonomic response which is the most severe problem, and it is possible that the other defects of face perception simply reflect anatomical proximity between the pathways involved in the different aspects of face perception—it would be unusual for brain malfunction to compromise one of these pathways without affecting the others to some extent.

The more serious issue concerns why people with Capgras delusion should arrive at such an unlikely account of their experiences as to think that relatives have been replaced. Why, for instance, don't they just accept that other people seem a bit strange for reasons they can't figure out? Two points seem pertinent here. First, it seems likely that many people who suffer this type of anomalous perceptual experience may well generate more plausible explanations of what has happened to them (see Gold and Hohwy, this volume; Langdon and Coltheart, this volume)—but those who do will not attract as much interest from psychiatrists or neurologists! Second, the suspiciousness noted in people with Capgras delusion may be one of the factors which limit the possibilities they consider to those which involve changes in other people rather than changes in themselves and dispose them to think they are the victims of some kind of trick.

There is some evidence suggesting that people with delusions may show reasoning biases which involve forming conclusions on the basis of less evidence than a non-deluded person would require. Huq, Garety and Hemsley (1988) found that people with delusions were more confident and requested less information than non-deluded people before reaching a decision in a probability judgement task. This is an intriguing finding because, superficially, probability judgements would seem to have nothing to do with the patients' delusions. The result is robust, having also been found in other studies (Dudley, John, Young and Over, 1997a, 1997b; Garety, Hemsley and Wessely, 1991; Huq et al., 1988).

Another factor favouring misinterpretation is an attributional bias. This has been noted in suspicious patients by Kaney and Bentall (1989) and Candido and Romney (1990), who found that people with persecutory delusions were inclined to attribute hypothetical negative events to *external* causes, whereas depressed people attributed them to *internal* causes. The persecutory delusions and suspiciousness that are often noted in Capgras cases may therefore contribute to the fundamental misinterpretation in which the patients mistake a change in themselves for a change in others.

My colleagues and I therefore think that the Capgras delusion reflects an unfortunate interaction of impairments involving anomalous perceptual experience and reasoning biases of the type noted in other people with delusions, and paranoid delusions in particular. We think that the Capgras delusion represents just one among a number of ways in which people might try to explain similar anomalous perceptual experiences to themselves, and that to properly understand this delusion we need to understand not just the perceptual anomaly but also the factors which create and sustain the relatively bizarre impostor explanation.

Whether the particular reasoning biases I have described, or even the concept of reasoning biases in general (Bentall, 1995) will prove adequate to sustain an interpretation of all aspects of the Capgras delusion remains to be seen. Langdon and Coltheart (this volume) mount a persuasive case based on psychological evidence pointing to the possibility that there is more going on, and Gold and Hohwy (this volume) show how a more philosophical approach to the idea of rationality also brings out features of delusions that will need to be carefully investigated. For now, though, the important points are that a single-factor account looks unlikely to be adequate and that plausible interacting contributory factors are beginning to be identified.

If one accepts the suggestion that the Capgras delusion reflects an attempt to account for an anomalous experience, it follows that the relative weighting of different contributory factors could be fairly elastic. For example, a person might have such a strongly anomalous experience that only a relatively minor form of reasoning bias would lead them to misinterpret it, whereas someone else might be in such a suspicious state that they arrive at a delusional account of a comparatively minor perceptual anomaly.

This seems to be the case—it is known that the relative balance of differing contributory factors may vary according to the aetiology underlying the delusion. Using a structured review of case reports of delusional misidentification (many of which were reports of Capgras delusion), Fleminger and Burns (1993) showed that paranoid delusions preceding the delusional misidentification were more commonly noted when there was no direct evidence of organic cerebral dysfunction. Further discussion of the implications of this finding can be found in Breen et al. (this volume).

Our working hypothesis is that the Capgras delusion may be due in part to impairment of the visual system. In effect, the patient's beliefs change because the evidence on which they are based has altered. If correct, this emphasizes the fundamental importance of vision as a source of evidence about the world.

The proposal that defective emotional reactions to familiar visual stimuli are implicated in the Capgras delusion was one which often found favour in early descriptions (Brochado, 1936), but other accounts of the impairment that underlies the Capgras delusion have also been suggested. Joseph (1986b) proposed a cerebral hemisphere disconnection hypothesis, in which each cerebral hemisphere independently processes facial information, and the Capgras delusion arises when the two processes fail to integrate. Cutting (1991) argued against a perceptual account, and thought that the delusion is due to a breakdown of the normal structure of semantic categories, leading to a disturbance in the judgement of identity or uniqueness. Staton et al. (1982) drew attention to the possibility of a memory deficit, in which the Capgras patient compares a present percept with an old representation of the face, and notes the mismatch. Feinberg and Shapiro (1989) noted a failure to register familiarity, and suggested that the Capgras delusion resembles a state of selective persisting *jamais vu*.

Some of these hypotheses are clearly incompatible with the model presented here, whereas others can be regarded as variants with a different emphasis. The important point, however, is that all of the accounts lead to testable predictions which can be investigated in future cases.

An interesting consequence of the idea that the Capgras delusion reflects interacting contributory factors is that it may also offer an account of the Cotard delusion. In the 1880s, Cotard described a syndrome of nihilistic delusions ('le délire de négation') in which everything seems so unreal that the patient thinks she or he has died (Cotard, 1880, 1882). Although a key feature of this syndrome was the delusion of being dead, Cotard had noted that there could be differing and fluctuating degrees of severity. Other florid symptoms associated with the Cotard syndrome included thinking that the entire world had ceased to exist, feelings of putrefaction of internal bodily organs, self-mutilating or (paradoxically) suicidal urges, and beliefs in the absence or (conversely) enormity of parts of the body. However, the patients reported in Cotard's (1882) key paper did not invariably display all of these accompanying features, which again brings into question the utility of the syndrome concept in cases presenting with the delusion of being dead, if by syndrome is meant a pattern of symptoms which will inevitably co-occur. For this reason, we have preferred to refer to the specific symptom of believing that you are dead as the Cotard delusion.

At first sight, the Cotard and Capgras delusions would seem to have little to do with each other, except that they both involve bizarre claims about existence (for self or others). On closer examination, however, there are other parallels. Both delusions can be produced by broadly similar types of brain injury (Drake, 1988; Young et al., 1992). For example, in a case we investigated, WI, the Cotard delusion followed contusions affecting temporoparietal areas of the right cerebral hemisphere and some bilateral frontal lobe damage (Young et al., 1992). Moreover, there are similarities in the cognitive impairments. WI not only became convinced that he was dead, but he also experienced difficulties in recognizing familiar faces, buildings and places, as well as feelings of derealization; all of which are often noted in Capgras cases. In fact, people suffering the Cotard delusion commonly report that they must be dead because they 'feel nothing inside', which presses the parallel with the hypothesized lack of affective reactions in Capgras cases still further. Young et al. (1992) therefore suggested that the underlying pathophysiology and neuropsychology of the Cotard and Capgras delusions may be related. Although these delusions are phenomenally distinct, they may represent the patients' attempts to make sense of fundamentally similar experiences.

The closeness of this link became really convincing for us when we studied a person who experienced both the Cotard and Capgras delusions in sequence (Wright, Young and Hellawell, 1993). This curious association of two unusual delusions has been reported in other cases too, and the key factor seems to be the patients' moods—when in a suspicious mood, they think that other people are impostors, when depressed they think they are dead. The underlying basis of both delusions could therefore be quite similar; a delusional interpretation of altered perception (especially loss of affective familiarity).

A clue to how this could happen comes from the studies which have shown that people with persecutory delusions tend to attribute negative events to external rather than internal causes, whereas depressed people tend to attribute them to internal causes (Candido and Romney, 1990; Kaney and Bentall, 1989). The relevance of these findings is that it is quite common for the Cotard delusion to arise in the setting of a depressive illness and for the Capgras delusion to be accompanied by persecutory delusions and suspiciousness (Enoch and Trethowan, 1991; Wright et al., 1993). Hence whilst the persecutory delusions and suspiciousness that are often noted in Capgras cases contribute to the patients' mistaking a change in themselves for a change in others ('they are impostors'), people who are depressed might exaggerate the negative effects of a similar change whilst correctly attributing it to themselves ('I am dead').

Of course, this may not be the only way to conceptualize the relation between the Capgras and Cotard delusions. Gerrans (this volume) suggests that the difference in content may result from the more global nature of the affective deficit in Cotard's delusion, noting that this is consistent with the idea that depression involves a neurochemical mechanism whose operation suppresses a wide range of affective and cognitive processes. A related proposal has been made by Ramachandran and Blakeslee (1998), who speculated that:

> Cotard's is simply an exaggerated form of Capgras' syndrome and probably has a similar origin. In Capgras', the face recognition area alone is disconnected from the amygdala, whereas in Cotard's perhaps all the sensory areas are disconnected from the limbic system, leading to a complete lack of emotional contact with the world (Ramachandran and Blakeslee, 1998, p. 167).

Ramachandran and Blakeslee (1998) pointed out that this predicts that people who experience the Cotard delusion will show a complete loss of skin conductance response (SCR) for all stimuli, whereas the SCR deficit accompanying Capgras delusion should be more circumscribed. In contrast, the attributional bias theory would tend to suggest that there should not be much difference between SCRs of Capgras and Cotard delusion patients. These ideas have yet to be tested, but they again show how the differences between theories can be turned into contrasting, falsifiable predictions.

We have thus arrived at the beginnings of an account of the Capgras and Cotard delusions which can make the strange content of these otherwise bizarre delusions at least partly intelligible, and which can generate non-trivial, testable and potentially falsifiable predictions. One of the features of the Capgras and Cotard delusions is that they can arise in the context of identifiable brain injury or in more 'functional' settings, and the account offered makes clear the potential interplay of organic and psychological factors. As well as scientific predictions, it may be possible further to test the account by developing forms of cognitive therapy targeted at the different contributory factors identified.

8. A Note of Caution

Although I have tried to show how we can begin to develop testable accounts of the factors involved in certain forms of delusion, I do not want to imply that cognitive neuropsychiatry will be easy. On the contrary, I think there is a widespread tendency to underestimate just how difficult it will be. This underestimation of the difficulties that lie ahead has arisen because the logic of extending the cognitive neuropsychological approach into the relatively unexplored territory of neuropsychiatry is appealing, and there have been sufficient successes in cognitive neuropsychology during the last 30 years that it is tempting simply to assume the same rate of progress can be achieved in the neuropsychiatric domain.

However, there are reasons for being less cheerful, and it is worth looking at these. Although cognitive neuropsychiatry is a new enterprise, two assumptions seem to be commonly used:

(1) The best way to understand neuropsychiatric phenomena is through a symptom-based approach.
(2) The logic and techniques of cognitive neuropsychology can be imported into the new domain of cognitive neuropsychiatry.

Neither is as straightforward as it seems.

The symptom-based approach has persuasive advocates, and it is also beginning to be used in related areas of clinical psychology and psychiatry (Bentall, 1995; Costello, 1992). The principal motivation for the symptom-based approach is that broadly based diagnostic categories like 'schizophrenia' group together people who may actually be very different from each other. For example, some people with schizophrenia have delusions, and some don't. If you want to understand how cognitive deficits relate to the abnormal experiences of people with schizophrenia, it doesn't seem a very good idea to average together results across people whose abnormal experiences may actually be markedly different.

Such arguments are now standard in cognitive neuropsychology, where careful investigations of individual cases have become a dominant research strategy. The rationale was clearly articulated in Coltheart's (1984) editorial introduction to the then new journal *Cognitive Neuropsychology*. Using the neurological syndrome of Broca's aphasia as an example, Coltheart (1984) argued that:

> Whilst syndromes conceived in this way may be useful in providing a vocabulary for communicating clinical impressions, they are not useful with respect to research in cognitive neuropsychology. The reason is simple. When syndromes are understood in this way, it will be possible for two patients to have different sets of symptoms yet still be assigned the same syndrome label. Because they have different symptoms, the explanations of their disorder in terms of defects within a model of the relevant cognitive system must be different (p. 6).

Using this approach, cognitive neuropsychology has rapidly advanced our understanding of a number of mental abilities; these include reading, object recognition, speech perception, and memory. But much of this progress has come from the careful investigation of people with stable deficits in what might be considered fundamental cognitive functions involved in sensory analysis, memory, and verbal or motor output. In contrast, the delusional beliefs discussed here are relatively unstable, and they do not obviously map directly to specific cognitive abilities. Often they are only held for a few weeks or even days. When the delusions change, patients may modify or abandon them as suddenly as they seemed to form them, or they may give them up much more slowly and reluctantly, saying things like 'it was as if X (the delusional event) happened. At the very least, this creates difficulties in the timing of investigations, and in interpreting the relation of deficits and symptoms which may be recorded on separate dates.

To make matters worse, there are difficult issues involved in determining what constitutes a symptom, which is not a theoretically neutral decision. For some researchers, having delusions forms a symptom that can be regarded as equivalent across different patients, whereas others prefer a subdivision into persecutory delusions, depressive delusions, and so on. Here, I have used an even finer-grained approach, looking at specific forms of delusional belief, such as thinking that a relative is an impostor. But why stop there? We could have equally well subdivided cases of Capgras delusion into those who only think they have a single duplicate relative versus those with multiple duplicates, or into patients who believe the impostors are robots, clones, Martians, and so on.

In practice, the decision about what specific subdivision to go for is based on a combination of preconception and hunch, and the only yardstick it can be evaluated against is whether or not it seems productive. This is by no means unworkable, but it is unwieldy and likely to lead to at least some blind alleys.

The idea of importing the logic and techniques of cognitive neuropsychology also runs into difficulties. I have sought to make clear how delusional beliefs which result from brain injury can be considered to reflect unfortunate interactions of more than one contributory factor. In particular, I have shown how patients might construct inadequate accounts of anomalous experiences. The implication is that the appropriate research agenda is not to seek *the* cause of delusion x, but instead to chart the various contributions which create and sustain the patient's idiosyncratic account of what has happened. A useful rule of thumb might instead be that the more bizarre the symptom, the more likely it is to reflect an interaction of underlying contributory factors.

In the pathogenesis of delusions, then, cognitive deficits that result from brain damage interact with things like reasoning biases. These biases may in turn be subject to major individual differences, where these individual factors may have been present before the injury, may be exacerbated by the injury (if you think for one moment that your wife is an impostor, you can rapidly become more generally suspicious), may be the result of general cognitive degeneration, may be the result of a distinct modular deficit, and so on.

This is quite different from the identification of single-component, dissociable deficits that characterizes so much cognitive neuropsychology, and it in turn implies that associations may have a more central role here than they at present have in cognitive neuropsychology. That is, in cognitive neuropsychiatry we should not always regard dissociations as the cardinal form of evidence—

there may be important implications to be derived from associations too. Examples where associations have been used here include the co-occurrence of perceptual anomalies and suspiciousness found in many people who experience the Capgras delusion, and the surprising co-occurrence of Capgras and Cotard delusions in some patients. If we attended only to dissociable delusions, we would conclude only that the Capgras and Cotard delusions are distinct, since each can occur without the other, and miss the implications of the fact that they can be associated. The key point is not that the interpretations offered here are necessarily correct, but that as a distinct discipline cognitive neuropsychiatry will need to develop its own rules and procedures.

This little catalogue of problems to be faced shows that advances in cognitive neuropsychiatry will be hard won. But it contains nothing to suggest cognitive neuropsychiatry is impossible, and given the interest and importance of the issues at stake, it should prove well worth the effort.

References

Alexander, M.P., Stuss, D.T. and Benson, D.F. 1979: Capgras syndrome: A reduplicative phenomenon. *Neurology*, 29, 334–9.

Anderson, D.N. 1988: The delusion of inanimate doubles. Implications for understanding the Capgras phenomenon. *British Journal of Psychiatry*, 153, 694–9.

Anton, G. 1899: Ueber die Selbstwahrnemung der Herderkrankungen des Gehirns durch den Kranken bei Rindenblindheit und Rindentaubheit. *Archiv für Psychiatrie und Nervenkrankheiten*, 32, 86–127.

Bauer, R.M. 1984: Autonomic recognition of names and faces in prosopagnosia: A neuropsychological application of the guilty knowledge test. *Neuropsychologia*, 22, 457–69.

Bauer, R.M. 1986: The cognitive psychophysiology of prosopagnosia. In H.D. Ellis, M.A. Jeeves, F. Newcombe and A. Young (eds.), *Aspects of Face Processing*. Dordrecht: Martinus Nijhoff, 253–67.

Bear, D.M. 1983: Hemispheric specialization and the neurology of emotion. *Archives of Neurology*, 40, 195–202.

Bentall, R.P. 1995: Brains, biases, deficits and disorders. *British Journal of Psychiatry*, 167, 153–5.

Berrios, G.E. 1991: Delusions as 'wrong beliefs': A conceptual history. *British Journal of Psychiatry*, 159, 6–13.

Berson, R.J. 1983: Capgras' syndrome. *American Journal of Psychiatry*, 140, 969–78.

Bisiach, E. 1988: Language without thought. In L. Weiskrantz (ed.), *Thought Without Language*. Oxford University Press, 464–84.

Bisiach, E. and Geminiani, G. 1991: Anosognosia related to hemiplegia and hemianopia. In G.P. Prigatano and D.L. Schacter (eds), *Awareness of Deficit after Brain Injury: Clinical and Theoretical Issues*. Oxford University Press, 17–39.

Bisiach, E., Vallar, G., Perani, D., Papagno, C. and Berti, A. 1986: Unawareness of disease following lesions of the right hemisphere: Anosognosia for hemiplegia and anosognosia for hemianopia. *Neuropsychologia*, 24, 471–82.

Brochado, A. 1936: Le syndrome de Capgras. *Annales Médico-Psychologiques*, 15, 706–17.

Bruyer, R. 1991: Covert face recognition in prosopagnosia: A review. *Brain and Cognition*, 15, 223–35.

Candido, C.L. and Romney, D.M. 1990: Attributional style in paranoid vs. depressed patients. *British Journal of Medical Psychology*, 63, 355–63.

Capgras, J. and Carrette, P. 1924: Illusion des sosies et complexe d'Oedipe. *Annales Médico-Psychologiques*, 12, 48–68.

Capgras, J. and Reboul-Lachaux, J. 1923: L'illusion des 'sosies' dans un délire systématisé chronique. *Bulletin de la Société Clinique de Médicine Mentale*, 11, 6–16.

Cappa, S.F., Sterzi, R., Vallar, G. and Bisiach, E. 1987: Remission of hemineglect and anosognosia after vestibular stimulation. *Neuropsychologia*, 25, 775–82.

Christodoulou, G.N. 1977: The syndrome of Capgras. *British Journal of Psychiatry*, 130, 556–64.

Collins, M.N., Hawthorne, M.E., Gribbin, N. and Jacobson, R. 1990: Capgras' syndrome with organic disorders. *Postgraduate Medical Journal*, 66, 1064–7.

Coltheart, M. 1984: Editorial. *Cognitive Neuropsychology*, 1, 1–8.

Costello, C.G. 1992: Research on symptoms versus research on syndromes. Arguments in favour of allocating more research time to the study of symptoms. *British Journal of Psychiatry*, 160, 304–8.

Cotard, J. 1880: Du délire hypocondriaque dans une forme grave de la mélancolie anxieuse. *Annales Médico-Psychologiques*, 38, 168–70.

Cotard, J. 1882: Du délire des négations. *Archives de Neurologie*, 4, 152–70, 282–95.

Cutting, J. 1991: Delusional misidentification and the role of the right hemisphere in the appreciation of identity. *British Journal of Psychiatry*, 159, 70–75.

David, A.S. 1993: Cognitive neuropsychiatry? *Psychological Medicine*, 23, 1–5.

de Pauw, K.W. and Szulecka, T.K. 1988: Dangerous delusions: violence and the misidentification syndromes. *British Journal of Psychiatry*, 152, 91–7.

de Pauw, K.W., Szulecka, T.K. and Poltock, T.L. 1987: Frégoli syndrome after cerebral infarction. *Journal of Nervous and Mental Disease*, 175, 433–8.

Dennett, D. 1981: *Brainstorms: Philosophical Essays on Mind and Psychology*. Brighton: Harvester.

Drake, M.E.J. 1988: Cotard's syndrome and temporal lobe epilepsy. *Psychiatric Journal of the University of Ottawa*, 13, 36–9.

Dudley, R.E.J., John, C.H., Young, A.W. and Over, D.E. 1997a: The effect of self-referent material on the reasoning of people with delusions. *British Journal of Clinical Psychology*, 36, 575–84.

Dudley, R.E.J., John, C.H., Young, A.W. and Over, D.E. 1997b: Normal and abnormal reasoning in people with delusions. *British Journal of Clinical Psychology*, 36, 243–58.

Ellis, H.D. 1998: Cognitive neuropsychiatry and delusional misidentification syndromes: An exemplary vindication of the new discipline. *Cognitive Neuropsychiatry*, 3, 81–9.

Ellis, H.D. and de Pauw, K.W. 1994: The cognitive neuropsychiatric origins of the Capgras delusion. In A.S. David and J.C. Cutting (eds), *The Neuropsychology of Schizophrenia*. Hove, E. Sussex: Lawrence Erlbaum, 317–35.

Ellis, A.W. and Young, A.W. 1988: *Human Cognitive Neuropsychology*. London: Lawrence Erlbaum.

Ellis, H.D. and Young, A.W. 1990: Accounting for delusional misidentifications. *British Journal of Psychiatry*, 157, 239–48.

Ellis, H.D., Young, A.W., Quayle, A.H. and de Pauw, K.W. 1997: Reduced autonomic responses to faces in Capgras delusion. *Proceedings of the Royal Society: Biological Sciences*, B264, 1085–92.

Enoch, M.D. and Trethowan, W.H. 1991: *Uncommon Psychiatric Syndromes*, 3rd edn. Oxford: Butterworth-Heinemann.

Feinberg, T.E. and Shapiro, R.M. 1989: Misidentification-reduplication and the right hemisphere. *Neuropsychiatry, Neuropsychology, and Behavioral Neurology*, 2, 39–48.

Fleminger, S. and Burns, A. 1993: The delusional misidentification syndromes in patients with and without evidence of organic cerebral disorder: A structured review of case reports. *Biological Psychiatry*, 33, 22–32.

Förstl, H., Almeida, O.P., Owen, A.M., Burns, A. and Howard, R. 1991a: Psychiatric, neurological and medical aspects of misidentification syndromes: A review of 260 cases. *Psychological Medicine*, 21, 905–10.

Förstl, H. and Beats, B. 1992: Charles Bonnet's description of Cotard's delusion and reduplicative paramnesia in an elderly patient (1788). *British Journal of Psychiatry*, 160, 416–18.

Förstl, H., Burns, A., Jacoby, R. and Levy, R. 1991b: Neuroanatomical correlates of clinical misidentification and misperception in senile dementia of the Alzheimer type. *Journal of Clinical Psychiatry*, 52, 268–71.

Förstl, H., Owen, A.M. and David, A.S. 1993: Gabriel Anton and 'Anton's symptom': on focal diseases of the brain which are not perceived by the patient (1898). *Neuropsychiatry, Neuropsychology, and Behavioral Neurology*, 6, 1–8.

Garety, P.A., Hemsley, D.R. and Wessely, S. 1991: Reasoning in deluded schizophrenic and paranoid patients: Biases in performance on a probabilistic inference task. *Journal of Nervous and Mental Disease*, 179, 194–201.

Halligan, P.W. and Marshall, J.C. 1994: Completion in visuo-spatial neglect: A case study. *Cortex*, 30, 685–94.

Halligan, P.W. and Marshall, J.C. 1995: Supernumerary phantom limb after right hemisphere stroke. *Journal of Neurology, Neurosurgery, and Psychiatry*, 59, 341–2.

Hirstein, W. and Ramachandran, V.S. 1997: Capgras syndrome: A novel probe for understanding the neural representation of the identity and familiarity of persons. *Proceedings of the Royal Society: Biological Sciences,* B264, 437–44.

Huq, S.F., Garety, P.A. and Hemsley, D.R. 1988: Probabilistic judgements in deluded and non-deluded subjects. *Quarterly Journal of Experimental Psychology*, 40A, 801–12.

Joseph, A.B. 1986a: Cotard's syndrome with coexistent Capgras' syndrome, syndrome of subjective doubles, and palinopsia. *Journal of Clinical Psychiatry*, 47, 605–6.

Joseph, A.B. 1986b: Focal central nervous system abnormalities in patients with mis-identification syndromes. *Bibliotheca Psychiatrica*, 164, 68–79.

Kaney, S. and Bentall, R.P. 1989: Persecutory delusions and attributional style. *British Journal of Medical Psychology*, 62, 191–8.

Lewis, S.W. 1987: Brain imaging in a case of Capgras' syndrome. *British Journal of Psychiatry*, 150, 117–21.

Maher, B.A. 1988: Anomalous experience and delusional thinking: The logic of explanations. In T.F. Oltmanns and B.A. Maher (eds), *Delusional Beliefs*. Chichester: Wiley, 15–33.

Marcel, A.J. 1993: Slippage in the unity of consciousness. In *Ciba Foundation Symposium No. 174: Experimental and Theoretical Studies of Consciousness*. Chichester: Wiley.

McGlynn, S. and Schacter, D.L. 1989: Unawareness of deficits in neuropsychological syndromes. *Journal of Clinical and Experimental Neuropsychology*, 11, 143–205.

Morrison, R.L. and Tarter, R.E. 1984: Neuropsychological findings relating to Capgras syndrome. *Biological Psychiatry*, 19, 1119–28.

Pick, A. 1903: Clinical studies: III. On reduplicative paramnesia. *Brain*, 26, 260–7.

Ramachandran, V.S. and Blakeslee, S. 1998: *Phantoms in the Brain: Probing the Mysteries of the Human Mind*. New York: William Morrow.

Reid, I., Young, A.W. and Hellawell, D.J. 1993: Voice recognition impairment in a blind Capgras patient. *Behavioural Neurology*, 6, 225–8.

Sass, L.A. 1994: *The Paradoxes of Delusion: Wittgenstein, Schreber, and the Schizophrenic Mind*. Ithaca, NY: Cornell University Press.

Shraberg, D. and Weitzel, W.D. 1979: Prosopagnosia and the Capgras syndrome. *Journal of Clinical Psychiatry*, 40, 313–6.

Silva, J.A., Leong, G.B., Weinstock, R. and Boyer, C.L. 1989: Capgras syndrome and dangerousness. *Bulletin of the American Academy of Psychiatry and the Law*, 17, 5–14.

Sims, A. 1988: *Symptoms in the Mind: An Introduction to Descriptive Psychopathology*. London: Baillière Tindall.

Staton, R.D., Brumback, R.A. and Wilson, H. 1982: Reduplicative paramnesia: A disconnection syndrome of memory. *Cortex*, 18, 23–6.

Stone, T. and Young, A.W. 1997: Delusions and brain injury: The philosophy and psychology of belief. *Mind and Language*, 12, 327–64.

Tranel, D. and Damasio, A.R. 1985: Knowledge without awareness: An autonomic index of facial recognition by prosopagnosics. *Science*, 228, 1453–4.

Tranel, D. and Damasio, A.R. 1988: Non-conscious face recognition in patients with face agnosia. *Behavioural Brain Research*, 30, 235–49.

Tranel, D., Damasio, H. and Damasio, A.R. 1995: Double dissociation between overt and covert recognition. *Journal of Cognitive Neuroscience*, 7, 425–32.

Tzavaras, A., Luauté, J.P. and Bidault, E. 1986: Face recognition dysfunction and delusional misidentification syndromes (DMS). In H.D. Ellis, M.A. Jeeves, F. Newcombe and A. Young (eds), *Aspects of Face Processing*. Dordrecht: Martinus Nijhoff, 310–16.

Van Lancker, D. 1991: Personal relevance and the human right hemisphere. *Brain and Cognition*, 17, 64–92.

Vogel, B.F. 1974: The Capgras syndrome and its psychopathology. *American Journal of Psychiatry*, 131, 922–4.

Von Monakow, C. 1885: Experimentelle und pathologisch-anatomische Untersuchungen Über die Beziehungen der sogenannten Sehsphäre zu den infracorticalen Opticuscentren und zum N. Opticus. *Archiv für Psychiatrie und Nervenkrankheiten*, 16, 151–99.

Wallis, G. 1986: Nature of the misidentified in the Capgras syndrome. *Bibliotheca Psychiatrica*, 164, 40–8.

Wilcox, J. and Waziri, R. 1983: The Capgras symptom and nondominant cerebral dysfunction. *Journal of Clinical Psychiatry*, 44, 70–2.

Wright, B., Mindham, R. and Burn, W. 1994: Canine Capgras. *Irish Journal of Psychological Medicine*, 11, 31–3.

Wright, S., Young, A.W. and Hellawell, D.J. 1993: Sequential Cotard and Capgras delusions. *British Journal of Clinical Psychology*, 32, 345–9.

Young, A.W. 1998: *Face and Mind*. Oxford University Press.

Young, A.W. and Burton, A.M. 1999: Simulating face recognition: Implications for modelling cognition. *Cognitive Neuropsychology*, 16, 1–48.

Young, A.W., Flude, B.M. and Ellis, A.W. 1991: Delusional misidentification incident in a right hemisphere stroke patient. *Behavioural Neurology*, 4, 81–7.

Young, A.W. and Leafhead, K.M. 1996: Betwixt life and death: Case studies of the Cotard delusion. In P.W. Halligan and J.C. Marshall (eds), *Method in Madness: Case Studies in Cognitive Neuropsychiatry*. Hove, E. Sussex: Psychology Press, 147–71.

Young, A.W., Leafhead, K.M. and Szulecka, T.K. 1994: The Capgras and Cotard delusions. *Psychopathology*, 27, 226–31.

Young, A.W., Reid, I., Wright, S. and Hellawell, D.J. 1993: Face-processing impairments and the Capgras delusion. *British Journal of Psychiatry*, 162, 695–8.

Young, A.W., Robertson, I.H., Hellawell, D.J., de Pauw, K.W. and Pentland, B. 1992: Cotard delusion after brain injury. *Psychological Medicine*, 22, 799–804.

3

Towards an Understanding of Delusions of Misidentification: Four Case Studies

NORA BREEN, DIANA CAINE, MAX COLTHEART,
JULIE HENDY AND CORINNE ROBERTS

Delusions of misidentification (DM) include a variety of fascinating disorders in which there is a mistaken belief in the identity of oneself, other people, places or objects. They include: Capgras syndrome—the belief that other people, often close relatives, have been replaced by doubles or impostors; Fregoli syndrome—the belief that strangers are in fact known people in disguise; intermetamorphosis—the belief that someone has changed physically and psychologically into another person; reverse intermetamorphosis—the belief that there has been a physical and psychological change of oneself into another person; and reduplicative paramnesia—the belief that there are doubles of known people or places. This last delusion (reduplicative paramnesia) differs from Capgras delusion in that while reduplication is believed to have occurred, there is no sense of replacement. Thus, the impostor claim is not made in cases of reduplicative paramnesia. Patients with DM traverse the boundaries of psychiatry, neurology and neuropsychology and have been studied from the perspective of all three disciplines.[1]

Cases of DM began to be published in the psychiatric literature in the early 1900s. The first extensive description of the Capgras syndrome was published by Capgras and Reboul-Lachaux in 1923 (Capgras and Reboul-Lachaux,

---

We are very grateful to TH, FE, DB, RZ and their families for their participation in this research. We would also like to thank Matthew Large for insightful discussion about the cases and referral of patient RZ, Virginia Arpadi for referring patient TH, David Sharpe for referring patient FE, and Robyn Langdon and Karalyn Patterson for helpful comments on an earlier draft of this chapter.

[1]   To date, the terminology used to describe these types of delusions has been 'delusional misidentification *syndromes* (DMS)'. A syndrome is defined by a cluster of symptoms, yet each type of delusional misidentification is defined by only a single particular symptom. Several authors have raised this issue (Young, 1998; Ellis and Young, 1990; Förstl et al., 1991) but have been reluctant to change the 'syndrome' terminology largely because the name is now entrenched in the literature. We strongly agree that use of the word 'syndrome' is inaccurate, and we have used instead the modified term 'delusions of misidentification' (DM). We hope that this term will be adopted in the future, as it maintains the familiar terminology, but is more accurately representative of the phenomenon.

1923).[2] The authors described a patient, Mme M., who believed her daughter, her husband, her doctors and nurses had been replaced by doubles. Mme M. used the term 'doubles' herself. In the original paper Capgras and Reboul-Lachaux proposed that the Capgras delusion arose due to a dissociation between recognition of the person and the lack of a feeling of familiarity for that person, leading to the patient recognizing the appearance of the person before them, but being unable to believe that they were truly who they seemed. However, this explanation was quickly overshadowed by the authors' subsequent psychodynamic theories regarding the Capgras delusion. For quite a number of years the predominant interpretation of Capgras delusion was that conflicting feelings of love and hate were resolved by the delusion, as the double could then be hated without guilt.[3]

More recently, the strategy of cognitive neuropsychology has been employed in the investigation of DM (Ellis and Young, 1990; Halligan and Marshall, 1996; Young, 1998). This approach involves developing models of normal mental processes by studying ways in which these processes break down after brain damage (Caramazza, 1986; Ellis and Young, 1996). As applied to disorders which have traditionally been labelled as 'psychiatric', the strategy has come to be termed cognitive neuropsychiatry. The work of Ellis and Young (1990; Young, 1998), in particular, has been influential in thinking about delusional beliefs within a cognitive neuropsychiatry framework. In much of the research investigating the cognitive processes underlying DM, the Capgras delusion has received the most attention (Young, 1998; Stone and Young, 1997). Young (1998) describes the Capgras delusion as a 'model delusion' in that it met the two psychiatric criteria for a delusional belief: the first being that other people with a similar cultural background would find the delusional belief unacceptable and implausible, and the second that the delusion is resistant to evidence to the contrary (p. 37).

Initially, a possible relationship between the Capgras delusion and face processing impairments was investigated by Young and colleagues (Ellis, Young, Quayle and de Pauw, 1997; Wright, Young and Hellawell, 1993; Young, Ellis, Szulecka and de Pauw, 1990; Young Reid, Wright and Hellawell, 1993). Across these four studies, eight patients who had experienced the Capgras delusion were tested on familiar face recognition, unfamiliar face matching and face memory. Seven of the eight patients were significantly impaired on at least one test, suggesting that face processing deficits commonly occurred in conjunction with Capgras delusion; however, there was a large amount of individual variability in the pattern of these deficits. Two patients had a deficit in recognizing familiar faces, two patients had a deficit in recognition memory

---

[2]   A complete translation into English of Capgras and Reboul-Lachaux's (1923) paper is provided by Ellis, Whitely and Luauté, 1994, pp. 117–46.

[3]   For a detailed description of the psychodynamic interpretation of the Capgras delusion prevalent in the early 1900s, see Enoch and Trethowan, 1979, pp. 8–13.

for faces, two patients had deficits in both recognition of familiar faces and unfamiliar face matching, one patient had deficits in all three areas of familiar face recognition, unfamiliar face matching and recognition memory for faces, and one patient performed in the normal range on all three face processing tests. This variability was also found by Silva et al. (1994) in their examination of face processing deficits in six patients who had experienced the Capgras delusion. Only one of the six patients had a deficit in unfamiliar face matching, while four out of the six patients had a deficit in recognition memory for faces.

Young et al. (1993) discussed the findings of face processing deficits in their Capgras patients in terms of a relationship between prosopagnosia (the inability to recognize previously known faces) and the Capgras delusion. They concluded that although there appeared to be some link between the two, the relationship must be subtle and not directly causal as 'prosopagnosic patients do not usually experience the Capgras delusion and, conversely, Capgras patients still can recognise a number of familiar faces' (Young et al., 1993, p. 697). Importantly, Capgras patients themselves often describe the misidentified person as a 'double' and state that the impostors are almost exact replicas of the originals. This indicates that the Capgras patient is not prosopagnosic since the patient remains able to recognize the face of the misidentified person, regardless of any specific deficit in face processing they may have.

Ellis and Young (1990) ingeniously reasoned that Capgras syndrome may be the mirror image disorder of prosopagnosia. They argued that face recognition consisted of two components: one which involved the overt recognition of familiar faces and a second which consisted of the emotional response one has to familiar faces. They proposed that in prosopagnosia there is a loss of the overt face recognition component, whereas in Capgras syndrome overt face recognition is relatively preserved, but there is a loss of the appropriate affective response to familiar faces. Ellis and Young (1990) suggested that when the Capgras patients receive this conflicting information—that is, they look at a known face and recognize it, but do not have the affective response normally associated with that face—they adopt some sort of rationalization in which the person is concluded to be an impostor or double.

This work by Ellis and Young (1990) was based in part on a two-route theory of face processing proposed initially by Bauer (1984, 1986), in which both a visual route (enabling overt visual recognition) and an affective route (enabling the association of an appropriate affective response to a known face) contribute to face recognition. Ellis and Young's adaptation of Bauer's two-route theory of face recognition enabled the specific prediction that Capgras patients would demonstrate relatively intact overt recognition of known faces but a reduced autonomic response, as measured by skin conductance response (SCR), to those same faces.[4] This prediction has now been validated by two

---

[4]   The skin conductance response (SCR) is a nonspecific physiological response that occurs when a subject is aroused. Arousal has an effect on the sympathetic nervous system, which

independent research groups (Ellis, Young, Quayle and de Pauw, 1997; Hirstein and Ramachandran, 1997). Ellis et al. (1997) measured the SCR of five Capgras patients using famous faces as the test stimuli. Hirstein and Ramachandran (1997) tested their patient, DS, using both famous and personally familiar faces, including those people about whom DS experienced delusions (father, mother, self). These findings indicate that Capgras patients are able to overtly recognize but have a reduced or absent SCR to either famous or personally familiar faces.[5] Hirstein and Ramachandran (1997) demonstrated further that DS's Capgras delusion was specific to the visual modality: he claimed his parents were impostors when looking at them, but not when speaking to them on the telephone.[6]

The significance of this lack of the usual affective accompaniment to seeing a known face in the formation of the Capgras delusion has been further developed by Stone and Young (1997), who described the delusional belief as occurring, in the first instance, when there are 'anomalous perceptual experiences created by a deficit to the person's perceptual system' (p. 327). It is important to note that Stone and Young used the term 'perceptual' rather broadly, not, as it is more usually used, to refer only to the processing of externally derived sensory information (visual, auditory, tactile) but also to include a disturbance in the affective experience, the processing of internally-derived (autonomic) information associated with a percept which, in this case, results in known faces failing to arouse the affective significance normally associated with them. An anomalous percept, in this highly particular sense, is taken to provide the precondition for the development of the misidentification delusion.

Why is it, however, that patients with the Capgras delusion interpret the absence of an affective response toward the misidentified person as signalling that the person is an impostor, a rather implausible belief to adopt? Why do patients not conclude that, since the person before them looks exactly like

---

is measurable as electrodermal activity in the skin of the fingers. In the experimental situation, interpretation of an SCR is dependent on whether or not a different response is elicited to contrasting stimuli. For example, when normal subjects view photographs of faces, they have a much larger SCR when they view known faces compared to when they view strangers' faces.

5   The five Capgras patients described by Ellis et al., 1997, were psychiatric patients who had additional persecutory delusions, and three of the patients had a formal diagnosis of schizophrenia. No information was provided with regard to neurological or imaging evidence of brain damage in these five patients. In contrast, the patient described by Hirstein and Ramachandran, 1997 had the onset of the Capgras delusion following a severe head injury. Although the total number of patients is very small, these results of these two studies indicate that a reduced SCR can occur in both patients with the delusion occurring as part of a primary psychiatric disorder (primary Capgras) and patients who have the Capgras delusion as the result of an identifiable neurological lesion (secondary Capgras).

6   Ellis and Young, 1990, also attempted to interpret the delusions of Fregoli and intermetamorphosis in terms of the cognitive modelling of face processing.

their spouse (or other relative, whatever the case may be), and has all the associated behaviours of that person, the lack of appropriate feeling (i.e. lack of affective response) on seeing them must be the result of some internal problem—for example, the loss of one's own ability to feel an emotional response to familiar people. Young et al. (1993) proposed that this more rational explanation does not occur in Capgras because the delusion arises specifically in the context of a paranoid, or at least intensely suspicious, mood state. Such a mood state leads the patient to misattribute a change in their internal world (loss of the normal affective significance that usually accompanies seeing a familiar face) to a change in their external world (the known person has been replaced by a double or impostor) (see also Ellis, Young, Quayle and de Pauw, 1997; Stone and Young, 1997). Ellis and Young (1990) suggest that the paranoid or suspicious mood of patients with the Capgras delusion can also result in their thinking of the doubles as evil or dangerous in some way.

Ellis and Young (1990) further argue that the loss of affective response to known faces in Capgras patients occurs in the context of a more general disturbance in affective responsiveness. Several authors have linked the Capgras delusion with generalized depersonalization or derealization (Merrin and Silverfarb, 1976; Christodoulou, 1977; Todd, Dewhurst and Wallis, 1981). Merrin and Silverfarb (1976) stated that 'a number of cases (of Capgras delusion) began with diffuse feelings of unreality or depersonalization, followed by indiscriminate misidentification and finally by the establishment of the Capgras delusion' (p. 968). In support of this connection between the Capgras delusion and depersonalization/derealization, Ellis and Young (1990) give the example of patients with DM who sometimes report that everything, not just the misidentified person, looks strange, that 'things may look painted or not natural and faces may look like masks or wax models or seem to have been changed by plastic surgery' (p. 241).

Patients with DM are highly resistant to the presence of contrary evidence. When challenged about the absurdity of their delusional belief, Capgras patients are often able to appreciate they are making a bizarre claim, yet the belief remains fixed. Young (1998) reports that 'if you ask (the Capgras patient) "what would you think if I told you my wife had been replaced by an impostor", you will often get answers to the effect that it would be unbelievable, absurd, an indication that you had gone mad. Yet these patients will claim that, none the less, this is exactly what has happened to their own relative' (p. 37). If the patient is asked to provide evidence that the misidentified person is an impostor, they will often report minor physical differences in support of their claim. In the original case described by Capgras and Reboul-Lachaux in 1923, Mme M. said that she identified people as being doubles by observing minor differences, and gave examples such as 'a little mark on the ear . . . a thinner face . . . the way of speaking . . . the way of walking' (Ellis, Whitley and Luauté, 1994, p. 129). Clifford Beers also described this method of detection in his retrospective account of his experience of the Capgras delusion in the early 1900s: 'Relatives and friends frequently called to see me. I spoke to none, not even to my mother and father. For, though they all appeared about as they used to do, I was able to detect some slight difference in look or gesture or intonation of voice, and this was enough to confirm my belief that they were impersonators' (Beers, 1953, pp. 62–3). In some cases the delusional belief is so strongly held that there is a risk of violence against the alleged impostor. A review of 260 reported cases of delusional misidentification by Förstl et al. (1991) found that physical violence had been noted in 46 cases (18%). In one extreme case, a young man with the Capgras delusion for his stepfather, accused him of being a robot, and subsequently decapitated him to look for batteries and microfilm in his head (de Pauw and Szulecka, 1988). While this degree of violence is relatively rare, it indicates how strong the delusion can be.

While DM have been described as transient phenomena (Ellis, Luauté and Retterstol, 1994), there are now reported cases where the delusion persisted for several weeks (Young, Reid, Wright and Hellawell, 1993; Collins, Hawthorne, Gribbin and Jacobson, 1990; Quinn, 1981) or indeed for months or years (Silva, Leong, Weinstock, Sharma and Klein, 1994; Frazer and Roberts, 1994; Todd, Dewhurst and Wallis, 1981; Hirstein and Ramachandran, 1997). Hirstein and Ramachandran, (1997) described patient DS, who had the Capgras delusion for his father for over two years. Silva et al. (1994) described Ms. A who fatally stabbed and shot her mother following a five-year period of believing that her parents were impostors. There are also reported instances in which the delusion recurred intermittently over long periods of time, such as the young man described by Mackie, Ebmeier and O'Carroll (1994), who stated that several times each day his parents or close relatives would be replaced by an impostor, and that this had gone on continually throughout the past year. It would therefore appear that DM can be highly variable with regard to both stability and duration.

All of the early reports of Capgras delusion were to be found in the psychiatric literature, but in 1971 a case of Capgras was described in a young man following a head injury, with no previous history of psychiatric disorder (Weston and Whitlock, 1971). This provided clear evidence that the Capgras delusion can occur after known neurological damage. Since then, many patients with DM have undergone more thorough neurological investigations, including brain imaging, as part of their medical investigations, and a number (but by no means all) of the reported cases have been found to have a cerebral pathology (Malloy, Cimino and Westlake, 1992; Fleminger and Burns, 1993).

Malloy et al. (1992) reviewed all of the published Capgras cases reported during the 10 year period 1979–89. Based on their analysis of 35 cases, Malloy et al. (1992) identified two categories of Capgras, depending on whether the delusion occurred as part of a primary psychiatric disorder, such as schizophrenia (primary Capgras) or as the result of an identifiable neurological correlate (secondary Capgras). Cases were assigned to the latter on the basis of positive neuroimaging, electroencephalogram (EEG), and/or neuropsycholog-ical findings. They found that 63% of cases had positive neurological findings but there was no uniform pattern of impairment in these secondary Capgras cases. Neuroimaging (CT or MRI scans) revealed right-hemisphere lesions in 46%, bilateral or diffuse abnormalities in 36%, and no abnormality in 18%. Of the cases with abnormal EEG, 53% had right-hemisphere abnormality predominantly, 40% had diffuse changes, and one case showed unilateral left-hemisphere electrophysiological abnormality. Only 35% of the secondary Capgras patients were reported to have had deficits on neurological examin-ation, but all of the positive findings indicated right-hemisphere involvement. Neuropsychological assessment revealed that the secondary Capgras patients tended to display executive, visuospatial and memory dysfunction or gen-eralized abnormalities.

Malloy et al. (1992) further distinguished primary from secondary Capgras delusion according to a number of clinical features. The average age of onset of the delusion was earlier in primary Capgras (mean age 32 years) than in secondary Capgras (mean age 48.5 years). Primary cases were more likely to have an insidious onset (90%) which evolved gradually, whereas secondary cases were more likely to have sudden onset delusions (56%). All of the primary cases displayed associated psychotic symptoms, with paranoia being the most prominent, whereas psychotic symptoms were only present in 62% of the sec-ondary cases. Capgras patients without apparent organic cerebral dysfunction were more likely to have experienced other psychiatric symptoms prior to the onset of the Capgras delusion (69% reported by Malloy et al; see also Fleminger and Burns,1993, who reported 95%) compared to those with organic cerebral dysfunction (36% reported by Malloy et al.; 28% reported by Fleminger and Burns).

In a similar review, but using slightly different selection criteria, Fleminger and Burns (1993) retrospectively analysed cases of delusional misidentification of persons (including the Capgras delusion *and* reduplicative paramnesia) pub-lished since 1977. Patients were classified into groups according to whether or not they had evidence of neurological disorder. The authors raise the point that some of the patients identified as having no neurological lesion might be found to have organic brain disease with more sophisticated imaging tech-niques or at post-mortem; however, they defend their study technique as it enabled groups with differing degrees of neurological impairment to be com-pared. Based on analysis of these 50 cases, Fleminger and Burns (1993) ident-ified a group of patients who fell between the categories of primary and sec-ondary Capgras defined by Malloy et al. (1992). This group of patients had some evidence of organic dysfunction (e.g. history, mental state examination, disorientation) but no evidence on clinical investigation (e.g. EEG or CT brain scans). This group also fell in the middle of the two distinct groups with regard to the presence of preceding paranoid delusions (69%). In addition, they found that patients with neurological impairments were more likely to regard the

Table 1 Summary of criteria for characterizing DM patients according to a spectrum of neurological–non-neurological aetiology, based on the findings of Malloy et al. (1992) and Fleminger and Burns (1993)

Delusions of misidentification: a neurological continuum	*No identified neurological lesion*	→ *Some evidence of neurological impairment*	→ *Identified neurological lesion*
Evidence of neurological lesion	No	Yes History Orientation Mental State Examination	Yes CT, MRI, EEG Neurology Neuropsychology
Mean age at onset	32 years		48.5 years
Type of onset	Insidious		Acute
Delusion interpretation	Threatening		Benign, Trickery
Associated psychotic symptoms†	100%		62%
Psychiatric symptoms preceding the DM	Majority 69%★ 94%★★	69%★★	Minority 36%★ 28%★★

†The most predominant associated psychotic symptom was paranoia.
★Results from Malloy et al. (1992)
★★Results from Fleminger and Burns (1993)

misidentification as benign or as due to trickery, whereas patients without evidence of neurological impairment were more likely to interpret the delusions as being threatening. These observations suggest that individuals with DM can be classified on a continuum from 'no identified neurological lesion' to 'identified neurological lesion', with many cases probably falling somewhere between the two poles. The differences between patients falling at different points along this continuum found by Malloy et al. and Fleminger and Burns are detailed in Table 1.

In summary, the key features currently considered to be critical to the development of the Capgras delusion, and possibly other DM, are as follows:

- There is an anomalous perceptual experience (considered by Ellis and Young, 1990; Young, 1998, to be the loss of the normal affective response to known faces, specifically) which is a precondition for the delusion.
- This disturbed perceptual experience is accompanied by a paranoid, or at least intensely suspicious, mood, which leads to misattribution of the anomalous perceptual experience (Stone and Young, 1997; Young, 1998).

- The loss of normal response to familiar faces occurs in the context of more generalized depersonalization-derealization (Young, 1990).

In addition there is often a deficit in visual face processing, although the patients are not prosopagnosic. To date, there has been no discussion as to whether the above features apply equally to primary and to secondary cases of Capgras.

Four case studies of DM will now be presented. Two cases are misidentification of the reflected self, one is that of a reverse intermetamorphosis and one is that of a reduplicative paramnesia. An outline of the particular delusional beliefs in each case will be presented, following which the cases will be discussed in the context of three levels of interpretation: the neurological level (the extent to which structural pathology is implicated in the delusional phenomenon and the implications of this); the cognitive level (what cognitive impairments appear to be implicated in DM formation); and the phenomenological level (the individual's experience of the delusion).

1. Case 1—Patient FE: Mirrored-Self Misidentification

FE, an 87-year-old man, had an unremarkable medical history until the age of 86 years, when he was briefly admitted to hospital after a suspected transient ischaemic attack.[7] Following his discharge home his family reported that he had occasional nocturnal hallucinations, but no other change in FE's behaviour or cognitive function was noticed until one year later, when they moved house. The family then noticed that FE was not able to recognize his own reflection in the mirror. He treated his own reflection as though it were another person who was following him around, not only in his own home but also in the car, shopping centres and even on an aeroplane! FE attempted to communicate with this *person* on numerous occasions by talking to him and by using sign language, and was a bit mystified as to why the *person* never spoke back to him. FE was not particularly worried about the *person* being in his own home, but did get upset on one occasion when he saw the *person* in bed with his own wife (their bed faced a full-length, wall-to-wall mirror). Nevertheless, FE showed no signs of paranoia about the *person* and denied that he believed the *person* intended to harm him or his family. FE's family tried on numerous occasions to dissuade him from his belief by providing him with evidence contrary to the delusion. FE would listen attentively to their arguments and often agreed with their logic, but his delusional belief remained steadfast.

---

[7] A transient ischaemic attack (TIA) is a temporary stroke that completely resolves, caused by a blockage of blood vessels in the brain.

FE had no previous psychiatric history. He presented as a well oriented man and was able to provide a detailed history including relevant names and dates throughout his life span. Neuropsychological testing revealed intact left hemisphere function (excellent language skills and verbal memory) but marked right hemisphere dysfunction (impaired copying, drawing, constructional skills and visual memory). At his initial presentation the delusional belief had been stable for 10 months, and it remained stable for the following two years. During the two-year follow-up period FE's overall intellectual function declined and a diagnosis of a progressive dementia of uncertain aetiology was made.

The following are excerpts of conversation with FE while he was standing in front of a mirror looking at his own reflection:

FE: That's not me! (*FE's initial response when he stepped in front of the mirror*).

Examiner: Who is that?

FE: That's not me. It hits me straight away. First of all I didn't like his face at all, but I've got used to his face and I'll have a smile with him if I am in the bathroom for a wash or something, but it's not me.

Examiner: It's not you.

FE: No

Examiner: So this is the person you see in your house.

FE: Yes

Examiner: And it's not you?

FE: No

Examiner: What does that person look like?

FE: Well, he looks very much like me. I guess he could pass for F_____ E_____.

Examiner: He does look like you.

FE: Yes, I see that. He's not a bad looking fellow.

Examiner: So what does he look like? Can you describe him?

FE: No better than that (*indicating toward his reflection in the mirror.*)

Examiner: Does he wear glasses?

FE: I think he does, I think he does. Yes, he does wear glasses. (*FE does wear glasses.*)

Examiner: What colour is his hair?

FE: I don't think he is as white as I am. (*FE has white hair and is balding.*)

Examiner: Is he going a bit bald, or does he have a full head of hair?

FE: Oh, I think he's about the same as mine as far as hair covering is concerned. (*FE then tilts his head forward so that the top of the head of the reflected image is visible.*)

Examiner: So this is the person that you see in your house . . .

FE: Mmm (*nods yes*).

Examiner: . . . and you saw in the plane that time . . .

FE: Mmm (*nods yes*)

Examiner: . . . and you see in the shopping centre.

FE: Mmm (*nods yes*).

Examiner: So this is the person that is following you around?

FE: Well, you come walk around here with me. (*FE walks away from the mirror so he can no longer see the mirror reflection.*)

Examiner: You want to walk around?

FE: Whether that will help or not.

Examiner: Help to do what?

FE: To show how he comes into the picture.

Examiner: Oh, right. So you leave the mirror, you come back here (*in front of the mirror*) and there he is back again.

FE: Yes, yes.

Examiner: Is he always dressed in the same clothes as you?

FE: Oh, I've never, oh, I think so. We both dress very similar. If you could step into another room, you'd see how quick it hits you. I think you can distinguish that it's not me, it's himself. He's got a personality himself.

Examiner turned FE away from the mirror and then slowly back to face it.

Examiner: Who is that? (*indicating towards FE's reflection*).

FE: I don't know his name.

Examiner: It's the person again?

FE: It's the person again, yes. When you look at the Greek or something or other, it's a reflection. We have to say, that the children have arrived at it, he's a non-entity because he is a shadow.

Examiner: So your children have told you he's a non-entity because he's a reflection and a shadow?

FE: They agree with that.

Examiner standing next to FE in front of a mirror, with the reflections of both the examiner and FE visible to FE.

Examiner: (*Pointing to her own reflection*) Who is this, next to the person?

FE: I don't know.

Examiner: Who does it look like? Have you seen this person in here before? (*pointing to the reflection of the examiner*).

FE: That's you.

Examiner: That's me?

FE: Yes.

Examiner: Me, here? (*pointing to herself*) What's my name?

FE: I don't know, oh yes, it's Nora.

Examiner: Nora, that's right. So that's me in the mirror?

FE: Yes.

Examiner: That's my reflection?

FE: Yes.

Examiner: And who is that? (*pointing to FE's reflection*).

FE: I don't know what you would call him. It makes me a bit sick because he moves about freely with us. I don't be too friendly because I don't see it does him any good.

FE's semantic knowledge regarding mirrors was intact. He was clearly able to define what a mirror was, what it was used for, and was able to identify several mirrors amongst a group of other objects without difficulty. He had no difficulty recognizing the reflected images of various objects in a mirror. His wife said that FE rarely used a mirror any longer, but did occasionally look in the mirror when using his electric shaver. When the authors observed FE shaving, he did look in the mirror, but he appeared to be shaving in an automatic manner, rather than using his own reflection for guidance. Interestingly, FE demonstrated some behavioural evidence of covert recognition that the reflected image he was looking at was in fact himself. When asked if the *person* was bald, FE tilted his head forward so that the top of his head would be visible in his reflected image in the mirror.

FE was well oriented to self, and there was no evidence to suggest general depersonalization or derealization. He denied feeling that family members or friends seemed strange in any way, or that there was anything in his environment, apart from the stranger he believed had moved into his life, that was not quite normal. He always insisted he did not know who the reflection was, and referred to it as *the person*, but never referred to it as an impostor or double. He did not express any paranoia in relation to his reflected image or in relation to anyone else. He did not act in a way that would suggest that he felt threatened by his mirror image and he never indicated that he felt the reflection was evil.

Ellis and Young (1990; Young, 1998) have suggested that patients with the Capgras delusion may have a pervasive feeling of strangeness and unfamiliarity that is important in the development of the delusional belief. We were interested to know if this applied to FE. We investigated whether FE had retained a feeling of familiarity in relation to his personal belongings. We assessed this by presenting him with sixteen items, half of them his own possessions and half of them objects he had never seen before. The items selected included eight salient personal belongings including his own cap, belt, Bible, cup, watch, tie, pen and cuff-links. All of these items were judged by his wife to have a strong significance for FE. Each of the eight personal items was matched with an object of the same type that was very similar in appearance. The items were presented in a random order, and the test was repeated on two occasions. When asked to classify the items as familiar or not, he scored 30/32 correct.

When asked to judge whether each object belonged to him, he scored 27/32 correct: his errors included one error in which he thought an unfamiliar object was his own, and four errors in which he thought familiar objects belonged to someone else.

FE had a marked disorder of face processing. He performed poorly on simple face matching tasks, including a straightforward matching of a sample face to an identical one in a set of four faces. When shown photographs of 51 famous faces, he correctly identified only one. In contrast, when given the names of famous people and asked to provide as much information about them as possible, FE did much better. In the majority of cases (75%) he demonstrated intact semantic knowledge regarding these people, such as their occupation or the reason for their being famous. When shown photographs of family members' faces, he correctly identified 16/20 as being familiar. He was able to identify by name the faces of himself, his wife and his son, but was inconsistent in his ability to identify his daughter's face by name, and extremely limited in his ability to identify by name other close relatives, stating that they 'looked familiar' but that he did not know who they were.

In addition to these failures of recognition, FE committed a number of errors of false recognition. He incorrectly identified many of the celebrities as being personally known to himself. Similarly, when shown faces of strangers, he often identified the faces as being personally known to him; for example, as someone he had previously worked with or as a relation. Thus, while FE did not suffer from a generalized sense of depersonalization/derealization or loss of affective responsiveness, his responses indicated a heightened sense of familiarity with regard to both previously known and previously unseen faces, and to unfamiliar objects, such that he reported personally knowing people who were complete strangers to him and reported feelings of familiarity regarding objects he had never seen before.

Some months after the onset of FE's mirrored-self misidentification, he expressed the delusional belief that his wife, Alison, was two people and that his son had a brother. (FE had one son and one daughter.) He said there were two Alisons, one was his wife and the other was the mother of his children. He confided in one of the examiners that he had unwittingly committed adultery on one occasion with *the other Alison*, and that he felt extremely guilty about this. His wife said that he spoke about *the other Alison* in her presence; for example, talking about her in the third person to their children, telling them things that she had said or done. Further investigation of the evolution of FE's DM was not possible beyond this point because of general deterioration in his intellectual function.

2. Case 2—Patient TH: Mirrored-Self Misidentification

TH, a 77-year-old man, also presented with delusional misidentification of his own reflection. At the time of presentation, TH's delusional belief had been stable for four months. He was well oriented, not confused, and did not have any other delusional beliefs. TH had a very similar neuropsychological profile to that of FE. He also demonstrated intact left hemisphere function but marked right hemisphere dysfunction. TH had no past psychiatric history.

Like FE, TH often attempted to talk to his own reflection, and thought that the 'other person' was quite rude as he never spoke back. TH said that he had first encountered the 'other person' at a bus stop, where he had just appeared one day. TH spoke of this *person* following him around; for example, appearing at the hospital during TH's appointments with the authors. TH described a trip that he and his wife had taken to the country during which they had encountered this *person* coming into a café just as they were leaving it (the door to the café was glass). TH said that this 'other person' must know what time he got up, as the 'other person' was always already in the bathroom when TH went in there in the morning, and, when TH got out of the shower, the 'other person' was waiting, undressed, presumably ready to have his own shower. When questioned, TH said that he had never been afraid of this *person*, and when asked what this *person's* personality was like, TH replied that the *person* had not given him any reason to be suspicious.

TH continued to have the delusional misidentification of his reflection for the 10-month period of follow-up investigation. Diagnosis of a progressive dementia of unspecified type was made.

The following are excerpts of conversation with TH while he was standing in front of a mirror looking at his own reflection:

Examiner: What do you see there?
TH: I see my face in there, a reflection of it.
Examiner: And can you describe what that reflection looks like?
TH: Just like that bloke there (*points to his own reflection*).
Examiner: What does he look like?
TH: What does he look like?
Examiner: Yes. How would you describe him?
TH: Well, the only way I could describe him is that he looks like me.
Examiner: He looks like you?
TH: Yes.
Examiner: Does he look a lot like you?
TH: A lot like me.
Examiner: Does he?
TH: Yes.
Examiner: Is he bald?
TH: Is he bald? (*Looks at own reflection.*) He'd have to be wouldn't he, or he wouldn't, it wouldn't . . . Yes, he'd have to be. He'd be a man as old as me. He used to watch down the corridor to see when you came out of your room, especially in the morning. I'd come out of the room to go to the toilet and he'd be looking

round the doorpost to see if I was coming. He'd be following me or I'd be following him. It was a little bit confusing at times. You'd look in the mirror and say 'Who's that?', looks like me. But people say 'It's not you, it's only a reflection in the glass that you can see'. It's only a reflection. But this man here (*pointing to his own reflection*), he's my twin brother if you wanted to match up two look-alikes.

Examiner: Because this fellow here (*pointing to TH's reflection*) looks so much like you?

TH: (*Pointing at his own reflection*) What do you say?

Examiner: (*Thinking the question has been addressed to her, the examiner replies to TH's question*) Yes, I would agree that he looks very much like you.

TH turns to examiner, looking puzzled as to why she responded to his question.

Examiner: Oh, you mean you were asking him, (*pointing to TH's reflection*) what does he think?

TH: Yes. I haven't been able to get him to talk since I met him and known him.

Examiner: Why is that do you think?

TH: I don't know.

Examiner: So when you ask him questions, he doesn't answer you?

TH: No, so I assume that he can't talk. He's the only one that could answer that question.

Examiner: Do you know what his name is?

TH: Tom. That's what he told me his name was. My name is Tom.

Examiner: Yes. That's a coincidence.

TH: He asked me what my name was when I met him and he said Tom. And I said 'That's good, I'm Tom too'.

Examiner: Were you ever worried by him that he might hurt you?

TH: No.

Examiner: He seems to be wearing the same clothes that you are wearing. Does that always happen?

TH: That always happens.

Examiner: How would you explain that?

TH: He's not changing his clothes. He'll walk out the door, come down the hall, and I'll be dressed like this (*pointing to himself*), and he'll come out the other door dressed exactly the same.

Examiner: Really?

TH: It doesn't matter how many times you did it, it would always come out that way.

Examiner: Right. So he'll always be wearing the same clothes that you are wearing.

TH: No. He's only wearing a reflection of the clothes that I am wearing.

Examiner: At the moment in your bathroom, you have the curtain over the mirror don't you?

TH: Yes. There is a curtain over all the mirrors in the house.

Examiner: So when you want to use the mirror, and you pull it up at the corner, pull the curtain up, what happens? What do you see?

TH: As soon as you lift the corner, you see him (*nodding his head at his reflection*).

Examiner: What happens when you shave?

TH: He'll get his razor and he'll be on the other side of the mirror, and I'll be on this side of the mirror, and we'll shave at the same time, sometimes.

Examiner: When you look in here (*indicating to the mirror*) tell me what you see?

TH: (*Looking at the examiner's reflection*) I can see a reflection, oh, are you talking to that gentleman or me? (*pointing to his own reflection*).

Examiner: (*Looking at TH*) I'm talking to you.

TH: To me (*pointing to his own chest*). I can see your reflection and I can see Tom's reflection.

Examiner: Tom who?

TH: I don't know his second name. He's been unable to tell me what his second name is apparently.

Examiner: Is that because he doesn't talk to you?

TH: He doesn't talk to anyone.

Examiner: Doesn't he?

TH: (*Looking at his own reflection*) Is that right? Do you talk to anyone? Can you talk? Can you talk or have you got trouble talking or you didn't learn to talk, you weren't taught? I don't know.

Examiner: Because he doesn't tell you.

TH: No. I don't think he can.

TH said that he had also seen the *person*'s wife, and that she looked quite like his own wife, and that the two women wore very similar clothes. When asked where this *person* and his *wife* lived, TH said that they lived in an adjoining unit located at the back of TH's home (there was no unit adjoining TH's home). On one occasion, one of the examiners was standing next to TH in front of a mirror, and he was asked to identify what he saw in the mirror. TH said that in addition to *the person*, he also saw *the woman* who had come with the examiner (the examiner had arrived on her own).

Like FE, TH also demonstrated some behavioural evidence of covert recognition that the reflected image he was looking at was in fact himself. TH repeatedly stated that the *person* he saw in the mirror never spoke to him, yet when asked what that *person*'s name was, TH said it was Tom. That is his own first name, implying some covert knowledge that this *other Tom* was actually his own reflection. In addition, when asked whether the *person* in the mirror was bald, TH replied 'yes, he'd have to be'. In fact, the *person* would only 'have' to be bald if TH was aware that what he was looking at was his own reflection.

Unlike FE, TH's face processing was substantially intact. He was able to match unfamiliar faces on both simple and difficult matching tasks. He was able to identify both personally familiar and famous faces. Similarly to FE, but to a much lesser extent, TH did make false positive identification of strangers' faces as familiar on 6/26 occasions.[8] TH's affective response to salient personal objects was also tested, in the manner described above for FE. Each of 10 of his own possessions was matched with an unfamiliar object of the same type. TH correctly identified, as his own, the objects he owned and he rejected all of the matched distracters.

During the last testing session, TH spontaneously recited the following poem:

> *When you get what you want in your struggle for self*
> *And the world makes you king for the day*
> *You go to the mirror and look at yourself*
> *And see what that man has to say.*
>
> *He's the fellow to please, never mind all the rest*
> *He's with you clear up to the end*
> *And you've passed the most difficult dangerous test*
> *If the man in the glass is your friend.*

He was able to recite the poem a second time to allow the examiner to transcribe it, stating that he had learned it many years ago.

In view of the absence of any significant face processing disorder in TH, we explored further his ability to interpret mirror-reflected space. To do this we devised an experiment based on that by Ramachandran, Altschuler and Hillyer (1997) who observed that patients with left visual neglect were unable to interpret mirror reflections of objects correctly when the reflection of the objects occurred in the neglected visual field. When shown an object on their left, the patients kept banging their hand into the mirror or groped behind it attempting to grab the reflection. Ramachandran, Altschuler and Hillyer (1997) named this deficit 'mirror agnosia' since the patient could see the mirror clearly but behaved as though it did not exist.

TH sat in a chair facing a mirror. Objects (for example, pen, stapler, key,

---

[8]   As a control comparison, TH's wife was administered the same tests of face recognition as TH. TH's wife had no difficulty correctly identifying all 26/26 strangers' faces as unfamiliar.

apple) were held up behind his left or right shoulder and he was asked first to name the reflected object. He was able to do this without difficulty. He was then asked to take the object in his hand. Instead of reaching behind the appropriate shoulder, TH reached towards the mirror on each occasion, scratching on the surface of the mirror or attempting to reach into or behind it to get the object. He repeated this behaviour time after time over 20 trials. Clearly the experience of his hand hitting the glass did not override his belief that the object was literally located in front of him (mirror agnosia), not withstanding that he was able to say what a mirror was and how one is used.

Consistent with these findings, TH was impaired on formal testing of visuo-spatial skills including copying, drawing, and block construction. In striking contrast, however, TH had no difficulty negotiating his way around the environment, including his home (which was quite hazardous as his wife often rearranged large piles of objects on the floor of their cluttered home), and several large hospital buildings. There was no evidence of apraxia on formal testing with TH.

TH developed an additional delusion, one of reduplication for place, seven months after the onset of the delusion of self-misidentification. The reduplication delusion occurred for the hospital to which TH had been admitted for further investigations. TH knew that he was in hospital B_____, but believed there was another hospital that was the same with the same name and there was a third hospital that was also the same but was named B_____ West.

3. Case 3—Patient DB: Reduplicative Paramnesia

DB had a sudden onset of reduplicative paramnesia following a right parietal stroke. She was a 76-year-old widow whose past medical history was unremarkable and there was no history of psychiatric illness. Following the stroke, DB was oriented for time, person and place. There was no evidence of dementia or amnesia, but, when interviewed, DB had a striking reduplicative paramnesia. In the course of the same interview, she clearly stated that her husband had died suddenly four year earlier and had been cremated (this was correct), but also that her husband was a patient on the ward in the same hospital.

Examiner: I believe your husband died some years ago.
DB: Four years ago.
Examiner: Could you tell me a little bit about that? What happened?
DB: He just collapsed when he was in the toilet on a Sunday after-
          noon. No doctors were available of course. We got the ambu-
          lance and they got the police because there was no doctor
          present. Then they held a post-mortem at a different hospital.
          They took the remains to a different hospital for the death cer-
          tificate and then we had a cremation. He was 76.

Examiner: How long had you been married?

DB: Up to now we've been married 57 years. In 1932 we got married.

Examiner: And he was cremated you said?

DB: Yes.

Examiner: You were telling me your husband was also at this hospital. Is that right?

DB: Yes, yes.

Examiner: What's he doing in this hospital?

DB: I don't know, I still can't find out.

Examiner: Is he staff or a patient?

DB: A patient.

Examiner: But you don't know why he's a patient here?

DB: I've been trying to find out. But I did hear when he was talking to some of the men that he had a stroke and he could feel it coming on.

Examiner: So he had a stroke as well you think?

DB: Probably. Can't you find that out yourself?

Examiner: Well, I'm not sure I understand quite what's going on. I thought you said your husband was dead. How can your husband be in this hospital if he is dead?

DB: That's what a lot of people say, 'don't you get worried about it?', and I said I'm not religious fortunately or I might be worried about it, you know.

Examiner: It strikes me as odd. If he was cremated, how could he still be here?

DB: Death is final isn't it, as a rule.

Examiner: Well, you would think so wouldn't you. How can you explain that he is still here if he has been cremated?

DB: Well, that's it. I think they took him to seven different hospitals to get a certificate.

Examiner: You're not mistaken? You're not mistaking someone else here for him are you?

DB: No.

Examiner: You're very sure it's him?

DB: Yes.

The patient also reduplicated other members of her family, including her two daughters, a grandson and the father-in-law of one of her daughters. Each of these was said to work at the hospital or to be a patient at the hospital. DB also had anosognosia for her left arm. The arm was paralysed after the stroke, but DB denied the paralysis and said that she still used the arm to feed herself. Testing revealed no prosopagnosia, but she did have many manifestations of a profound right-hemisphere syndrome including left visual neglect and impaired visuospatial processing.

DB was reviewed 19 months after the stroke, at which time she was living in a nursing home. At that time the reduplicative paramnesia regarding her husband persisted. DB did not believe her husband to be in the nursing home with her, but she did state that he had been to see her daughters. She was not sure where he was now living. She was a little concerned about his financial status, as she had stopped his pension when he had died! DB also had reduplicative paramnesia for other members of her family including her grandson (who had been reduplicated during the initial hospital admission) and various other grandchildren. In addition, she expressed reduplication for place, stating that the nursing home had taken over her house in Sydney as an annexe.

4. Case 4—Patient RZ: Reverse Intermetamorphosis

RZ, a 40 year old woman, had the delusional belief that she was a man. This had been a stable delusion for two months prior to our assessment with RZ. During most of that two months she had believed that she was her father, but occasionally she would state that she was her grandfather. At the time we saw RZ, she had taken on the persona of her father. She would only respond to her father's name, and she signed his name when asked to sign any forms. She consistently gave her father's history when questioned about her personal history. For example, when asked her age she said she was in her 60s.

In order to make sense of the dialogue below, the following family history is provided. RZ (also, for clarity, sometimes referred to as Roslyn) is one of seven children and her siblings include Sharon, Beverley, Greg, Wayne, Jodie and Michelle. Roslyn's parents are Douglas (also called Doug and Dougie) and Lil. Roslyn's paternal grandparents are Matt and Georgie. Roslyn has two children, Philip and Leah. Roslyn was married for four years in her early twenties, and is now divorced and not in a relationship.

The following excerpts are from an interview with RZ. Throughout the interview, RZ's mother, Lil, was sitting beside her.

Examiner: Could you tell me your name?
RZ: Douglas.
Examiner: And your surname?
RZ: B_____.
Examiner: And how old are you?
RZ: I don't remember.
Examiner: Roughly how old are you?
RZ: Sixty-something.
Examiner: Sixty-something. And are you married?
RZ: No.
Examiner: No. Have you been married?

RZ: Yes.

Examiner: What was your partner's name?

RZ: I don't remember. Lil.

Examiner: Lil. And you have children?

RZ: Four.

Examiner: And what are their names?

RZ: Roslyn, Beverley, Sharon, Greg.

Examiner: And where do you live?

RZ: In G_____ (*correctly named hospital she was currently in*).

Examiner: At the moment that's right. Where do you normally live when you are not here?

RZ: _____Rd, W_____. (*This was the correct address for her father's property, where she was staying prior to the hospital admission.*)

Examiner: And is that a property?

RZ: Yes.

Examiner: And do you own that property?

RZ: Yes.

Examiner: You own it?

RZ: Yes.

Examiner: So it's yours?

RZ: Yes.

Examiner: Who else lives on that property?

RZ: Lil (*nodding toward her mother, Lil, who was sitting next to her*), the bloke with blue eyes who I don't know, Doug or whoever he is, and Wayne.

Examiner: And so Lil is who? Lil who lives on the property, is she related to you?

RZ: No.

Examiner: No. Who is your wife?

RZ: Georgie. (*At this point in the interview, Roslyn has taken on the identity of her paternal grandfather, Matt.*)

Examiner: Georgie, right. So Lil who lives on the property is not related to you?

RZ: No, she's related by marriage.

Examiner: By marriage.

RZ: Yes.

Examiner: So who has she married? Lil is married to who?

RZ: Doug.

Examiner: And is Doug related to you?

RZ: Yes.

Examiner: Who is he?

RZ: Son.

Examiner: He's your son?

RZ: Yes.

Examiner: So what is your name again?

RZ: This is ridiculous.

Examiner: It's getting confusing, isn't it? I'm sorry, I'm having trouble following. So, your name is . . .

RZ: Dougie. (*Roslyn has switched back to the identity of her father, Doug.*)

Examiner: Dougie. And do you have a son Doug?

RZ: No.

Examiner: You are Doug?

RZ: Yes.

Examiner: So who is Lil?

RZ: She is married to the bloke on the farm, with Wayne.

Examiner: So who is the bloke on the farm?

RZ: I don't know.

Examiner: Someone you don't know?

RZ: Yes.

Examiner: But he's married to Lil?

RZ: Yes.

Examiner: Who is this sitting next to you?

RZ: Lil.

Examiner: Lil.

RZ: Yes.

Examiner: Who is she?

RZ: She is Roslyn, Beverley, Sharon, Greg, Wayne, Michelle and Jodie's mother.

Examiner: Right. So is she related to you? Is this woman here related to you?

RZ: No.

Examiner: No. Why do you think she has come in to see you?

RZ: Because I'm sick.

Examiner: Right. But if she's not related to you why do you think she would have come in? How does she know you?

RZ: She just does. She knows who I am.

Examiner: She knows who you are. Is she related to you in some way?

RZ: No.

Examiner: She's not?

RZ: No.

Examiner: I was talking to Lil before and Lil actually said that she was your mother.

RZ: No, she's not my mum.

Examiner: Is that not right?

RZ: No.

Examiner: So when you look at this woman next to you, you don't think that is your mother?

RZ: (*Turned to look at her mother*) No, it's not my mother.

Examiner: Who is your mother? What's her name?
RZ: I don't remember.
Examiner: You don't remember. Do you know what her name was?
RZ: She died years ago.
Examiner: Right. What about your father?
RZ: He's dead too.
Examiner: Right. Do you remember his name?
RZ: Matt.

The examiner then asked Roslyn's mother, Lilian, to state the members of her family and Roslyn's place in the family.

Examiner: So what do you think about this? (*referring to her mother's account of the family.*)
RZ: (*Shakes her head 'no'.*)
Examiner: Do you think this woman is just making that up?
RZ: Yes. Because I have a man's voice and I've got man's legs so I can't be female, because Dr R_____ gave me injections in the arm to grow breasts, and they castrated me about, in the hospital when I had a hydatid cyst or something they said I had, but they, I don't remember it. I just remember going with Wayne and whoever is out on the farm, Doug, I remember going with him to C_____ and having an operation and I woke up, I think it was C_____ or S_____, and I said 'oh yes, it's been done'. They were my first words when I woke up.
Examiner: So before that time do you think you were a woman?
RZ: No.
Examiner: So you think you have always been a man?
RZ: Yes.
Examiner: And you're a man now?
RZ: No, I'm a female.
Examiner: You're a female now are you? Or a man?
RZ: Well, I've got a man's voice and a female body.
Examiner: Right. So how has that happened?
RZ: Through operations. The doctors did it. They experimented with me or something, because I must have said I wanted to be a female or something, so they experimented with me.
Examiner: So you were a man?
RZ: Yes.
Examiner: And your name was Doug?
RZ: No, Doug's on the farm. I'm just confused because I don't remember. It feels like they've taken my brain out and I don't even have a brain. (*At this point, the delusional identity briefly breaks down.*)

Examiner: What name do the people who work here (*at the hospital*) call you?
RZ: Roslyn.
Examiner: Why do you think they call you Roslyn?
RZ: Because something happened years ago. I kicked Roslyn out of the house when she was living out there with Philip and Leah.
Examiner: Who are Philip and Leah?
RZ: Roslyn's kids.
Examiner: Where is Roslyn these days?
RZ: I don't know. Don't ask me because I wouldn't have a clue. She might be working at N_____ St. She moved out of S_____ Rd and went to live somewhere else.
Examiner: Right. So you know her?
RZ: Yes.
Examiner: But you don't know where she is?
RZ: No.
Examiner: And so you know her children as well?
RZ: Yes, because they come to visit.
Examiner: They come to visit you?
RZ: Yes.
Examiner: Right. How come they come to visit you?
RZ: Just for something to do, or just to come and say hello.
Examiner: How do they know you?
RZ: From years ago. When they were little.
Examiner: Did you know them then?
RZ: Yes.
Examiner: When they come to see you, what do they call you?
RZ: Mum. But I'm not their mum.

RZ standing in front of a mirror looking at her own reflection.

Examiner: When you look in the mirror there, who do you see?
RZ: Dougie B_____ (*her father's name*).
Examiner: What does that reflection look like?
RZ: His hair is a mess, he has a beard and a moustache and his eyes are all droopy.
Examiner: So is that a man or a woman?
RZ: A man.
Examiner: How old is Dougie?
RZ: Sixty-something.
Examiner: And does that reflection you are looking at now look like a sixty-something person?
RZ: Yes.
Examiner: It looks that old does it?

RZ: Yes.
Examiner: Do you think that a sixty-something year old man would have grey hair?
RZ: Well, I haven't worried a lot over the years so my hair didn't go grey.
Examiner: So it's not grey?
RZ: No. It's brown.

RZ was diagnosed with schizophrenia when she was 23 years of age. She had three hospital admissions during her 20s about which little information was available. She was then well until one year before the current admission. At that time she was reported as having chronic negative symptoms and delusional beliefs, including the belief that she was a man. During that admission, severe hirsutism was noted but extensive testing did not reveal the cause. At the time of the current assessment with RZ the hirsutism remained, and was severe enough to warrant RZ shaving her face. RZ reported the fact that she needed to shave as evidence of the truth of her delusional belief that she was a man.

When questioned, RZ continually elaborated her delusional belief. She said that she had some womanly traits because she was given injections by doctors and psychologists that made her grow breasts and she was castrated. This might suggest some paranoia regarding medical staff; however, when questioned specifically, RZ denied having any paranoia or suspiciousness regarding her family, friends or hospital staff, or her environment.

RZ found it difficult to maintain the delusion when she was interviewed and asked persistent questions about her identity. During the course of the interview she switched identity from her father to her grandfather and then back to her father. At another point her delusional identity broke down completely, and she said 'I'm just confused. It feels like they've taken my brain out and I don't even have a brain'.

Testing revealed no face processing deficits. She was able to match unfamiliar faces, was able to recognize famous faces and correctly rejected stranger's faces as being unfamiliar. Her primary visual perceptual ability was normal. In contrast to these areas of preserved cognitive function, RZ's presentation was dominated by flattened affect, consisting of monotonic speech and reduced social responsiveness.

5. Discussion

These four cases are amongst the most detailed studies of DM yet reported. We have made a thorough investigation of the history and symptomatology, including the neurological status, the delusional phenomenology and the neuropsychological profiles of all four patients. Whereas previous studies have sought the common denominator amongst cases of DM, we have examined the differences amongst the cases under study. It is precisely these differences that have allowed us critically to examine current interpretations of DM, to identify aspects of those interpretations that we consider to be problematic and to point the way towards future research. Here we consider the cases from three different perspectives.

5.1 Interpretation of DM at a Neurological Level

Although there has been considerable interest in the fact that DM can have a neurological basis, little attention has been paid, in most case studies, to the actual neurological status of patients under investigation. The reviews of Malloy et al. (1992) and Fleminger and Burns (1993) have demonstrated the need to address this question centrally in considering patients with DM, and have provided a basis for classifying these patients. In Table 1 we have summarized the findings of Malloy et al. (1992), and Fleminger and Burns (1993) which we have interpreted as defining a neurological continuum ranging from 'no identifiable neurological lesion' at one end through to a 'clearly identified neurological lesion' at the other, along which cases of DM may be usefully considered. (See Table 1.)

In applying this continuum to the four patients described above, DB would be positioned at the 'identified neurological lesion' end of the continuum, as her stroke was clearly the precipitating event in the sudden onset of a reduplicative paramnesic belief in a patient with no previous psychiatric history. FE and TH's mirrored-self misidentification had less sudden onset but both men had gross deficits on neuropsychological testing indicative of organic dysfunction, and neither had any record of past psychiatric history. Both men went on to develop more extensive dementing syndromes. FE and TH would both also meet the criteria to be classified at the 'neurological lesion' end of the continuum.[9] Consistent with the finding that delusions with an underlying neurological lesion have a later age of onset, FE, TH and DB had onset at ages 87, 77 and 76 years respectively. FE, TH and DB all interpreted the delusion as benign, were not threatened by it and had no associated psychotic symptoms, consistent with the summary of findings for cases with identified neurological lesions presented in Table 1.

In contrast, while no information was available regarding the onset of RZ's delusion of reverse intermetamorphosis, she had a long psychiatric history, no clearly defined neurological cause for her delusional belief and no striking abnormality on neuropsychological investigation. She would therefore lie at the 'no identified neurological lesion' end of the continuum. As her delusional

---

[9]   Misidentification of one's own mirror image has been infrequently reported. In the small number of cases in the literature, it has occurred in the context of advanced global dementia (Foley and Breslau, 1982; Mendez et al., 1992), atrophy (Gluckman, 1968), and right-hemisphere dysfunction (Feinberg, 1997; Spangenberg, Wagner and Bachman, 1998), providing further support for a neurological role in the development of the delusion.

belief involved a change of her own identity, the characteristic of finding the misidentified person threatening is not applicable to RZ, although she had some evidence of mild paranoia associated with the delusion (a belief that medical staff had given her an operation and injections to turn her into a male). The onset of RZ's delusional belief occurred when she was 40 years of age, markedly earlier than in the cases of DB, TH and FE, and consistent with the findings of an earlier age of onset in cases which do not have an identified underlying neurological lesion. This distinction between cases at a neurological level provides a basis for interpreting differences both in the cognitive antecedents of DM and in the phenomenological experience of DM.

5.2 Interpretation of DM at a Cognitive Level

It has been argued that a precondition for the Capgras delusion is an underlying perceptual deficit, specifically loss of the appropriate affective accompaniment to seeing a known face. As noted in the introduction, the notion of an 'anomalous perceptual experience' has been used rather broadly in this context to refer to a reduced affective responsiveness to known faces. We consider that the use of the term 'perceptual' in this way confounds two separable components of the cognitive deficits contributing to the delusional belief. One of these is a 'perceptual' component, in the more usual sense of that term, that is a disturbance in the processing of externally derived (sensory) information. The other is a disturbance in the affective (autonomic) responsiveness to such incoming sensory information.

5.2.1 The Role of Perceptual Experience   TH, DB and FE all demonstrated profound perceptual deficits, not in the sense of the deficit in affective response to familiar faces described by Ellis and Young (1990; Young 1998) and Stone and Young (1997) but in the more usual sense of a disturbance in the processing of incoming sensory information. TH had mirror agnosia, FE had severe visual face processing deficits and DB had primary visuospatial deficits and left visual neglect.

It seems highly likely that there was a direct link between TH's inability to interpret reflected space and his DM. TH, placed in front of a mirror, interpreted the reflected image as real, treating the mirror as though it were a window through which one were seeing, or could reach into, a real, rather than a reflected, world. TH's DM involved the belief that the person perceived to be in that space was someone other than himself, a real person, a person who looked very much like himself, and who was following him around.

On first thought, it seems equally likely that FE's striking visual face processing deficit underlay the development of his mirrored-self misidentification. If it were the case that this deficit caused him to be unsure of whether the face he was seeing in the mirror was his face, this might have given rise to the hypothesis that the person he was viewing was a stranger and so directly contribute to his DM. Appealing as this interpretation is, it runs afoul of one fact: despite FE's inability to recognize famous faces and the faces of many close relatives, and his misidentification of unfamiliar faces, he remained able to recognize and discriminate his own face in photographs surprisingly well. Given this, it is hard to argue that a difficulty in recognizing his own face in the mirror was a contributing cause of his DM. Since FE is no longer available for testing, we cannot seek additional data to help us here. All we can do is mention two possible ways out of this dilemma.

The first is to consider whether the identification of a face in a mirror might differ in important ways from identification of a face in a photograph. Identification of a photograph of oneself involves recognizing a past representation, whereas mirrored-self recognition involves knowing that the reflection is a concurrent representation of oneself in present time. It is not clear why the latter might be more compromised than the former by the presence of a face processing impairment; but if that were so, then FE's face processing impairment could play a causal role in his DM. The finding that intact recognition of oneself in photographs can coexist with the inability to recognize one's own mirror image has been reported in another case of mirrored-self misidentification. Phillips, Howard and David (1996) reported patient EF who, like FE, was unable to recognize her own reflection in the mirror and demonstrated face processing deficits on formal testing but remained able to identify photographs of herself. This finding, now documented in two mirrored-self misidentification cases, supports the idea that recognition of oneself in a mirror and a photograph are dissociable and that failure to recognize oneself in the mirror does not mean that recognition of oneself in photographs must necessarily be compromised.

The second possibility is that FE may have suffered from mirror agnosia just as TH did, so that the two patients' DMs have the same underlying perceptual impairment. We were unable to test for the presence of mirror agnosia in FE, and so we cannot rule out this explanation. According to this interpretation, FE's visual face processing deficits were coincidental rather than causal with respect to his DM, in the same way that Young and colleagues (Young, Reid, Wright and Hellawell, 1993; Ellis, Young, Quayle and de Pauw, 1997) have proposed that visual face processing deficits are coincidental in the Capgras delusion.

DB's perceptual deficits—a profound disturbance of spatial awareness—did not appear to be associated with the development of her DM, reduplicative paramnesia for several family members. Instead, DB's reduplicative paramnesia appeared more likely to have resulted from an anomalous affective experience.

5.2.2 The Role of Anomalous Affective Experience   DB's paramnesic delusion involved the false attribution of a sense of personal familiarity to a recent remembered experience. For example, she accurately remembered seeing people visiting the patient in the next bed the day before, but mistakenly

believed that it was her husband that the people were visiting. DB's inappropriately heightened affective responsiveness resulted in her interpreting events or people with whom she was not involved as having to do with her personally. Similarly, both FE and TH had a tendency to judge unknown faces as being personally familiar, which also suggests hyperfamiliarity. All three patients thus demonstrated a tendency towards a *heightened* affective responsiveness, such that events bearing only a passing resemblance to prior experience (e.g. looking at photographs, a gathering of people in close proximity) seemed to evoke an inappropriate feeling of familiarity. This reading of these delusional experiences has some resonance with Ellis and Young's notion of a disturbance in the affective response to perceptual experience, but whereas they have focused exclusively on the *loss* of the affective response, these cases raise the possibility that an *excess* of the affective response equally may underlie the formation of a misidentification delusion.

Together, these three cases—FE, TH and DB—provide convincing evidence that an anomalous perceptual and/or affective experience, which the patient feels compelled to explain, underlies the formation of some DM, but that no single perceptual or affective anomaly is capable of explaining all forms of DM. These cases suggest that the disturbance in affective response may be either deficient or excessive and may be associated with any aspect of perception or memory but is not necessarily a generalized disturbance in affect as described by Ellis and Young (1990).[10] We speculate that the particular aspect of cognition that is affected (for example, the particular perceptual or affective deficit involved or the combination of these) may determine the specific form of the delusion, as also argued by Langdon and Coltheart (this volume).

We are not suggesting that perceptual or affective deficits of the kind that we observed in FE, TH and DB, are sufficient explanation of their delusions of misidentification. Rather, we are proposing that such deficits may provide necessary antecedents to the formation of DM in some patients. Further, our observations suggest that in addition to a defective percept and/or a disturbance in the affective responsiveness to the environment, there is also a failure to be influenced by, or give weight to, evidence which for a normal person would override the influence of the anomalous percept or affective experience in the production and maintenance of belief. It is this failure which enables the DM to be accepted. As a result, all three patients (FE, TH and DB) were able to give untroubled expression, in a single narrative or conversation, to ideas

---

[10] An alternative view might be that the inappropriate affective response is caused by the misidentification, rather than being the cause of it. We would argue against this view on the basis that patients who have severe face processing perceptual impairments, including prosopagnosic patients (who can no longer recognise any previously known faces), do not develop delusions of misidentification. Therefore, it cannot be argued that the perceptual impairment alone causes a delusion of misidentification which then causes the inappropriate affective response.

which would be completely contradictory, and therefore troubling, to any cognitively intact person. Garety (1991; Garety and Hemsley, 1994) has argued that reasoning impairments are necessary components in the formation of delusions in general. The nature of possible reasoning deficits in patients with DM is an area which remains to be explored.

Unlike the other three cases, RZ did not have any evidence of a perceptual disorder, her visual face processing ability was normal, and there was no evidence of an affective impairment in relation to face recognition. Rather, in the context of a long psychiatric history, RZ presented with an actual physical abnormality in the form of hirsutism. That is, in her case, there may have been an anomalous physical rather than perceptual or affective defect which was the crucial contributing factor in the development of the delusion that she was a man. She certainly invoked this physical abnormality as evidence to defend her delusional belief. RZ's intense discomfort when challenged about her belief and her continual elaboration of her belief in response to interview questions may be interpreted as indications of insight into the implausibility of her DM or, alternatively, as discomfort due to knowing that the examiner found the DM implausible. Either way, there would appear to be a degree of insight into the implausibility of her belief and a concern that she convince others of her belief, that was not evident in the other three cases.

5.3 Interpretation at a Phenomenological Level

The difference in neurological classification and cognitive interpretation between the three patients FE, TH and DB and the fourth patient, RZ, was also apparent with regard to the patients' phenomenological experience of their delusional beliefs, including the strength with which the belief was held, and the fixity of the belief.

5.3.1 Strength of the Delusional Belief

With regard to the strength of their delusional beliefs, FE held his delusional belief with the most conviction. FE never wavered in his belief that his reflection was another person, no matter how much evidence to the contrary was presented to him. He never described his own reflected image as being a reflection. TH also held steadfastly to his delusional belief regarding his reflection, despite occasionally slipping between describing his reflected image as a reflection and as a person. The behaviour of both FE and TH toward their own reflected image, in repeatedly attempting to engage in conversation with their reflection, indicated that overtly both men believed the reflection to be a real person who should be capable of independent speech. DB's experience of reduplicative phenomena was stable and persistent but it was a characteristic of the phenomenon in her case that the details of the delusion varied depending on the events around her that seemed to precipitate them. For instance, a gathering of people around another patient in the ward preceded the delusion that it was her husband that these people were visiting. In the face of contradictory evidence, however, DB doggedly adhered to her delusional beliefs without altering the content of the belief in any way, indicating that her delusional beliefs were strong. A noteworthy feature of the behaviour of FE, TH and DB was the way in which they replied to questions regarding their delusions. Their replies were immediate, and they never attempted to convince the interviewer of the validity of their delusional belief. If a question were put to them that they could not explain, they simply admitted it. For example, FE and TH both agreed that it was strange that the *other person* was in their own homes but neither man felt any obligation to provide an explanation for it.

In contrast, RZ's delusional belief appeared to be much less resilient. She found it difficult to maintain the delusion under the pressure of intensive questioning regarding her personal history, and indeed the delusional belief shifted during the course of the interview from her identity being that of her father, to that of her grandfather, and then back again to her father. She was often slow to reply to questions, no doubt due to the effort required to remember the details of her father's history and his relationships with family and friends. At one stage during the interview, RZ exclaimed, 'I'm just confused because I don't remember it. It feels like they've taken my brain out and I don't even have a brain', outwardly indicating the struggle it was to maintain the delusion when under pressure. This breakdown in the delusional belief during the course of an interview never occurred in the other three patients.

5.3.2 The Fixed Nature of the Delusional Belief The delusions of FE, TH and DB were all very fixed. Despite detailed questioning and direct challenges regarding the content of their delusional beliefs, neither FE nor TH elaborated their belief about the *person* who they believed was following them around. Neither man attempted to explain why or how the other *person* was in their home or following them around, why that person behaved the same way they did or was dressed the same, or why other family members did not attempt to talk to the *person*. In the two-year follow-up period after the initial presentation of the mirrored-self misidentification, both men developed other delusional beliefs and, again, the fixity of their beliefs was striking. For example, FE developed the additional delusional belief that his wife was two people, but he never elaborated the belief to provide an explanation of how or why this had happened. TH went on to develop the delusional belief that there were duplicates of the hospital he was staying in, but he did not elaborate this belief to incorporate how or why this had occurred. Neither man developed a wide web of delusional beliefs in which their delusional misidentification became embedded. In both cases the delusional beliefs remained isolated from a more rational belief system which was operative in other cognitive domains. DB was reviewed 19 months after her stroke. At that time she maintained the delusional belief that various family members were in the institution she found herself in, and she had also developed a reduplicative delusion for place. Like FE and TH, DB's delusions of misidentification were striking due to the fixity of the beliefs.

In complete contrast, RZ did not display the fixity of belief that was the prominent feature of the delusions of FE, TH and DB. RZ constantly elaborated her belief when she was challenged about it, the content of the delusional belief changed during the course of one interview (RZ swapped between assuming her father's identity and her grandfather's identity) and at one point the delusional belief broke down entirely. Qualitatively, the strength and fixity of the delusional beliefs were striking features that set RZ apart from the other three patients.

5.3.3 Paranoia/Suspiciousness

As previously discussed, it has been suggested that a mood of paranoia or suspiciousness may be crucial to the formation of the Capgras delusion, and in particular crucial to the individual's attribution of anomalous experiences (e.g. perceptual, affective) to an external cause rather than an internal problem (Young et al., 1993; Ellis et al., 1997). However, paranoia was not a feature in any of the four cases we have presented. Both FE and TH were a little disgruntled to find that a complete stranger had taken up residence in their lives, but neither of them regarded the misidentified image as evil or harmful. Similarly, DB was faintly puzzled that her long dead husband should have reappeared, but she did not attribute any malevolent intent to him, or indeed any intent on his part in relation to herself. Finally, although RZ's delusion revolved around her family, at no time did she express concern about the behaviour of any family member to herself. Therefore, while paranoia may form a core component specifically of the Capgras delusion, it clearly is not helpful in accounting for why FE, TH, DB or RZ developed or maintained their DM. We propose that factors other than a negative mood are necessary for the development of DM in the patients we have presented, and, in particular, other cognitive factors, as previously discussed.

5.3.4 Depersonalization/Derealization

It has also been suggested that the Capgras delusion occurs in conjunction with depersonalization and/or derealization. None of these patients had either of these features as defined by *DSM-IV* (American Psychiatric Association, 1994). Depersonalization is defined as 'an alteration in the perception or experience of the self, so that one feels detached from, and as if an outside observer of, one's mental processes or body' (*DSM-IV*, p. 766). Although RZ had an altered experience of the self, she actually believed that she was her father, or grandfather, and so did not meet the criteria of feeling detached from her own mental processes or body. In this strict sense then, she did not have depersonalization despite her experience of the self being abnormal.

6. Conclusions

In summary, we have presented four cases of DM in the context of three levels of interpretation: neurological, cognitive and phenomenological. There were striking similarities amongst three of the patients (FE, TH and DB) at all three of the levels of interpretation, whereas one case, RZ, was very different from the others on the three levels. FE, TH and DB all met the criteria to be classified at the 'neurological lesion' end of the continuum. All three cases had marked perceptual deficits and/or a disturbance in affective response to environmental stimuli. It is likely that each also had some form of reasoning deficit that enabled them to accept the DM without evaluating its implausibility, although this was not explored in this study. These deficits appeared to underlie the formation of the DM in each of these cases. In addition, in all three cases the delusion was fixed and strongly held, and the patient was unconcerned as to whether other people accepted their belief. In contrast, RZ was classified at the 'no neurological lesion' end of the continuum. She had no perceptual or affective cognitive deficit, but did have a physical abnormality which she invoked in defending her delusion. RZ's discomfort when challenged, her shifting delusional content and her elaboration of the delusion in response to interview questions were all features that were absent in the other three cases, and possibly suggest a degree of insight into the implausibility of her DM.

Despite their differences in these areas, the three cases FE, TH and DB did not greatly differ from RZ with regard to mood state. None of the four patients attributed evil or harmful intentions to the misidentified person. None of the patients had depersonalization or derealization, although RZ described an abnormal experience of self. Therefore, the role of paranoia does not appear to be crucial in the development of the three variants of DM we have presented.

When we first assessed FE and TH, we considered whether their mirrored-self misidentification was a delusion in its own right or whether it was a variant of the Capgras delusion, as had been previously reported (Gluckman, 1968). The two delusions may be considered similar in that they both involve a type of person misidentification. There are, however, many ways in which the Capgras delusion and mirrored-self misidentification are very different. The Capgras delusion is the belief that *doubles* have *replaced* people, usually close relatives, whereas the delusion of mirrored-self misidentification does not involve doubles or replacement. In addition, Capgras patients tend to be paranoid or intensely suspicious, the doubles are often thought of as evil or dangerous and the delusion often occurs in the context of depersonalization or derealization. In contrast, FE and TH were not paranoid or suspicious, did not believe that the *person* (their misidentified reflected self) was evil or intended them harm, and the delusion did not arise within a context of depersonalization or derealization.

To date, most cognitive investigation of DM has focused on the Capgras delusion. These studies have resulted in the important finding that a deficit in the normal affective response to familiar faces is a contributing factor in that particular delusion, and have led to important refinements in the modelling of normal face processing (Breen, Caine and Coltheart, in press). The four cases that we have presented suggest that it is unlikely that this particular deficit can be applied across the board to other DM. We consider that thorough understanding of these disorders will depend on investigation of the differences amongst patients and their particular delusional phenomena, in much the same way as has been done so successfully with language and memory disorders. In the same way that a cognitive model of reading can suggest a variety of ways in which normal reading might be disrupted, resulting in different types of dyslexia, a model of belief formation might also indicate a number of sources of disruption, resulting in a range of disorders including different types of delusions. Investigation of the particular disruption underlying different types of delusion, such as we have presented for three different forms of DM in this chapter, enables a rich understanding of DM. Such investigations of DM may also contribute further to an understanding of the role of affect in relation to cognitive processes other than face processing.

References

American Psychiatric Association 1994: *Diagnostic and Statistical Manual of Mental Disorders*, Fourth Edition (*DSM-IV*). Washington, DC: American Psychiatric Association.

Bauer, R. 1984: Autonomic recognition of names and faces: A neuropsychological application of the Guilty Knowledge Test. *Neuropsychologia*, 22, 457–69.

Bauer, R. 1986: The cognitive psychophysiology of prosopagnosia. In H. Ellis, M. Jeeves, F. Newcombe and A. Young (eds), *Aspects of Face Processing*. Dordrecht and Lancaster: Martinus Nijhoff, 253–67.

Beers, C.W. 1953: *A Mind that Found Itself: An Autobiography*, 7th edn. New York: Doubleday & Co. Inc.

Breen, N., Caine, D. and Coltheart, M. In Press: Models of face recognition and delusional misidentification: A critical review. *Cognitive Neuropsychology*.

Capgras, J. and Reboul-Lachaux, J. 1923: L'illusion des 'sosies' dans un délire systématise. *Bulletin de la Société Clinique de Médecine Mentale*, 11, 6–16.

Caramazza, A. 1986: On drawing inferences about the structure of normal cognitive systems from the analysis of patterns of impaired performance: The case for single-patient studies. *Brain and Cognition*, 5, 41–66.

Christodoulou, G.N. 1977: The syndrome of Capgras. *British Journal of Psychiatry*, 130, 556–64.

Collins, M.N., Hawthorne, M.E., Gribbin, N., and Jacobson, R. 1990: Capgras' syndrome with organic disorders. *Postgraduate Medical Journal*, 66, 1064–7.

de Pauw, K. and Szulecka, T.K. 1988: Dangerous delusions: Violence and the misidentification syndromes. *British Journal of Psychiatry*, 152, 91–6.

Ellis, H.D., Luauté, J.P., and Retterstol, N. 1994: Delusional misidentification syndromes. *Psychopathology*, 27, 117–20.

Ellis, H.D., Whitley, J. and Luauté, J.P. 1994: Delusional misidentification: The three original papers on the Capgras, Fregoli and intermetamorphosis delusions. *History of Psychiatry*, 5, 117–46.

Ellis, H.D., and Young, A.W. 1990: Accounting for delusional misidentifications. *British Journal of Psychiatry*, 157, 239–48.

Ellis, A.W., and Young, A.W. 1996: *Human Cognitive Neuropsychology: A Textbook with Readings*. Hove, E. Sussex: Psychology Press.

Ellis, H.D, Young, A.W., Quayle, A.H. and de Pauw, K.W. 1997: Reduced autonomic responses to faces in Capgras delusion. *Proceedings of the Royal Society: Biological Sciences*, B264, 1085–92.

Enoch, M.D. and Trethowan, W.H. 1979: *Uncommon Psychiatric Syndromes*, 2nd edn. Bristol: John Wright and Sons Ltd.

Feinberg, T.E. 1997: Some interesting perturbations of the self in neurology. *Seminars in Neurology*, 17, 129–35.

Fleminger, S. and Burns, A. 1993: The delusional misidentification syndromes in patients with and without evidence of organic cerebral disorder: A structured review of case reports. *Biological Psychiatry*, 33, 22–32.

Foley, J.M. and Breslau, L. 1982: A new syndrome of delusional misidentification. *Annals of Neurology*, 12, 76.

Förstl, H., Almeida, O.P., Owen, A., Burns, A. and Howard, R. 1991: Psychiatric, neurological and medical aspects of misidentification syndromes: A review of 260 cases. *Psychological Medicine*, 21, 905–10.

Frazer, S.J. and Roberts, J.M. 1994: Three cases of Capgras' syndrome. *British Journal of Psychiatry*, 164, 557–9.

Garety, P.A. 1991: Reasoning and delusions. *British Journal of Psychiatry*, 159 (supplement 14), 14–18.

Garety, P.A. and Hemsley, D.R. 1994: *Delusions: Investigations into the Psychology of Delusional Reasoning*. Maudsley Monographs, Number 36. Hove, E. Sussex: Psychology Press, Taylor and Francis.

Gluckman, L.K. 1968: A case of Capgras syndrome. *Australian and New Zealand Journal of Psychiatry*, 2, 39–43.

Halligan, P.W. and Marshall, J.C. (eds) 1996: *Method in Madness: Case Studies in Cognitive Neuropsychiatry*. Hove, E. Sussex: Psychology Press.

Hirstein, W. and Ramachandran, V.S. 1997: Capgras syndrome: A novel probe for understanding the neural representation of the identity and familiarity of persons. *Proceedings of the Royal Society: Biological Sciences*, B264, 437–44.

Mackie, J., Ebmeier, K.P. and O'Carroll, R.E. 1994: An MRI, SPECT and neuropsychological study of a patient presenting with Capgras syndrome. *Behavioural Neurology*, 7, 211–15.

Malloy, P., Cimino, C. and Westlake, R. 1992: Differential diagnosis of primary and secondary Capgras delusions. *Neuropsychiatry, Neuropsychology and Behavioral Neurology,* 5, 83–96.

Mendez, M.F., Martin, R.J., Smyth, K.A. and Whitehouse, P.J. 1992: Disturbances of person identification in Alzheimer's disease: A retrospective study. *Journal of Nervous and Mental Disease,* 180, 94–6.

Merrin, E.L. and Silverfarb, P.M. 1976: The Capgras phenomenon. *Archives of General Psychiatry,* 33, 965–8.

Phillips, M.L., Howard, R. and David, A.S. 1996: 'Mirror, mirror on the wall, who. . .?': Towards a model of visual self-recognition. *Cognitive Neuropsychiatry,* 1, 153–64.

Quinn, D. 1981: The Capgras syndrome: Two case reports and a review. *Canadian Journal of Psychiatry,* 26, 126–9.

Ramachandran, V.S., Altschuler, E.L. and Hillyer, S. 1997: Mirror agnosia. *Proceedings of the Royal Society: Biological Sciences,* B264, 645–7.

Silva, J.A, Leong, G.B, Garza-Trevino, E.S., Le Grand, J., Oliva, D., Weinstock, R. and Bowden, C. 1994: A cognitive model of dangerous delusional misidentification syndromes. *Journal of Forensic Sciences,* 39, 1455–67.

Silva, J.A., Leong, G.B., Weinstock, R., Sharma, K.K. and Klein, R.L. 1994: Delusional misidentification syndromes and dangerousness. *Psychopathology,* 27, 215–19.

Spangenberg, K.B., Wagner, M.T. and Bachman, D.L. 1998: Neuropsychological analysis of a case of abrupt onset mirror sign following a hypotensive crisis in a patient with vascular dementia. *Neurocase,* 4, 149–54.

Stone, T. and Young, A.W. 1997: Delusions and brain injury: The philosophy and psychology of belief. *Mind and Language,* 12, 327–64.

Todd, J., Dewhurst, K. and Wallis, G. 1981: The syndrome of Capgras. *British Journal of Psychiatry,* 139, 319–27.

Weston, M.J. and Whitlock, F.A. 1971: The Capgras syndrome following head injury. *British Journal of Psychiatry,* 119, 25–31.

Wright, S., Young, A.W. and Hellawell, D.J. 1993: Sequential Cotard and Capgras delusions. *British Journal of Clinical Psychology,* 32, 345–9.

Young, A.W. 1998: *Face and Mind.* Oxford University Press.

Young, A.W., Ellis, H., Szulecka, T.K. and de Pauw, K.W. 1990: Face processing impairments and delusional misidentification. *Behavioural Neurology,* 3, 153–68.

Young, A.W. Reid, I., Wright, S. and Hellawell, D.J. 1993: Face processing impairments and the Capgras delusion. *British Journal of Psychiatry,* 162, 695–8.

4

Refining the Explanation of Cotard's Delusion

PHILIP GERRANS

An elegant theory in cognitive neuropsychiatry explains the Capgras and Cotard delusions as resulting from the same type of anomalous phenomenal experience explained in different ways by different sufferers. 'Although the Capgras and Cotard delusions are phenomenally distinct, we thus think that they represent patients' attempts to make sense of fundamentally similar experiences' (Young and Leafhead, 1996, p. 168). On the theory proposed by Young and Leafhead, the anomalous experience results from damage to an information processing subsystem which associates an affect of 'familiarity' with overt recognition of faces, and, sometimes, scenes and objects. When the normal affect of familiarity is absent the subject experiences an unusual feeling of derealization or depersonalization. The Cotard and Capgras patients adopt different, delusional, explanations of this unusual qualitative state, for reasons to do with 'attributional style'.

It is part of this attribution hypothesis that delusional subjects, like normal people, interpret perceptual phenomena in the light of a set of background beliefs whose structure is a product of social/contextual influences and individual psychological dispositions. That structure predisposes people to reason in certain ways, to discount or reinterpret evidence and to favour certain hypotheses: that is to have an attributional style. Perhaps what we encounter in delusion is extreme cases of attributional style in conjunction with bizarre qualitative states for which there is no precedent in normal experience. The Cotard patient, whose attributional style is introjective, interprets strange sensations of depersonalization or derealization in terms of a change in herself. The Capgras patient, whose attributional style[1] is to seek external explanations, interprets her unsettling experience in terms of a change in the external world.

I suggest that the difference between the Capgras and Cotard delusions cannot be explained solely in terms of different attributional styles applied to

---

I would like to thank Martin Davies for comments and suggestions, Andy Young and the organizers of the Theory of Mind workshops at Macquarie, Adelaide and Tasmania.

[1] Attributional style plays the same role here as the notion of bias in Langdon and Coltheart, this volume, who contrast bias and deficit explanations of delusional reasoning. They use the expression 'attributional bias' to capture a preference for types of explanation within a normally functioning reasoning system. The notion of deficit refers to abnormal function of the reasoning system.

essentially the same affective deficit. The Cotard delusion, in its extreme form, is a rationalization of a feeling of disembodiment based on global suppression of affect resulting from extreme depression. In the Capgras case the affective deficit is more localized, confined to familiars. So, in that respect, their aetiologies and qualitative features differ significantly. While is quite possible that someone whose global affective processes were suppressed would experience the local deficit which generates the Capgras delusion, we would not expect that local affective deficit to generate the Cotard response.

The attribution hypothesis seems closely tied to a view (explained in more detail below) that normal and delusional patients are reasoning in essentially the same ways. I suggest that, in Cotard patients at least, we are looking at seriously distorted reasoning processes which invite a version of the reasoning deficit hypothesis proposed by Langdon and Coltheart (this volume). The Cotard subject seems to have lost a very basic aspect of normal rationality, the ability to recognize oneself as the owner of one's experiences. As Langdon and Coltheart, and Gold and Hohwy (this volume) point out, schizophrenic delusions of thought insertion seem irrational for the same reason. The origin of the deficit in the Cotard delusion results from the dual role played by affective processing. Affective processes on which qualitative experiences depend signal, not only changes in body state, but that the experience is occurring *in one's own body*. Thus, when global affect is absent, flattened or distorted, the delusion of disembodiment, while irrational given one's background knowledge, is a natural way to explain the consequent derealization. The 'naturalness' or 'observational adequacy' of the explanation, however, does not indicate normality of the reasoning which generates it.

1. Routes to Recognition and Cognitive Impenetrability

In order to examine these ideas more closely, consider the explanation of these two delusions by Young and Leafhead. It builds on a theoretically elegant and empirically powerful neuropsychological theory of face recognition. According to that theory, developed over the last 15 years, face recognition involves an affective component together with a cognitive component that enables overt recognition to take place (Bauer, 1984; Ellis and Young, 1990; Young et al., 1993, 1994; Ellis et al., 1997).

The independence of the mechanisms responsible for overt recognition and affect is suggested by double dissociation effects following localized neurological damage. Young and collaborators refer to a series of cases in which subjects have overt recognition of faces but no affective response to them, or else intact affective response to faces without overt recognition (a result observed in some, though not all, cases of prosopagnosia). Of course, the mere occurrence of these types of dissociation does not, in itself, necessitate an explanation in terms of independent mechanisms of affect and overt recognition. In part the explanation depends on an overall theory of modular cognitive function into which the explanation of the dissociation phenomenon fits (Fleminger, 1992; Stone and Young, 1997; Shallice, 1988). On that model, dissociation of deficits is taken to indicate the independent (i.e. modularized) functioning of mechanisms whose damage produces the deficit.

The commitment of cognitive neuropsychiatry to the modular explanation of dissociation effects is shown, not just by its explanation of selective damage, but via its endorsement of Pylyshyn's (1984) thesis of cognitive impenetrability. That thesis states that the functioning of a modularized subsystem cannot be affected by the subject's beliefs. Although there is evidence of cross-talk, recurrence, feedback and feedforward interaction and top-down processing between and within modules, modules cannot be affected by the subject's acquisition or loss of beliefs (Coltheart, 1999). Modules deliver inputs to the belief system, their function being unaffected by its operations. Famously, the belief system is, in Fodor's words, a domain-general Central Processor whose functioning is 'Quinean and isotropic'. The CPU is holistic (domain-general) in its operations, whereas the modules which feed information to it are restricted in their operations to specific domains.

Capgras delusion arises in cases where the affective component of the face processing module is damaged, leaving overt recognition unimpaired. The subject sees someone who appears, in all respects, identical to the familiar person but the subject does not experience the normal affective response. Thus she has an uncanny phenomenal sensation based on the absence of an affect whose normal production is automatic and instantaneous. The Capgras delusion is an attempt to explain that uncanny feeling. The subject adopts the hypothesis that the familiar has been replaced by an identical replica, an inference which would explain why everything looks the same but 'feels' strange.

> They [delusional subjects] receive a veridical image of the person they are looking at, which stimulates all the appropriate overt semantic data held about that person but they lack another, possibly confirming, set of information which, as Lewis (1987) and Bauer (1986) have suggested, may carry some sort of affective tone. When patients find themselves in such a conflict (that is receiving some sort of information which indicates that the face in front of them belongs to X, but not receiving confirmation of this) they may adopt some sort of rationalisation strategy in which the individual before them is deemed to be an imposter, a dummy, a robot, or whatever extant technology may suggest (Ellis and Young, 1990, p. 244).

The operation of the affective component of the face processing subsystem, whether intact or impaired, is not cognitively penetrable by the rest of the agent's beliefs. In the Capgras delusion the subject believes that familiar persons have been replaced by identical replicas. The Capgras subject neither revises her other beliefs to make the new belief consistent with the others she already holds, nor rejects this inconsistent belief. Typically, Capgras delusion is associated with localized paranoia, but, once again, the paranoid beliefs do not prompt the type of systematic belief revision required by holistic rationality. As an example of this kind of inferential isolation, Stone and Young (1997) quote this record made by Alexander of a conversation with a Capgras patient:

> E: Isn't that [two families] unusual?
> S: It was unbelievable!
> E: How do you account for it?
> S: I don't know. I try to understand it myself, and it was virtually impossible.
> S: What if I told you I don't believe it?
> E: That's perfectly understandable. In fact, when I tell the story, I feel that I'm concocting a story . . . It's not quite right. Something is wrong.
> E: If someone told you the story, what would you think?
> S: I would find it extremely hard to believe. I should be defending myself.
>
> (Alexander et al., 1979, p. 335)

Rationality is a normative constraint of consistency and coherence on the formation of a set of beliefs and thus is *prima facie* violated in two ways by the delusional subject. Firstly she accepts a belief which is incoherent with the rest of her beliefs, and secondly she refuses to modify that belief in the face of fairly conclusive counter-evidence and a set of background beliefs which contradict the delusional belief. Why not then explain delusion as a failure of rationality, of the system which adopts and maintains beliefs on the basis of their coherence with the rest of the agent's belief set? The answer in the case of Capgras, and other delusions of misidentification, is that the patient's irrationality, despite local paranoia, is confined to a single domain: the response to familiars. In the rest of her life and cognitive activities, the patient's reasoning ability is undisturbed. Hence the idea that the delusion is best explained in terms of localized discrepant input to the reasoning system, not the malfunction of the reasoning system itself. Maher (1974, p. 103) summarizes the approach of cognitive neuropsychiatry thus:

> Strange events, felt to be significant, demand explanation . . . In brief, then, a delusion is an hypothesis designed to explain unusual perceptual phenomena and developed through the operation of *normal cognitive processes.*

2. Are Delusional Subjects Reasoning Normally?

Note here that this way of describing things does not attend to an important distinction between forming a delusional belief ('belief formation') and failing to revise it once formed ('belief maintenance'). The account of the Capgras delusion just considered accords with the idea that the delusion is largely to be explained as the result of normal processes of belief formation. Stone and Young (1997) discuss the notion of an observationally adequate belief, one fixed on the basis of perception rather than extensive further theorizing. The Capgras patient has a veridical perceptual image and a 'feeling' of unfamiliarity. The replication hypothesis preserves the veridicality of both aspects of her experience. In that sense it is like an observationally adequate belief, one whose content is normally fixed on the assumption of veridical experience.

The notion of observational adequacy thus preserves the normality of belief formation. It does seem, though, that observational adequacy cannot explain the failure to revise a delusional belief. However, one way to resist this conclusion is to appeal to the notion of modularity. In cases of visual illusion, although the subject believes that her percept is non-veridical, she cannot alter it. Similarly, in the case of the Capgras delusion, the uncanny experience which generates the delusion, because it is the output of a modularized affective subsystem, is cognitively impenetrable. The patient therefore explains her intractable experience by generating a delusional observational belief consistent with that experience. Exactly which belief is generated depends on the patient's cognitive resources. In cultures like ours it is unsurprising that the beliefs would advert to robots or dummies, in other cultures perhaps one might expect hypotheses of possession or 'soul migration':

> the content of the patient's perceptions and his thought will be determined by the psychology of the patient and his circumstances, but the original offending misperception appears likely to be triggered by an organic process (Spier, 1992, p. 283).

The idea that the exact content of the belief (i.e. which observationally adequate hypothesis is chosen) depends on psychological and sociological factors is the 'attribution hypothesis' and once again it preserves the normality of the cognitive function of the delusional subject. Normal reasoners also bring to bear background hypotheses which are a result of their own idiosyncratic personal and environmental histories. Everyone has some bias in their reasoning system which leads them to prefer some hypotheses, discount others and reinterpret evidence and, perhaps, the Capgras patient is merely bringing to bear her reasoning bias on a deeply disturbing and intractable phenomenal state. The attribution hypothesis together with the notion of observationally adequate belief and the impenetrability of the damaged system combine to give the most plausible possible explanation of the Capgras delusion within the framework established by Maher.

Within that framework, given that the deficit in the Cotard and Capgras cases is described by Young and Leafhead as 'essentially similar', the difference in the content of the delusions must be accounted for in terms of differences in the background psychology and circumstances of the patient, and this, following Cotard himself, is the explanation given by Young and Leafhead. The classic Cotard subject forms the belief that she is dead, a belief which *prima facie* is even more difficult to incorporate than the replication hypothesis of the Capgras patient. The crucial difference is that the Cotard patient is typically extremely (often psychotically) depressed (Berrios and Luque, 1995a). Noting this, Young and Leafhead pursue a theory (Beck, 1989; Candido and Romney, 1990) about attributional styles in depressive patients to the following conclusion:

> while depressed patients tend to attribute negative events to internal causes, people with persecutory delusions tend to attribute them to external causes . . . the persecutory delusions and suspiciousness often noted in Capgras cases may therefore contribute to the patents mistaking a change in themselves for a change in others ('they must be imposters'), whereas people who are depressed exaggerate the effect of a similar change whilst correctly attributing it to themselves ('I must be dead') (Young and Leafhead, 1996, p. 167).

3. Cotard Delusion: Attribution or Deficit?

The involvement of depression in the Cotard delusion is extremely significant, so let us distinguish three possible ways of linking depression to the delusion:

(1) Attribution Hypothesis. A person with a depressive tendency and associated attributional style suffers selective damage to a modularized affect-of-familiarity-system, the experiential effects of which she then rationalizes in the way described above.

(2) The localized damage and consequent loss of localized affect *cause* the depression and its associated tendency to internal attribution. After all, it is not inconceivable that someone who recognized her family members but no longer felt any of the familiar emotions in their presence would become depressed.

(3) The neurochemical substrate of psychotic depression causes generalized loss of affect, including the local affect of familiarity. Here there are two possibilities:

    (a) The global affective deficit is then rationalized using normal attributional style.

    (b) Deficit Hypothesis. The global affective deficit is rationalized using reasoning processes which are abnormal. An intuitively plausible consideration in favour of this hypothesis over the Attribution hypothesis is given by Langdon and Coltheart (this volume, p. 200): 'If the formation of a delusional belief were just a question of bias, then surely the weight of counter-arguments would eventually tip the scales in favour of rationality'. They conclude that delusions maintained in the face of mounting counter-evidence must involve reasoning deficits as well as perceptual malfunction and attributional biases.

I shall try and show that, for Cotard cases, the deficit hypothesis (3b) is the best candidate. The abnormality or reasoning deficit is the subject's failure to acknowledge at the level of rationality that her experiences are her own. This is seen most clearly in the extreme cases described by Enoch and Trethowan (1991), but less extreme cases fall on a continuum from death to non-existence in which the patient seeks to explain her experience without implicating herself in it (Berrios and Luque, 1995b). Both Langdon and Coltheart, and Gold and Hohwy (this volume) discuss this 'ownership' issue in the context of schizophrenia. Langdon and Coltheart, for example, discuss the possibility that the failure in the schizophrenic case is the result of failure of a metarepresentational capacity, whereas I am claiming that in the Cotard case failure of affective processing is the causal origin of the deficit. However, in both cases, the failure to implicate oneself in one's experiences, evidenced by the nature of the delusions (thought insertion in schizophrenia, of bodily inexistence in Cotard), is evidence of a reasoning deficit, rather than a matter of attributional style.

Recall the important difference between the Cotard and Capgras cases. In the Capgras cases the paranoia is presented as a rationalization of localized feelings of unfamiliarity, depersonalization or derealization in relation to a particular person, place or object. The patient is otherwise unaffected and one is left with the impression that disruption of all affective responses has not occurred. In the Cotard case, however, it seems likely that normal affective links to a wide range of perceptual and cognitive experiences have been suppressed. Furthermore, there are good reasons to think that the mechanisms of suppression may be the neurochemical mechanisms involved in depression, which have a global effect, not only on subtle affective responses like familiarity, but on more florid ones like elation and even, on some theories, on cognitive processes (Panskepp, 1982). In such a case, the lack of emotional responses, feelings of emptiness and derealization would be the result of global affective suppression or damage rather than of localized organic damage interpreted within a depressive mindset.

That affect can be suppressed globally as well as locally by neurochemical processes associated with depression is a well supported hypothesis. Mood states induced in this way have complex feedback relations with both cognitive and affective processing because they are

neurochemical states which act to modify the activity of broad areas of the central nervous system . . . [The] effect [of such a state] may be diffuse, affecting the whole system, or specific, affecting the various emotional responses differently. In addition to its effects on the affect program system in the limbic brain, the same chemical condition may affect higher areas of the brain and thus affect emotional phenomena involving higher cognition and higher cognitive phenomena generally (Griffiths, 1997, p. 256).

My suggestion is that in some Cotard cases the depression causes a global affective deficit with the type of diffuse effects cited by Griffiths. Our phenomenal experiences, whether subtle, persistent and global in the case of moods, or florid, instantaneous and localized as in fright, are instances of conscious awareness of processes, themselves inscrutable to introspection, which regulate body state. Depression is a global suppression of affect, which because of its complex interdependence on levels of chemicals like serotonin and noripinephrine is something which can occur in degrees. The point I wish to emphasize is that, at the limit, as in the Cotard cases, there is good reason to think that it would be experienced as disembodiment, because its physiological basis is global suppression of all mechanisms by which we achieve phenomenal awareness of our body state.

I note here that, in the course of a discussion of the role of affect, Ramachandran reaches a similar conclusion about the essential link between the global nature of affective suppression and the content of the delusion:

> In Cotard's all the sensory areas are disconnected from the limbic system . . . I would predict that Cotard's syndrome patients will have a complete loss of GSR for all external stimuli—not just faces (Ramachandran and Blakeslee, 1998, p. 167).

Supporting evidence comes from those cases of extreme depression, accompanied by delusion, which can, apparently, occur without a history of the type of organic accident cited by Young and Leafhead. Cases of the Cotard delusion have been reported (Enoch and Trethowan, 1991) in which the subject proceeds beyond reporting her rotting flesh or her death to the stage of describing the world as an inert cosmos whose processes she merely registers without using the first-person pronoun.[2] In this type of case the patient conceives of herself as nothing more than a locus, not of experience—because, due to the complete suppression of affect, her perceptions and cognitions are not annexed to her body—but of the registration of the passage of events. She has effectively effaced herself from the universe: nothing which occurs is of any significance to her and, hence, she describes the world without implicating

---

[2]   Although it should be noted that in such cases organic damage of the type referred to by Young and Leafhead cannot be ruled out. The Enoch and Trethowan cases predate PET investigation for example.

herself in that description. Few such cases are reported nowadays because that level of depression is recognized as preceding suicide and attracts pharmacological intervention, or, in extreme cases, ECT, at an earlier stage. However, their occurrence does strongly suggest that, in the absence of affective processing, perception and cognition have no bodily consequences and thus are not 'felt' at the phenomenal level to belong to the agent.[3] The patient does not recognize experiences as significant for her because, due to the global suppression of affect, she has no qualitative responses to the acquisition of even the most significant information. These extreme cases of the Cotard delusion are those in which neural systems on which affect depends are suppressed and, as a consequence, it seems to the patient as if her experiences do not belong to her. Thus the patient reports, not changes in herself, but changes in the states of the universe, one component of which is her body, now thought of as another inert physical substance first decomposing and finally disappearing.[4]

If this is the case, then perhaps the Capgras and Cotard delusion may result from affective damage with quite different aetiologies. Of course this possibility does not invalidate the basic picture of normal and abnormal recognition. In both cases the patient generates a delusional belief to explain feelings of unreality or abnormality which arise following disruption to subpersonal mechanisms of affect. In the Capgras case, the absence of affect is confined to quite specific eliciting situations. In cases associated with psychotic depression, the suppression of affect is general and it is thus unsurprising that the Cotard delusion would be experienced initially as disembodiment and finally as absence from the physical world.

Exactly how different are the Capgras and Cotard delusions? Young (this volume) rightly warns of the danger that a dissociation effect (some people have the Capgras but not the Cotard and others have the Cotard but not the Capgras delusions) might lead us to assume that the Capgras and Cotard delusions are independent, conceptually and neurologically. Young reminds us of the cases of association, such as that described by himself and Leafhead. But although he is prepared to associate the delusions in some cases, Young would not go along with Ramachandran who describes the Cotard delusion as 'simply an exaggerated form of Capgras' syndrome and probably has a similar origin' (Ramachandran and Blakeslee, 1998, p. 167). If this is taken to mean that the loss of affect is global in the Cotard and local in the Capgras, then it

---

[3]   My claim here is not that the mechanisms involved in bodily monitoring no longer function. The patient can still detect perceptual stimuli and the movements of her limbs, but the those mechanisms of detection no longer give rise to their normal consciously experienced phenomenal correlates.

[4]   Although note once again that these cases precede the ability to detect neurological damage by PET scan. Enoch and Trethowan give psychodynamic explanations which, as Stone and Young, 1997, point out, have been superseded.

is true. However, as stated, it implies that there are no significant differences in causal origin or reasoning strategy between the Capgras and Cotard patients.

I distinguished possible aetiologies of affective suppression and claimed that in the Cotard case there is an essential link between that aetiology and the content of the delusion. I also suggest that the neurochemical substrate of psychotic depression introduces more than normal bias into the subject's reasoning, it creates a deficit. It is part of normal rationality to self impute one's experiences, and the Cotard subject can no longer do this. Thus I incline toward the deficit hypothesis as an explanation of the Cotard delusion.

This endorsement of the deficit hypothesis requires elaboration to explain a type of case discussed by Young in support of the attribution hypothesis. He and his collaborators have reported a case of alternation between these delusions, following a neurological accident, which appeared to coincide with switches in attributional style (Young et al., 1993). As Young (this volume, p. 65) explains it:

> the key factor seems to be the patients' moods—when in a suspicious mood, they think that other people are impostors, when depressed they think they are dead. The underlying basis of both delusions could therefore be quite similar; a delusional interpretation of altered perception (especially loss of affective familiarity).

Can the deficit hypothesis accommodate these types of case? The best explanation appeals to the distinction between forming and revising a belief. I said earlier that the attribution hypothesis accords best with the idea that the delusional and the normal subject are not reasoning differently. This may well be the case in the formation of the belief: a discrepant experience is rationalized according to attributional style, which may fluctuate.

However in psychotic depression the mood is not transient but deeply entrenched. And, characteristically, depressive hypotheses are quite immune to revision. Once depression has set in it functions to maintain the delusional hypothesis in the face of pressure from the rest of the agent's beliefs and accumulating counter-evidence. My suggestion is that the maintenance of a belief like the Cotard delusion requires a reasoning deficit. And the effect of psychotic depression is to introduce that rigidity by making it impossible for the agent to feel as if her experience is her own.

This is not inconsistent with the alternation between the delusions in cases where the depression waxes and wanes. In those cases, if the depression is a matter of relatively transient mood it could account for fluctuation between attributional styles which suggest alternative observationally adequate hypotheses of death or replication. However, where depression is deeply entrenched and psychotic it produces a deficit of reasoning which makes it impossible for the subject to bring countervailing knowledge to bear. Thus I suggest that the deficit hypothesis as it applies to the Cotard case is best thought of as a deficiency in belief revision rather than formation.

References

Alexander, M.P., Stuss, D.T. and Benson, D.F. 1979: Capgras' syndrome: A reduplicative phenomenon. *Neurology*, 29, 334–9.

Bauer, R.M. 1984: Autonomic recognition of names and faces: A neuropsychological application of the guilty knowledge test. *Neuropsychologica*, 22, 457–69.

Bauer, R.M. 1986: The cognitive psychophysiology of prosopagnosia. In H.D. Ellis, M.A. Jeeves, F. Newcombe and A.Young (eds), *Aspects of Face Processing*. Dordrecht: Martinus Nijhoff, 253–67.

Beck, A.T. 1989: *Cognitive Therapy and the Emotional Disorders*. Harmondsworth: Penguin.

Berrios, G.E. and Luque, R. 1995a: Cotard's syndrome: Analysis of 100 cases. *Acta Psychiatrica Scandinavica*, 91, 185–8.

Berrios, G.E. and Luque, R. 1995b: Cotard's delusion or syndrome? A conceptual history. *Comprehensive Psychiatry*, 36, 218–23.

Candido, C.L. and Romney, D.M. 1990: Attributional style in paranoid vs depressed patients. *British Journal of Medical Psychology*, 63, 355–63.

Coltheart, M. 1999: Modularity and cognition. *Trends in Cognitive Sciences*, 3, 115–20.

Ellis, H.D. and Young, A.W. 1990: Accounting for delusional misidentifications. *British Journal of Psychiatry*, 157, 239–48.

Ellis, H.D., Young, A.W., Quayle, A.H. and de Pauw, K.W. 1997: Reduced autonomic responses to faces in Capgras delusion. *Proceedings of the Royal Society: Biological Sciences,* B264, 1085–92.

Enoch, M.D. and Trethowan, W.H. 1991: *Uncommon Psychiatric Symptoms*, 3rd edn. Oxford: Butterworth-Heinneman.

Fleminger S. 1992: Seeing is believing: The role of preconscious perceptual processing in delusional misidentification. *British Journal of Psychiatry*, 160, 293–303.

Griffiths, P. 1997: *What Emotions Really Are: The Problem of Psychological Categories*. University of Chicago Press.

Lewis, S.W. 1987: Brain imaging in a case of Capgras' syndrome. *British Journal of Psychiatry*, 150, 270–1.

Maher, B. 1974: Delusional thinking and perceptual disorder. *Journal of Individual Psychology*, 30, 98–113.

Panskepp, J. 1982: Towards a general psychobiological theory of emotion. *Behavioural and Brain Sciences*, 5, 407–43

Pylyshyn, Z. 1984: *Computation and Cognition: Towards a Foundation for Cognitive Science*. Cambridge, MA: MIT Press.

Ramachandran, V.S. and Blakeslee, S. 1998: *Phantoms in the Brain: Human Nature and the Architecture of the Mind*. London: Fourth Estate.

Shallice, T. 1988: *From Neuropsychology to Mental Structure*. Cambridge University Press.

Spier, S. 1992: Capgras syndrome and the delusions of misidentification. *Psychiatric Annals*, 22, 279–85.

Stone, T. and Young, A.W. 1997: Delusions and brain injury: The philosophy and psychology of belief. *Mind and Language*, 12, 327–64.

Young, A.W. and Leafhead, K.M. 1996: Betwixt life and death: Case studies of the Cotard delusion. In P. Halligan and J. Marshall (eds), *Method in Madness: Case Studies in Cognitive Neuropsychiatry*. Hove, E. Sussex: Psychology Press.

Young, A.W., Leafhead, K.M. and Szulecka, T.K. 1994: The Capgras and Cotard delusions. *Psychopathology*, 27, 226–31.

Young , A.W., Reid, I., Wright, S. and Hellawell, D.J. 1993: Face-processing impairments and the Capgras delusion. *British Journal of Psychiatry*, 162, 695–8.

Young, A.W., Robertson, I.H., Hellawell, D.J., de Pauw, K.W. and Pentland, B. 1992: Cotard delusion after brain injury. *Psychological Medicine*, 22, 799–804.

5

Insights into Theory of Mind from Deafness and Autism

CANDIDA C. PETERSON AND MICHAEL SIEGAL

Researchers in the field of developmental psychology have devoted consider-able attention in recent years to the question of how children come to under-stand their own and others' behaviour by acquiring a theory of mind, in other words, the awareness that the human action is governed by covert mental states that do not always match objective reality (Butterworth, Harris, Leslie and Wellman, 1991; Perner, 1991; Wellman, 1990). The discovery of an atypi-cal developmental course for autistic children who are faced with the problem of understanding other minds has extended this explosion of scientific investi-gation to the field of developmental psychopathology as well (Baron-Cohen, Tager-Flusberg and Cohen, 1993).

Defined in this way, a theory of mind is thought to confer the ability to impute mental states like beliefs, intentions, memories and desires to self and others 'as a way of making sense of and predicting behaviour' (Baron-Cohen, Tager-Flusberg and Cohen, 1993, p. 3). As such, its development is an important cornerstone of social, communicative, and affective life. A practical understanding of mental states enables children to appreciate that their own and others' behaviour may be shaped by cognitive abstractions that are not part of the immediately perceptible world. The awareness that beliefs may be false is crucial to sophisticated interactions with others, both negative ones like trickery and deceit, and positive ones including empathy, joking, or make-believe. The merging of one's own thoughts with others' in conversation, play, reminiscence, and mutual insight also becomes possible when mental states are discovered (Mitchell, 1997).

Children who, through failure to develop a theory of mind, are 'mindblind' (Baron-Cohen, 1995) are likely to be handicapped when it comes to appreciat-ing others' emotions and viewpoints. They are likewise uniquely vulnerable to the devious manipulations of their thoughts by those who would deceive, cheat or betray them. A theory of mind is essential for effective communication

This chapter was prepared with the support of the Australian Research Council. Thanks are due to Helen Bosisto, Margaret Gore, Gail Follett, Alexa Hinze, Wendy Newman, and James Peter-son for their assistance with data collection and to all the children who took part, their parents, and teachers.

(Frith and Happé, 1999). Indeed, according to Wellman (1993), once a person develops a theory of mind, 'the assumption is that this understanding guides all social action and interaction' (p. 10).

1. The False Belief Paradigm and its Historical Antecedents

Piaget (1929) proposed that children under the age of 7 years were 'mental realists' whose cognitive egocentrism blinded them to the mental life of others. Consequently, before this age, he believed children were incapable of grasping the distinction between objective reality and human cognitive representations of it. This set the stage for one line of inquiry into the growth of concepts of mind. Piagetian interviews probed children's understanding of processes like thinking, dreaming or memory. Tests of cognitive role-taking were also administered in which the mental perspectives of individuals in different situations had to be considered.

The term 'theory of mind' was introduced by Premack and Woodruff (1978) along with their proposition that chimpanzees possessed one. Their method entailed presenting videotapes about human problem-solving (e.g. food retrieval) to a language-trained chimpanzee (Sarah) and then attributing mental 'role-taking' when Sarah chose a still photo of a correct solution (e.g. a person raking bananas to the cage with a stick) in preference to an irrelevant behaviour (e.g. climbing). This procedure has generated continuing controversy (see Heyes, 1998, for a recent review) and some have argued that a theory of mind cannot be unequivocally demonstrated in humans or other organisms unless verbal tests are used (Slaughter and Mealey, 1998).

In a critique of Premack and Woodruff's (1978) conclusions, Dennett (1978) offered a hypothetical sketch of what has since become the contemporary 'litmus test' for theory of mind, namely the inferential false belief paradigm in which subjects are required to make inferences about the behaviour of actors whose beliefs about objective reality have been rendered false (e.g. they do not know that an object they saw in one place has since been moved). Because correct inferences about actors' behaviour requires acknowledgement of their mental states, the false belief paradigm offers stronger evidence for the presence of a theory of mind than Premack and Woodruff's approach (Slaughter and Mealey, 1998).

Two versions of the false belief paradigm have together generated a large volume of recent research with normally developing and atypical children. The first of these, the inferential false belief test based on changed location (e.g. 'Sally-Ann': Baron-Cohen, Leslie and Frith, 1985), presents a sequence of events in a way that would enable an astute observer to infer a person's (or story's character's) mental state (e.g. a doll puts her ball in a basket and closes the lid, leading to the inference that she thinks the ball is in the basket despite the fact that she can no longer see it). Then the surreptitious transformation of reality is engineered so as to contradict the original belief (while the doll is away, someone moves the ball to a covered box). The subject is then asked about the original character's beliefs either directly ('Where does she think the ball is?') or by demanding a further inference about ensuing behaviour ('Where will she look for her ball?'). A stringent two-trial version of the task requires a second inference under similar circumstances to rule out chance success through guessing. When given false-belief tests in this format, most 3-year-olds fail by responding as Piagetian realists with the true location of the object (Perner, Leekam and Wimmer, 1987). But from the age of 4 or 5 years, evidence of an inferential theory of mind emerges in the vast majority of normal children, who are able to state that the character will search in the original, now false, location. Similarly, in a misleading appearance (or 'deceptive container') version of the task, a person or story character is shown an object (e.g. a rock or an apple) or a container (e.g. a Smarties or M&Ms box or teapot) that, on superficial inspection, has one obvious interpretation. The subject is then made privy to contradictory information (the rock, when touched, reveals itself as a sponge; the apple, when lighted, is really a candle; the Smarties/M&Ms box is opened and shown to contain pencils). An uninformed other is then introduced, followed by a test question about beliefs ('What will she think is in the box before I open it?') or behaviour ('When I ask him what this is before he touches it, will he say it is a rock or a sponge?'). Sometimes representational change questions are also included. In these, the subject is quizzed about his or her own beliefs before being made privy to the deceptive information ('When you first saw this, before I lit it, did you think it was a candle or an apple?'). As with changed location false belief tasks, most normally developing 4- and 5-year-olds correctly ascribe mistaken beliefs to uninformed others and to the self. However, children who are younger than 4 years generally fail to acknowledge the possibility of beliefs that are presently patently false. They therefore respond to test questions by stating the true nature, location, identities or contents of the stimuli.

2. Autism and False Belief

The success that is displayed by most normally developing 4-year-olds on false belief tests is in sharp contrast to the performance of autistic individuals, who typically continue to fail both changed location and misleading appearance tests into their teens and adulthood and at mental ages well beyond 4 years (e.g. Baron-Cohen et al., 1985; Eisenmajer and Prior, 1991; Leslie and Frith, 1988; Reed and Peterson, 1990). However, mentally retarded children without autism often succeed on false-belief tests at lower mental ages, ruling out simple cognitive deficits as an explanation for the delays that are observed in the case of autism (e.g. Baron-Cohen et al., 1985; Perner, Frith, Leslie and Leekam, 1989). Furthermore, autistic children's failure to grasp the concept of false belief appears to be specific to representations that arise in the mental domain. For example, Baron-Cohen, Leslie and Frith (1986) found that autistic young people who succeeded readily in arranging pictures to record sequences of physical events and overt behaviours were selectively incapable of performing the same task when the stimuli depicted mental states. Similarly, Reed and Peterson (1990) found that autistic children and adolescents did as well as mentally retarded and normal preschool children at making inferences about visual perception. But even though they could not only infer *invisibility* based on blocked line of sight, but also identify the varying *percepts* of viewers observing the same scene from different vantage points, they routinely failed corresponding tests that differed only in being cognitive. Thus they could neither infer *ignorance* based on blocked informational access, nor *false belief* based on the faulty mental input available to another mind.

It is conceivable that autistic children may possess an even better understanding of some forms of non-mental representation than normal preschoolers of comparable mental age. Using normally developing children aged 4 and 5 years as subjects, Zaitchik (1990) pioneered a photographic misrepresentation task that was closely parallel to inferential tests of false belief. With tight controls for comprehension, memory and attention, she discovered that normal children were no better than chance at predicting what would appear in a polaroid snapshot of a scene that had been transformed in a salient manner after the photo was taken, even though they routinely passed two corresponding narrative tests of false-belief understanding. Leekam and Perner (1991) presented a simplified version of Zaitchik's task to a group of able autistic teenagers. Subjects were shown a doll who had changed her dress either after the photo was taken, or after another doll had left the room. Only 27 per cent of the diagnosed autistic adolescents replied correctly to the question: 'What colour does (the other doll) think Judy is?' Yet 14 of these 15 autistic subjects displayed an accurate understanding of photographic misrepresentation by naming the original colour when asked: 'In the picture, what colour is Judy?' Similar results were obtained by Leslie and Thaiss (1992) on tasks assessing the understanding of two different types of mental and photographic representation (place change and identity change). Despite the fact that the vast majority of the intelligent autistic children in their sample accurately understood both types of photographic misrepresentation, only 23 per cent of them displayed a correspondingly accurate understanding of false belief. Leslie and Thaiss concluded that 'a specialized cognitive mechanism which subserves the development of folk psychological notions . . . is dissociably damaged in autism' (p. 229).

3. Deafness and False Belief

The question of whether a failure to grasp concepts of false belief at an advanced mental age is a problem unique to autism, or shared by children from other clinical populations, has considerable theoretical significance

(Baron-Cohen, 1995). Autism is known to be a 'biologically-based neurodevelopmental disorder' (Bailey, Phillips and Rutter, 1996) that is diagnosed when a child displays a triad of impairments in imagination, language, and social relatedness (Frith, 1989). Evidence of a genetic link, along with general agreement on its biological basis, suggests that the root cause for these diagnostically significant behavioural manifestations of autism resides in an abnormality of the central nervous system (CNS). One theoretical possibility is that the same CNS disturbance also explains autistic children's delayed development of a theory of mind. However, if other populations are impaired in understanding a theory of mind without the clinical manifestation of autism, this would argue against attributing both abnormalities to a single CNS disruption.

Initial empirical evidence supported the notion of autism specificity. In addition to mentally retarded children, subjects with emotional disturbance (Siddons, Happé, Whyte and Frith, 1990), like those with specific language disorders (Leslie and Frith, 1988; Perner et al., 1989) and with the cognitive deficits of Williams Syndrome (Tager-Flusberg, 1995) have been shown to succeed more readily on false-belief tests than children with autism. More recently, however, another diagnostic group has been discovered that appears to share autistic children's extreme delays on tests of an inferential theory of mind.

In particular, the results of a number of recent studies show that profoundly deaf children who grow up in hearing families often lag several years behind hearing children in their development of an understanding of false belief, even when care is taken to include only children of normal intelligence and social responsiveness in the deaf samples (Deleau, 1996; Peterson and Siegal, 1995, 1997, 1998; Russell, Hosie, Gray, Scott and Hunter, 1998; also see Table 1). For example, Peterson and Siegal (1995) and Russell et al. (1998) each observed that only a minority of deaf children aged 5 to 12 years passed a standard two-trial (Sally-Ann) false-belief test based on changed location (see above for a detailed description), and it was not until aged 13 to 16 that deaf children's success rates were seen to approximate those of normally developing 4-year-olds (Russell et al., 1998).

Furthermore, the delays observed among deaf children also resemble those displayed by autistic children in being specific to concepts of mind, rather than pertaining to false representation more generally. In two experiments, Peterson and Siegal (1998) presented matched groups of children from three populations: (1) autistic children, (2) normal preschoolers, and (3) signing deaf primary school children from hearing families, with standard tests of false mental and photographic representation, using a within-subjects design. The results of the first study, which borrowed Leekam and Perner's (1991) and Leslie and Thaiss's (1992) procedures, replicated these authors' findings (see above) of significantly better performance by autistic children on Zaitchik's (1990) false-photo task than on a comparable two-trial false-belief test (Baron-Cohen et al., 1985). Exactly the same pattern of differential success and failure was observed among the normally intelligent severely and profoundly deaf children in the sample who came from hearing families and had acquired signed communication belatedly upon school entry. Furthermore, the levels of success by deaf and autistic children were almost identical to one another.

The second study, which used a nonverbal response mode, essentially replicated these results. Deaf and autistic children performed similarly, each showing better understanding of false photographic than false mental representation. Incidental linguistic or conversational differences between mental and photographic tasks were ruled out in this study, since all aspects of the two types of task, apart from the locus of the obsolete representation in a camera or a human mind, were carefully equated.

Nevertheless, deaf and autistic children displayed chance accuracy on the belief task, while exceeding chance on the comparable photographic version. No such domain-specific dissociation emerged in normally developing preschoolers in the second experiment, where all linguistic and conversational demands of the tasks had been minimized and carefully equated. Four-year-olds were near ceiling on both tasks, while 3-year-olds were no better than chance with either false mental, or false photographic, representation. (In line with these findings for normal children, it is worth noting that other recent studies have similarly contradicted Zaitchik's (1990) original suggestion that normal developers find false photographs harder to understand than false beliefs (e.g. Slaughter, 1998).

Peterson and Siegal's (1995, 1997, 1998, 1999) findings regarding Australian deaf children's poor performance on theory of mind tests have been widely replicated. Table 1 displays a summary of the results of 11 separate investigations that have examined the performance of independent samples of severely and profoundly deaf children from several different cultures and educational systems on standard test of false-belief understanding. (See Happé, 1995, for a similar tabulation of studies of false-belief understanding in subjects with autism).

Taken collectively, the populations of deaf children that have been assessed in these studies are impressively varied, and can be seen to represent a wide range of family circumstances, preferred communication modalities, and approaches to deaf education. A broad span of ages has also been encompassed, and a range of techniques for measuring false-belief understanding has been used. Overall, the results of these studies provide consistent support for the proposition that signing deaf children from hearing families are seriously delayed in acquiring a theory of mind.

The results of the studies that are summarized in Table 1 reinforce the similarities noted earlier between deaf and autistic children, indicating that even in the presence of normal intelligence, these groups are likely to continue through adolescence to fail the simple tests of false-belief understanding that are passed by most normally developing preschoolers at age 4. Furthermore,

Table 1 Summary of 11 studies of deaf children's understanding of false belief

Investigations	Subjects	Mean Age	False-Belief Tasks	Results
Courtin & Melot (1998)	N = 79 French deaf children, including 13 native signers, 22 signers from hearing homes and 44 oral deaf	Signers and oral from hearing homes: 7.5 years; native signers: 5.4 years	Three (unspecified) first-order tasks	Native signers aged 5 outperform older oral and signing deaf from hearing homes; less than half in the latter two groups pass at least two of three tasks after age 7 years
Deleau (1996)	N = 48 French signing deaf children	Unspecified: range passing control questions: 5–8 years	One-trial changed location task	Only 60% pass at ages 6 to 8 years; hearing controls outperform
de Villiers et al. (1997)	N = 22 USA orally trained deaf from hearing homes	7.6 years	Two-trial narrative changed location task	Only 54% pass
Peterson & Siegal (1995)	N = 26 Australian severely and profoundly deaf signers aged 8 to 13 years from hearing homes	10.6 years	Two-trial changed location (Sally–Ann) task	Only 35% pass
Peterson & Siegal (1997)	N = 35 deaf Australian total communication pupils: 25% native signers; 74% from hearing homes	8.9 years	Two-trial changed location (Sally–Ann) task	Native signers: 89% pass Signers from hearing homes: 46% pass
Peterson & Siegal (1998); Experiment 1	N = 30 Australian deaf signers from hearing homes	8.4 years	Two-trial changed location (Sally–Ann) task	Only 40% pass

Table 1 Continued

Peterson & Siegal (1998); Experiment 2	N = 24 Australian signing deaf children from hearing homes	9.3 years	One-trial changed appearance task with nonverbal response option	Only 54% pass
Peterson & Siegal (1999)	N = 59 Australian deaf children (58% signers from hearing homes; 19% native signers; 23% oral)	9.4 years	Three tasks (1) Two-trial Sally-Ann (2) Smarties (3) Changed appearance	Most oral deaf and native signers pass all tasks and outperform signers from hearing homes, less than half of whom pass
Remmel, Bettger & Weinberg (1998)	N = 12 USA signing prelinguistic deaf children; 5 with signing deaf parents and 7 with hearing parents	8.7 years	Three-question misleading appearance task	Native signers: M = 2.5/3 correct; deaf from hearing: M = 1.1/3 correct
Russell et al. (1998)	N = 32 Scottish severely and profoundly deaf children: 2 native signers and 30 signers from hearing families	10.7 years	Two-trial changed location task	Age 6: 17% pass Age 10: 10% pass Age 15: 60% pass Total: 28% pass
Steeds, Rowe & Dowker (1997)	N = 22 English profoundly deaf children	9.7 years	One-trial changed location task	33% fail control questions; 70% (including control-question failers) pass false-belief

the one published study that followed a substantial group of deaf children into late adolescence (Russell et al., 1998) suggested that it was not until after the age of 15 years that a slight majority (60 per cent) of normally intelligent deaf students from hearing households displayed a consistently accurate understanding of false belief. However, deaf adults are found to organize cognitive verbs in a similar manner to hearing adults (Clark et al., 1996), consistent with presence of a functional theory of mind in maturity.

4. Differences among Deaf Groups in Rates of Theory of Mind Development

Interestingly, the results of the studies summarized in Table 1 also combine to suggest that the ease with which deaf children develop a theory of mind may be related to the nature and extent of their exposure to conversation at home while growing up as preschoolers. Three separate groups of preschool deaf children can be identified on the basis of their access to signed or spoken conversation with family members who are able to communicate in these modalities with varying degrees of fluency. Profoundly deaf children of signing deaf parents, along with those who have another native speaker of sign language in their immediate household (e.g. a signing deaf grandparent or an older deaf sibling who has become a fluent signer at school), can be dubbed 'native signers' owing to their access, throughout their growing up, to a natively fluent conversational partner with whom they are able to share a common first language, such as Australian Sign Language (Auslan), American Sign Language (ASL) or signed English. Another group consists of orally trained deaf children who, with the help of amplifying hearing aids, have been taught to speak and to comprehend spoken language. (Though not always successful in children with serious hearing losses, oral training does enable some deaf children to participate in family conversation through the spoken modality). The third group consists of severely and profoundly deaf children who eventually acquire their preferred medium of communication, sign language, in school after varying periods of conversational deprivation while growing up in families without any fluently signing members.

When tested during their early years of primary school, severely and profoundly deaf children who are native signers are found to differ markedly in their performance on false-belief tests from their signing severely and profoundly deaf classmates who have grown up in exclusively hearing homes. Deaf native signers appear to develop concepts of false belief at the same age as do children of normal hearing. But belatedly signing deaf children from hearing families are consistently found to do worse than native signers on false-belief tasks (Courtin and Melot, 1998; Peterson and Siegal, 1999; Remmel et al., 1998). Furthermore, these differences are not transitory, but can be observed throughout the age period from 5 through to 16 years (Peterson and Siegal, 1997, 1999; Russell et al., 1998).

When a child is born deaf into a hearing family (which is the case for the vast majority of deaf schoolchildren today), there are likely to be many departures from the normal course of development of language, social experience and conversation (Marschark, 1993; Vaccari and Marschark, 1997). Even when hearing parents make extensive efforts to learn to communicate in sign with their profoundly deaf children, the result is apt to be disappointing. According to Vaccari and Marschark: 'over 90 percent of deaf children have hearing parents, the majority of whom either do not know sign language or have relatively little skill in that domain' (1997, p. 793).

In contrast to parents who are deaf native signers, hearing parents typically report difficulties in communicating with their deaf children even about familiar everyday routines and have extreme difficulty sharing their thoughts, memories, intentions, and beliefs (Meadow, 1975). In many hearing families with a deaf child, any signs or communicative gestures that are produced by parent or child are restricted to topics in the immediately perceptible visual field, leaving parents and offspring alike unclear about one another's needs, desires, beliefs and capabilities (Vaccari and Marschark, 1997). Hearing mothers are found to share their emotions and intentions rarely, if at all, with their deaf offspring and may adopt a didactic role which discourages playful or inquisitive conversational exchange (Courtin and Melot, 1998).

Consequently, most deaf adults who eventually become fluent users of sign language acquire this language belatedly after varying periods of restricted conversation in their hearing families of origin. For example, when Power and Carty (1990) surveyed deaf native speakers of Auslan, they discovered an unusual linguistic background in that 'in 90 percent of cases Auslan is learnt not from parents within a family setting, but from other deaf students, usually in school' (p. 223). This means that until they enter a signing (or Total Communication) primary school, many profoundly deaf children have no readily available means of conversing with any of their hearing family members, especially about topics like mental states which may have no obvious visual referent. This is consistent with research showing that 'a deaf child of hearing parents may have no language in the sense of a code shared by many users' (Charrow and Fletcher, 1974, p. 436) until school entry at the age of 5 or 6 years.

Vaccari and Marschark (1997) noted that even mothers who make considerable effort to learn sign language frequently report difficulties in gaining the child's attention and conversing about unobservable thoughts and feelings. Morford and Goldin-Meadow (1997) studied four profoundly deaf children who were not exposed to a usable conversational language, but managed to express themselves at home by means of idiosyncratic systems of gestures known as 'homesign' (p. 420). Only one of them made spontaneous references to fantasy, hypothetical ideas or future events in conversation. Initiations of communication about the non-present by their caregivers were even less frequent. According to Marschark (1993): 'Deaf children are less likely than hearing children to receive explanations from their parents concerning emotions, reasons for actions, expected roles and the consequences of various behaviours' (p. 60). Similarly, Meadow (1975) concluded from one observational study of hearing families with a deaf child that: '95 percent of deaf children and their parents limited communication to topics with a visual referent' (p. 489), while the results of another study (Collins, 1969, cited in Meadow, 1975, p. 489) showed that 81 per cent of hearing mothers complained that 'they could communicate with their preschool deaf child only about things or events that were present in the time and/or space' (p. 489). If the spoken language skills of children with serious hearing impairments are poor, these unique features of conversation in hearing families might well limit deaf children's opportunities to gain insight into other people's thought processes. In the absence of a shared representational language, it is only in obvious cases when both conversational partners are looking at the objects they are thinking and talking about that a meeting of minds can take place.

In the case of oral deaf children with some residual hearing who are taught in spoken language classrooms with the aid of amplification, there is a possibility (not always actualized) of achieving fluent communication with hearing family members using speaking and listening. Consequently, for oral deaf children, any departure from the normal course of theory of mind development is likely to depend on the level of language proficiency. As shown in Table 1, Peterson and Siegal (1999) found that a group of orally trained Australian deaf pupils in a Total Communication primary school (who had enough spoken language fluency to cope readily with theory of mind tasks presented in an exclusively oral modality) performed near ceiling, and on a par with normally developing children and deaf native signers. But de Villiers et al. (1997) found that approximately half of their sample of 7-year-old orally taught North American deaf children failed standard false-belief tasks, and those who passed had significantly better language skills (such as vocabulary and verb complementation) than those who failed. Thus spoken language ability, a factor influencing access to family conversation at home, may also be central to oral deaf children's mastery of concepts of the mind. This is understandable, since spoken language may not only provide insight into the thought processes of peers and family members, but may also help to determine an oral deaf child's ability to display mental-state understanding when presented with standard tests of false belief.

5. Nature and Nurture in Theory of Mind Development

The difference in performance on false-belief tasks between native signers and deaf children from hearing families implicates family conversation in the growth of a theory of mind. Deaf children of hearing parents who lack an early conversational partner with whom to discuss imaginary, false, or abstract ideas and beliefs may miss out on a necessary source of cognitive input. The situation can be different for oral deaf with sufficient spoken language to discuss their beliefs with their family members in speech. Natively signing deaf children of deaf parents are similarly likely to gain conversational insight, via sign, into family members' mental states. Meadow, Greenberg, Erting and Carmichael (1981) discovered that deaf native signers converse as fluently in sign about non-present ideas, objects and events with their signing deaf relatives as hearing children with their hearing parents in spoken language.

Children with autism are as likely as signing deaf children from hearing families to miss out on these formative early conversational experiences, though for different etiological reasons. As noted above, a diagnosis of autism entails a triad of impairments in (1) imagination, (2) spoken language ability and (3) social relatedness (Frith, 1989). Consequently, a child with autism is likely to remain socially aloof from family members, to have too few linguistic skills to be fully able to engage in sophisticated family conversations about abstract ideas, and to have too little imagination to appreciate another person's imaginary, or false, beliefs. A deficit of pragmatic communication skill has been reliably identified with autism, beginning in infancy with absences of joint attention and directive pointing, and evolving, as vocabulary develops, into deficits in narrative fluency and such pragmatic conversational tactics as maintaining relevance and responding to questions (Bruner and Feldman, 1993). The relatively few autistic subjects who manage to pass false-belief tests display better language skills than those who fail (Happé, 1995). But a direction of causality for these results is difficult to determine. Conceivably, a basic theory of mind deficit may delay the development of language and pragmatic communication skills which are acquired through social interaction. Alternatively, a more basic language processing deficit may block the autistic child's access to the verbal, syntactic, and conversational information that is necessary in order to develop a theory of mind. Still a third possibility is that some core deficit in a different area of 'interpersonal–affective relatedness' (Hobson, 1993, p. 216) may underpin both the linguistic and the mentalistic deficits observed in individuals with autism. The empirical evidence to date does not enable a conclusive choice among these alternatives.

Nevertheless, there is convincing empirical support for the propositions both (1) that autistic children suffer conversational deprivation at home during the age period from 2 to 5 years when their peers without autism are developing an awareness of false belief, and (2) that conversation in families where a child has autism is selectively restricted when it comes to talking about mental states like intentions, beliefs, false ideas, or imaginary thoughts. Tager-Flusberg (1993) compared the conversations that arose spontaneously over a two-year period between mothers and preschoolers in households where the child either had autism or mental retardation owing to Down's syndrome. The children were matched for levels of productive language skill and were simply observed as they engaged in everyday interaction with their mothers over cooking, play, snacks and so on. A number of striking differences arose when the dialogues were analysed. None of the retarded children made pronoun reversal errors (e.g. saying 'you' to describe self while speaking) but all of the autistic did so at least some of the time, suggesting their confusion over the pragmatic roles of speaker and listener in a conversational exchange. In addition, autistic children asked fewer questions than retarded children and were less likely to expand, continue or oppose a topic their mother had introduced. Their dialogues were especially striking for their virtual absence of references to mental states like knowledge and belief. Indeed, while retarded and autistic children were no different in their talk about perception, desire, and facially visible emotions (e.g. happy, scared, angry), references to cognitive mental states (e.g. believe, dream, forget, guess, trick, wonder, pretend, etc.) almost never arose in the autistic children's conversations.

Tager-Flusberg concluded that: 'One of the primary functions of language, to serve as a major source of knowledge, is impaired in autistic children even in the prelinguistic period. It is this impairment which links deficits in joint attention, later problems with communication, and the understanding of belief' (p. 153). Bruner and Feldman (1993) also noted that one of the consistent differences between autistic children and both retarded and normally developing children of similar mental age is lack of pragmatic skill in conversation. Autistic children have difficulty sustaining a conversational exchange with another person. As Bruner and Feldman (1993) explained: 'In dialogue, autistic speakers seem unable to extend the interlocutor's previous comment' (p. 274). In addition, they appear to suffer a narrative deficit which leaves them unable to construct a coherent story line and deprives them of the ability to 'make new comments on a topic in discourse' (p. 275). A narrative deficit may combine with the diagnostic indicator of impaired imagination to interfere with the autistic child's capacity to engage in pretend play, while both pragmatic conversational problems are likely to limit autistic children's access to the kinds of social input through dialogue that might yield insight into the workings of other people's minds.

A conversational account of theory of mind development that ascribes deaf, and possibly autistic, children's difficulties with concepts of false belief to selective deprivation of conversational access to other people's intangible mental states is consistent with studies of individual differences in the rate at which young normal children develop an understanding of the mind. Though most normally developing preschoolers have a firm grasp of false belief by the age of 4 to 5 years, a more precocious understanding by 3-year-olds has been linked with these children's exceptionally rich and varied exposure to dialogue and conversation in early family life. For example, using a longitudinal methodology, Dunn, Brown, Slomkowski, Tesla and Youngblade (1991) found that the breadth and depth of the conversational exchanges involving mental-state information that took place spontaneously between 33-month-olds and their mothers and siblings predicted these children's aptitude for standard theory of mind tasks some seven months later. Those subjects who, as 40-month-olds, displayed a sufficiently advanced grasp of mental-state concepts to be able to explain story characters' behaviour in terms of false belief had talked more with their mothers and siblings about emotions and desires at age 2 than their peers who failed. In addition, those with a precocious understanding of false belief had more frequent discussions with their mothers about psychological causality (e.g. 'Why don't you like to eat ice-cream before dinner?') than failers, even when matched for age and overall verbal fluency. Brown, Donelan-McCall and Dunn (1996) likewise found that 4-year-olds' successful performance on theory of mind tests was correlated with frequent use of mental-state terms when playing and talking with their siblings and peers, suggesting that spontaneous mention of mental contents may trigger the growth of the level of understanding that is assessed in structured tests. Indeed, these authors argued that children become motivated to think about their own and other people's abstract ideas, and mistaken or pretend beliefs, 'not as solitary cognitive exercises, but while negotiating the social interactions in which these cognitive states are shared' (p. 848).

The importance for theory of mind development of engaging in conversations and playful interactions with varied partners may also underpin discoveries both that children with larger numbers of siblings develop concepts of false belief at a significantly earlier age than singletons (Jenkins and Astington, 1996; Perner, Ruffman and Leekam, 1994) and that children in broad extended family networks who are regularly exposed to talk with adults and older children inside and outside home are more adept at understanding false belief than those whose familiar range of conversational partners is narrow (Lewis et al., 1996).

For profoundly deaf children in exclusively hearing families, as for socially aloof autistic children, these important sources of insight into the minds of friends and kin may be relatively inaccessible. According to Nelson (1996) this may preclude both the basis and the necessity for developing a theory of mind. As she explained:

> Individual organisms without communicative capacities for exchanging information about what they think, feel, and desire must remain in a solipsistic state, implicitly assuming that other individuals seek, know, act and desire the same things they themselves do . . . Engaging in the exchange of thoughts and feelings through language with other humans enables the move to a new level of understanding others as different from oneself (p. 134).

Conversational accounts like these belong to a broad category of 'cultural' explanations for theory of mind (Lillard, 1997) that ascribe the mastery of mental-state understanding to the forces of social interaction. According to Smith (1996), 'Young incipient mind-readers need to be supported in their ontogenetic development of mind-reading skills. We need to consider as pre-requisites *both* individuals who can develop mind-reading, *and* enculturation within a community which mind-reads' (p. 353). Children may entertain a wide variety of explanations for human behaviour initially on the basis of their direct observations of the world, only narrowing these down to a mentalistic source subsequently if they happen to grow up in a social environment where people converse freely about psychological states and in a culture that ascribes human action to such mentalistic causes as false beliefs.

This emphasis on culture and conversation in the development of a theory of mind contrasts with an alternative explanation for autistic children's false-belief difficulties in terms of genetic or prenatal damage to a modular, neurological mechanism for processing information about the mind (Baron-Cohen, 1995; Fodor, 1987; Frith, Morton and Leslie, 1991; Leslie and Thaiss, 1992). While differing in detail, these nativist neurobiological approaches share the view that a specialized cognitive mechanism with a distinctive architecture and circumscribed function becomes dissociably damaged in autism, accounting not only for the difficulties that autistic individuals have on tests of false belief, but also for their triad of diagnostically significant impairments in everyday language, imagination and sociability (Frith, 1989).

To the extent that impaired social relatedness is deemed a necessary off-shoot for autism as a disorder and for the neurobiological damage that is held by the nativist approach to be jointly responsible for children's problems with concepts of mental state, it is hard to reconcile the poor false-belief understanding that is consistently observed in deaf children with this account, as summarized in Table 1. When attending schools and units where sign language is used, these deaf children are commonly observed to enjoy normal levels of social interaction with their deaf classmates (Marschark, 1993; Power and Carty, 1990). Very few of them could be described as socially aloof or deviant, or as aligning themselves in other ways with the diagnostic criteria for autism.

In addition, it is well known that no single identifiable neurological or traumatic process accounts for all cases of childhood deafness (Marschark, 1993). For example, although some children in the Peterson and Siegal (1998) sample had lost their hearing as fetuses through rubella infection, others had become deaf postnatally (though prelinguistically) through illnesses and accidental injuries specific to the peripheral auditory system. Yet these latter children performed similarly on false-belief tests to those who were known or suspected to have suffered prenatal brain damage. In addition, the fact that the replication studies reported in Table 1 predominantly involved deaf children with no known or suspected serious clinical diagnoses apart from hearing impairment rules out the pervasive congenital neurological impairments that have been implicated in the case of autism. Thus it would be seen that a nativist account, while potentially applicable to autistic children's problems with concepts of false belief, cannot effectively be generalized to deafness for the following reasons:

(1) Deaf children from hearing families consistently fail theory of mind tasks at advanced chronological and mental ages, performing on a par with autistic children of similar mental age.

(2) Deaf children are unlikely to be neurologically damaged with respect to the theory of mind modules that are postulated by a nativist account as the explanation for the delays connected with autism.

(3) Deaf children's failure of false-belief tests could conceivably reflect their deficient early conversational interaction in hearing families where absence of a shared language restricts discussion of beliefs and other mental states.

(4) Natively signing deaf children with signing deaf family members develop concepts of false belief at a normal age, a pattern that is more consistent with a conversational than a neurobiological account of other deaf children's difficulties.

If a conversational explanation for deaf children's delayed development of a theory of mind is entertained, the question of whether this account might also be applicable to autism naturally arises. Of course, it is conceivable that older deaf and autistic children could display similar problems with false-belief understanding for quite different reasons. On the other hand, as Tager-Flusberg's (1993) research has shown, autistic children do resemble deaf children in their selective deprivation of talk about mental states at home while growing up. Consequently, the conversational account may provide a parsimonious explanation for the similarities displayed by deaf and autistic children on false-belief tests, but also for their equally inferior performance to normal developers and retarded children of lower verbal mental age, who enjoy fluent dialogue about mental states with family members at home (Tager-Flusberg, 1989, 1993). In other words, deaf children and autistic children may both be delayed in developing a theory of mind owing to their restricted early conversational exposure at age 2 to 3 years due to hearing impairment and lack of a shared language in the one case and to social aloofness and language difficulties in the other.

6. Deafness and Neurobiological Development

On the other hand, there may be a neurobiological basis for the performance of deaf children as a result of differential patterns of brain development following hearing loss. Indeed, congenitally deaf children with limited conversational exposure in purely oral families have been observed, in adulthood, to display patterns of language-related brain activity that differ in salient ways both from those of hearing adults from oral households and from those of deaf native signers from signing families (Marschark, 1993; Neville, Coffrey, Lawson, Fischer, Emmorey and Bellugi, 1997).

In this respect, in keeping with recent findings that have shown that the brain seems to have evolved systems dedicated to different features of the social world, areas of the right hemisphere may be implicated in understanding that involves a theory of mind. Between 3 and 4 years, children undergo a developmental change leading to accurate responses to theory of mind tests that require the ability to follow pragmatic implications of conversation, questions and other features of social interactions (Siegal and Beattie, 1991; Surian and Leslie, in press). This development occurs at the same time as the spurt of right-hemisphere growth at around 4 years of age that has been reported by Thatcher (1992).

There are grounds to believe that these findings cannot be dismissed as simply reflecting an anatomical coincidence. First, adult stroke patients who have suffered right-hemisphere (RH) damage share similar difficulties with young children in interpreting the conversational implications of questioning in theory of mind tasks (Siegal, Carrington and Radel, 1996). These patients often succeed on conversationally explicit versions of the false-belief questions (e.g. when asked 'Where will Sally look first', rather than 'look for' the hidden object, so as to distinguish clearly between searching and successful retrieval). Such results are consistent with reports that RH damage is associated with substantial impairment in pragmatic understanding (Molloy, Brownell and Gardner, 1990).

To complicate matters, however, pragmatic modifications of the wording of false-belief questions (e.g. 'look first'), though shown to assist RH stroke patients, fail to benefit either deaf children (Peterson and Siegal, 1995) or autistic children (Surian and Leslie, in press). Furthermore, deaf and autistic children are found to differentially fail false-belief tasks but not false-photographic tasks even when identically worded test questions are used with each task (Peterson and Siegal, 1998). These findings suggest that the pragmatic deficit implicated in the case of children with autism and deafness is not restricted to simple misunderstanding of specific questions during the standard false-belief testing situation. Furthermore, to the extent that a theory of mind is a necessary component of a skilled conversationalist's pragmatic understanding of an interlocutor's mind and intentions, impairments in pragmatic skill and mental state understanding are likely to be reciprocal and inextricably interconnected.

Nevertheless, the possibility that delayed exposure to conversation may influence patterns of right-hemisphere brain development in deaf children warrants further investigation, as does the question of how similar these children are to RH stroke patients in terms of awareness of conversational pragmatics and theory of mind. The latter have suffered impairments through a cerebrovascular accident to areas of the right hemisphere whose activation is associated with conversational awareness, whereas the former have had a restricted access to conversation in the first place owing to the language patterns of their families. This restricted conversational access may even limit theory of mind understanding in response to situations in which the need to follow inferences in conversation is eliminated, perhaps owing to a failure of the mutual representation of contexts between speakers and listeners that is essential for effective comprehension (Clark et al., 1996).

Furthermore, there is evidence that right-hemisphere activation is more central to the general interpretation of language in deaf native signers than in hearing persons who use speech. Neville et al. (1997) have shown that reading messages in sign language involves the activation of parietal and temporal cortices in the right-hemisphere as well as the traditional left-hemisphere language areas. The greater theory of mind proficiency that we have found in deaf native signers than in delayed signers from hearing homes is consistent with the increased right-hemisphere activation among children in the former group that may also assist them in their skilled interpretation of conversationally sophisticated questioning when being tested on theory of mind tasks. Whether native signers perform better than hearing preschoolers on false-belief tests at age 3 to 4 years is an interesting question that awaits further research.

Indeed, very little work has so far directly compared social and neurobiological influences on mental-state understanding in groups of children as diverse as autistic, deaf and normally developing children. Further study of these influences and their interconnections is urgently needed, as is continued investigation of the conversational and pragmatic distinctions between signed and spoken languages. Though, for example, it has been noted that sign language involves a special awareness of nonverbal communication cues and social cognition (Emmorey, 1993), its role in cognitive development has rarely been studied.

Finally, of course, it is conceivable that a critical level of conversational input about mental states is necessary to trigger neurobiological development and hemispheric specialization, so that biological and social-experiential accounts of theory of mind development need not be mutually exclusive. Whatever their interpretation, the results we report from our own and others' investigations of deaf children's performance on tests of false belief underscore the likely role of early family conversation in developing an awareness of the mind, while also highlighting the need for further research to clarify the degree to which cognitive representations of mental states are influenced by biological and cultural factors.

References

Bailey, A., Phillips, W. and Rutter, M. 1996: Autism: Towards an integration of clinical genetic, neuropsychological and neurobiological perspectives. *Journal of Child Psychology and Psychiatry*, 37, 89–126.

Baron-Cohen, S. 1988: Social and pragmatic deficits in autism: Cognitive or affective? *Journal of Autism and Developmental Disorders*, 18, 379–402.

Baron-Cohen, S. 1992: The theory of mind hypothesis of autism: History and prospects of the idea. *The Psychologist*, 5, 9–12.

Baron-Cohen, S. 1995: *Mindblindness: An Essay on Autism and Theory of Mind*. Cambridge, MA: MIT Press.

Baron-Cohen, S., Leslie, A.M. and Frith, U. 1985: Does the autistic child have a 'theory of mind'? *Cognition*, 21, 37–46.

Baron-Cohen S., Leslie, A.M. and Frith U. 1986: Mechanical, behavioural and intentional understanding of picture stories in autistic children. *British Journal of Developmental Psychology*, 4, 113–25.

Baron-Cohen, S., Tager-Flusberg, H. and Cohen, D. 1993: *Understanding Other Minds: Perspectives from Autism*. Oxford University Press.

Brown, J.R., Donelan-McCall, N. and Dunn, J. 1996: Why talk about mental states? The significance of children's conversations with friends, siblings and mothers. *Child Development*, 67, 836–49.

Bruner, J. and Feldman, C. 1993: Theories of mind and the problem of autism. In S. Baron-Cohen, H. Tager-Flusberg and D. Cohen (eds), *Understanding Other Minds: Perspectives from Autism*. Oxford University Press, 267–91.

Butterworth, G., Harris, P., Leslie, A. and Wellman, H. 1991: *Perspectives on the Child's Theory of Mind*. Oxford University Press.

Clark, M. Schwanenflugel, P., Everhart, V. and Bartini, M. 1996: Theory of mind in deaf adults and the organization of verbs of knowing. *Journal of Deaf Studies and Deaf Education*, 1, 179–89.

Courtin, C. and Melot, A.M. 1998: Development of theories of mind in deaf children. In Marschark (ed.), *Psychological Perspectives on Deafness*. Malwah, NJ: Erlbaum, 79–102.

Deleau, M. 1996: L'attribution d'etats mentaux chez les enfants sourds et entendants: Une approche du role de l'expérience langagière sur une théorie de l'esprit. *Bulletin de Psychologie*, 5, 48–56.

Dennett, D. 1978: *Brainstorms*. Montgomery, VT: Bradford.

de Villiers, P., Hosler, B., Miller, K., Whalen, M. and Wong, J. 1997: Language, theory of mind and reading: A study of oral deaf children. Paper Presented at Society for Research in Child Development, Washington, DC, April.

Dunn, J. 1994: Changing minds and changing relationships. In C. Lewis and P. Mitchell (eds), *Origins of an Understanding of Mind*. Hove, E. Sussex: Erlbaum, 297–310.

Dunn, J., Brown, J., Slomkowski, C., Tesla, C. and Youngblade, L. 1991: Young children's understanding of other people's feelings and beliefs: Individual differences and their antecedents. *Child Development*, 62, 1352–66.

Eisenmajer, R. and Prior, M. 1991: Cognitive linguistic correlates of theory of mind ability in autistic children. *British Journal of Developmental Psychology*, 9, 351–64.

Emmorey, K. 1993: Processing a dynamic visual-spatial language: Psycholinguistic studies of American sign language. *Journal of Psycholinguistic Research*, 22, 153–87.

Fodor, J. 1987: *Psychosemantics: The Problem of Meaning in the Philosophy of Mind*. Cambridge, MA: MIT Press.

Frith, U. 1989: *Autism: Explaining the Enigma*. Oxford University Press.

Frith, U. and Happé, F. 1999: Theory of mind and self consciousness: What is it like to be autistic? *Mind and Language*, 14, 1–22

Frith, U., Morton, J. and Leslie, A. 1991: The cognitive basis of a biological disorder: Autism. *Trends in Neuroscience*, 10, 433–8.

Happé, F. 1995. The role of age and verbal ability in the ToM performance of subjects with autism. *Child Development*, 66, 843–55.

Heyes, C.M. 1998: Theory of mind in non-human primates. *Behavioural and Brain Sciences*, 21, 101–48.

Hobson, R.P. 1993: *Autism and the Development of Mind*. Hove, E. Sussex: Erlbaum.

Jenkins, J.M. and Astington, J.W. 1996: Cognitive factors and family structure associated with theory of mind development in young children. *Developmental Psychology*, 32, 70–78.

Leekam, S.R. and Perner, J. 1991: Do autistic children have a metarepresentational deficit? *Cognition*, 40, 203–18.

Leslie, A.M. 1994: ToMM, ToBy and Agency: Core architecture and domain specificity. In L.A. Hirschfeld and S.A. Gelman (eds), *Mapping the Mind: Domain Specificity in Cognition and Culture*. Cambridge University Press, 119–48.

Leslie, A.M. and Frith, U. 1988: Autistic children's understanding of seeing, knowing and believing. *British Journal of Developmental Psychology*, 6, 315–24.

Leslie, A.M. and Thaiss, L. 1992: Domain specificity and conceptual development: Neuropsychological evidence from autism. *Cognition*, 43, 225–51.

Lewis, C., Freeman, N., Kyriakidou, C., Maridaki-Kassotaki, K. and Berridge, D.M. 1996: Social influences on false belief access: Specific sibling influences or general apprenticeship? *Child Development*, 67, 2930–47.

Lillard, A.S. 1997: Other folks' theories of mind and behavior. *Psychological Science*, 8, 268–74.

Marschark, M. 1993: *Psychological Development of Deaf Children*. Oxford University Press.

Meadow, K.P. 1975: The development of deaf children. In E.M. Hetherington (ed.), *Review of Child Development Research, Volume 5*. Chicago: University of Chicago Press, 441–508.

Meadow, K.P., Greenberg, M.T., Erting, C. and Carmichael, H. 1981: Interactions of deaf mothers and deaf preschool children: Comparisons with three other groups of deaf and hearing dyads. *American Annals of the Deaf*, 126, 454–68.

Mitchell, P. 1997: *Acquiring a Concept of Mind: A Review of Psychological Research and Theory*. Hove, E. Sussex: Psychology Press.

Molloy, R., Brownell, H.H. and Gardner, H. 1990: Discourse comprehension by right-hemisphere stroke patients: Deficits of prediction and revision. In Y. Joanette and H.H. Brownell (eds), *Discourse Ability and Brain Damage: Theoretical and Empirical Perspectives*. New York: Springer-Verlag, 113–30.

Morford, J.P. and Goldin-Meadow, S. 1997: From here and now to there and then: The development of displaced reference in Homesign and English. *Child Development*, 68, 420–35.

Nelson, K. 1996: Four-year-old humans are different. Why? *Behavioral and Brain Sciences*, 19, 134–5.

Neville, H. 1993: Language, modality, and the brain. In M.H. Johnson (ed.), *Brain Development and Cognition*. Cambridge, MA: Blackwell, 424–48.

Neville, H., Coffrey, S.A., Lawson, D.S., Fischer, A., Emmorey, K. and Bellugi, U. 1997: Neural systems mediating American sign language: Effects of sensory experience and age of acquisition. *Brain and Language*, 57, 285–308.

Perner, J. 1991: *Understanding the Representational Mind*. Cambridge, MA: MIT Press.

Perner, J., Frith, U., Leslie, A.M. and Leekam, S.R. 1989: Exploration of the autistic child's theory of mind: Knowledge, belief, and communication. *Child Development*, 60, 689–700.

Perner, J., Leekam, S.R., and Wimmer, H. 1987: Three-years-olds' difficulty with false belief: The case for a conceptual deficit. *British Journal of Developmental Psychology*, 5, 125–37.

Perner, J., Ruffman, T. and Leekam, S.R. 1994: Theory of mind is contagious: You catch it from your sibs. *Child Development*, 65, 1228–38.

Peterson, C.C., and Peterson, J. 1990: Sociocognitive conflict and spatial perspective taking in deaf children. *Journal of Applied Developmental Psychology*, 11, 267–81.

Peterson, C.C. and Siegal, M. 1995: Deafness, conversation and the theory of mind. *Journal of Child Psychology and Psychiatry*, 36, 459–74.

Peterson, C.C., and Siegal, M. 1997: Psychological, biological, and physical thinking in normal, autistic, and deaf children. In H.M. Wellman and K. Inagaki (eds), *The Emergence of Core Domains of Thought*. San Francisco: Jossey-Bass (New Directions for Child Development Series, no. 75).

Peterson, C.C. and Siegal, M. 1998: Changing focus on the representational mind: Concepts of false photos, false drawings and false beliefs in deaf, autistic and normal children. *British Journal of Developmental Psychology*, 16, 301–20.

Peterson, C.C. and Siegal, M. 1999: Representing inner worlds: Theories of mind in deaf, autistic and normal hearing children. *Psychological Science*, 10, 126–9.

Power, D. and Carty, B. 1990: Cross-cultural communication and the deaf community in Australia. In C. Hendrick and R. Holton (eds), *Cross-Cultural Communication and Professional Education*. Adelaide: Flinders University Centre for Multicultural Studies.

Premack, D. and Woodruff, G. 1978: Does the chimpanzee have a theory of mind? *Behaviour and Brain Sciences*, 4, 515–26.

Reed, T. and Peterson, C.C. 1990: A comparative study of autistic subjects' performance at two levels of visual and cognitive perspective-taking. *Journal of Autism and Developmental Disorders*, 20, 555–67.

Remmel, E., Bettger, J.G., and Weinberg, A. 1998: The impact of ASL on theory of mind. Paper presented at TIRSL 6. Washington, DC, November.

Russell, P.A., Hosie, J.A., Gray, C., Scott, C. and Hunter, N. 1998: The development of theory of mind in deaf children. *Journal of Child Psychology and Psychiatry*, 39, 903–10.

Siddons, F., Happe, F., Whyte, R. and Frith, U. 1990: Theory of mind in everyday life: An interaction-based study with autistic, retarded and disturbed children.

Paper presented at European Developmental Psychology Conference, Stirling, Scotland.

Siegal, M. 1997: *Knowing Children: Experiments in Conversation and Cognition*. Hove, E. Sussex: Psychology Press/Taylor & Francis.

Siegal, M. and Beattie, K. 1991: Where to look first for children's understanding of false beliefs. *Cognition*, 38, 1–12.

Siegal, M., Carrington, J., and Radel, M. 1996: Theory of mind and pragmatic understanding following right hemisphere damage. *Brain and Language*, 53, 40–50.

Siegal, M. and Peterson, C.C. 1994: Children's theory of mind and the conversational territory of cognitive development. In C. Lewis and P. Mitchell (eds), *Origins of an Understanding of Mind*. Hove, E. Sussex: Erlbaum, 427–55.

Smith, P.K. 1996: Language and the evolution of mindreading. In P. Carruthers and P.K. Smith (eds), *Theories of Theories of Mind*. Cambridge University Press, 344–54.

Slaughter, V. and Mealey, L. 1998: Seeing is not (necessarily) believing. *Behavioral and Brain Sciences*, 25, 130.

Steeds, L., Rowe, K. and Dowker, A. 1997: Deaf children's understanding of beliefs and desires. *Journal of Deaf Studies and Deaf Education*, 2, 185–95.

Surian, L., and Leslie, A.M. In press: Competence and performance in false belief understanding: A comparison of autistic and three-year-old children. *British Journal of Developmental Psychology*.

Tager-Flusberg, H. 1989: A psycholinguistic perspective on the autistic child. In G. Dawson (ed.), *Autism: Nature, Diagnosis and Treatment*. New York: Guilford.

Tager-Flusberg, H. 1993: What language reveals about the understanding of minds in children with autism. In S. Baron-Cohen et al. (eds), *Understanding Other Minds*. Oxford University Press.

Tager-Flusberg, H. 1995: Language and the acquisition of theory of mind: Evidence from autism and Williams syndrome. Paper presented at Society for Research in Child Development, Indianapolis.

Thatcher, R.W. 1992: Cyclic cortical reorganization during early childhood. *Brain and Cognition*, 20, 24–50.

Vaccari, C. and Marschark, M. 1997: Communication between parents and deaf children: Implications for social-emotional development. *Journal of Child Psychology and Psychiatry*, 38, 793–801.

Wellman, H. 1990: *The Child's Theory of Mind*. Cambridge, MA: MIT Press.

Wellman, H. 1993: Early understanding of mind: The normal case. In S. Baron-Cohen, H. Tager-Flusberg, and D. Cohen (eds), *Understanding Other Minds: Perspectives from Autism*. Oxford University Press, 10–39.

Wood, D., Wood, D., Griffith, A. and Howarth, I. 1986: *Teaching and Talking with Deaf Children*. London: Wiley.

Zaitchik, D. 1990: When representations conflict with reality. *Cognition*, 35, 41–68.

6
Rationality and Schizophrenic Delusion
IAN GOLD AND JAKOB HOHWY

1. Introduction

The investigation of rationality is both normative and empirical. It is normative because it deals with the standards according to which one *ought* to act if one is to count as rational; it is empirical because we take it to be a conceptual truth that rationality is a property of actual reasoning and behaving agents, and a theory of rationality has to be a theory that some such agents do in fact satisfy. The study of rationality is thus one of the many places where a priori philosophy meets psychology and the other human sciences.

A good deal of the theory of rationality has been devoted to conceptual, rather than empirical, investigation. It has focused on rules of various kinds—those of logic, decision-theory, rational choice theory, and the like—in an effort to articulate the ideals of rational thought and behaviour. More recently, however, the relevance of empirical psychology, particularly the psychological theory of reasoning, has been recognized as significant (see Harman, 1986). We follow this development by arguing that the study of psychopathology is also relevant to the theory of rationality. We argue that the case of schizophrenic delusion does not fit into the traditional branches of the theory of rationality and propose, therefore, what Lewis (1986) calls a new 'department' of rationality.

It is not our intention to develop a complete theory of delusion in schizophrenia, much less a general theory of delusion (see Breen et al., and Langdon and Coltheart, both in this volume). Rather, we aim to offer an account of a subset of the delusions of schizophrenia and explore their implications for the study of rationality. We claim that schizophrenic delusion is a paradigm case of irrationality and, based on a discussion of a leading theory of delusion—that of Christopher Frith (1987, 1992)—we hypothesize that it is brought about by a violation of a constraint on rational thought we call *egocentricity*, a thought's manifesting itself in consciousness as having originated in one's own mind. Our account of schizophrenic delusion attempts to explain the empirical facts and to be consistent with what is known about schizophrenia. Our

We are very grateful to Max Coltheart, Martin Davies, Joel Gold and Natalie Stoljar for many helpful comments on earlier drafts of this chapter.

approach to the irrationality of delusion is thus naturalistic. We argue that neither of the traditional conceptions of rationality offers a successful account of schizophrenic delusion[1] and conclude that a new branch of the theory of rationality is required. Because this branch deals with the rationality of experience, we call it *experiential rationality*.

2. The Traditional Departments of Rationality

2.1 Procedural Rationality

The study of rationality since Hume has concerned itself primarily with modes of reasoning and its behavioural consequences. A wide variety of types of reasoning has been investigated, including instrumental reasoning, utility-maximization, and the like, but in all cases the focus has been on the properties of the reasoning rules, algorithms, or, as we will say, *procedures* (Brown, 1988). Some theories have explicated procedures as ideals, whereas others have attempted to be more psychologically realistic, but, according to the vast majority of these theories, rationality is a matter of rule-satisfaction. As Brown (1988) puts it:

> Rules are at the heart of our classical model of rationality: if we have universally applicable rules, then all who begin from the same information must indeed arrive at the same conclusion (p. 19).[2]

On the procedural account, therefore, one is *irrational* if one's thoughts or actions fail to be governed by the relevant ideal, rule, or reasoning procedure.[3] For example, a paradigm case of procedural irrationality is being susceptible to what philosophers call 'Dutch books' (Skyrms, 1986)—arguments that reveal one's behaviour to be logically equivalent to a betting strategy that guarantees financial loss.

Central to the procedural account is the claim that the particular contents

---

[1] The psychological theory of delusion is obviously distinct from the theory of delusional irrationality. However, it will become clear below that the typical psychological accounts of delusion fall quite straightforwardly into the traditional branches of the theory of rationality. For this reason, we consider both the theory of the delusion and the theory of delusional irrationality together.

[2] Cf. also Rescher, 1988, who emphasizes that the rational is distinguished from individual, idiosyncratic or subjective desires and intentions: 'Above all, reason is systematic: it requires us to pursue intelligently adopted objectives in intelligent ways, acting on principles that make sense in a systematic way and whose appropriateness other agents can in principle also determine . . . Rationality demands: consistency, uniformity, coherence, simplicity, economy' (pp. 16–18).

[3] For various approaches to the procedural account of rationality, see, for example, Cherniak, 1986; Kaplan, 1996; Rescher, 1988. For a discussion of rationality that takes psychological reality into account, see Kahneman, Slovic and Tversky, 1982.

of one's thoughts are *not* in general relevant to the analysis of rationality. As Hume (1888/1978) famously remarked "Tis not contrary to reason to prefer the destruction of the whole world to the scratching of my finger' (p. 416). These contents are the contents of desires (which Hume called the 'passions') and beliefs, and they form no part of this domain of rationality: 'Reason is, and ought only to be the slave of the passions, and can never pretend to any other office than to serve and obey them' (p. 415).

2.2 Content Rationality

This is not to say, however, that the content of belief and desire is not a matter of rationality but only that it belongs to a different branch of its study.[4] David Lewis (1986) puts this view as follows:

> instrumental [i.e. procedural] rationality, though it is the department of rationality that has proved most tractable to systematic theory, remains only one department among others. We think that some sorts of belief and desire (or, of dispositions to believe and desire in response to evidence) would be unreasonable in a strong sense—not just unduly sceptical or rash or inequitable or dogmatic or wicked or one-sided or short-sighted, but utterly unintelligible and nonsensical. Think of the man who, for no special reason, expects unexamined emeralds to be grue.[5] Think of Anscombe's (1957) example (in *Intention*, section 37) of someone with a basic desire for a saucer of mud. These beliefs and desires are unreasonable; though if twisted desire is combined with correspondingly twisted belief, then it may be that the failing lies entirely outside the purview of the department of instrumental rationality. So I say that other departments of rationality also may have a constitutive role. What makes the perversely twisted assignment of content incorrect, however well it fits the subject's behavior, is exactly that it assigns ineligible, unreasonable content when a more eligible assignment would have fit behavior equally well (pp. 38–9).

We agree that there are kinds of irrationality that can be traced to the contents of particular beliefs and desires. We argue, however, that there are cases of

---

[4] We do not mean to suggest that the departments of procedural and content irrationality never intersect, or that there are never ambiguous cases. A familiar example of such an intersection is the case of a belief with a self-contradictory content. The content of the belief is irrational because it exemplifies a procedural violation. (We are grateful to Martin Davies for alerting us to this issue.)

[5] 'Grue' is the gerrymandered property of being green if examined before some time, *t*, in the future and blue if examined thereafter (see Goodman, 1973). The gerrymandered quality of the property is what makes a belief that emeralds are grue ineligible.

irrationality that represent neither procedural failings nor beliefs or desires with ineligible content in Lewis's sense. These cases are delusions.

3. A Case of Irrationality: Delusion in Schizophrenia

3.1 Delusion

Delusion is one of the five characteristic symptoms identified by the American Psychiatric Association's *Diagnostic and Statistical Manual of Mental Disorders* (*DSM-IV*, 1994) the presence of which can lead to a diagnosis of schizophrenia. Indeed, delusion is a pervasive and highly typical symptom of schizophrenia, though by no means unique to it (see Breen et al.; Gerrans; and Young, all in this volume). Some of the characteristic delusions of schizophrenia include *thought broadcasting*, the belief that one's thoughts are being heard by others; *thought insertion*, the belief that some of one's thoughts are being inserted into one's mind from an outside source; *delusions of control*, the belief that one is being controlled by an external force; *delusions of reference*, the belief that the actions of others have a special reference to oneself; and *delusions of persecution*, the belief that one is the target of the malicious actions of others (Cutting, 1990).

To an outside observer, delusions are, first and foremost, bizarre and wildly improbable:

> Delusions of being wired or radio controlled are relatively common [in schizophrenia]. Often it is the FBI or the CIA which is the suspected perpetrator of the scheme. One patient was convinced that he had a radio sewn into his skull when he had had a minor scalp wound sutured and had tried to bring legal suit against the FBI innumerable times. Another man, at one time a highly successful superintendent of schools, became convinced that a radio had been implanted in his nose. He went to dozens of major medical centers, even to Europe, seeking a surgeon who would remove it. He even had an X-ray of his nose showing a tiny white speck which he was convinced was the radio (Torrey, 1995, p. 54).

From a theoretical point of view, however, what is more significant than the bizarreness of delusion is the fact that, in the delusional state, the patient's mind seems invaded by an alien force. The classic description of the phenomenology of delusion by Kraepelin (1919) conveys this well:

> People speak to the patient in his thoughts, guide them, contradict him, 'offer' him thoughts, suggest them to him, transfer to him words, thoughts, pictures, smells and feelings. A patient said, 'My senses don't belong to me any more, they are being unlawfully taken from me.'

Strangers send him thoughts silently and speak in his head, it is 'a remembrance, a memory a memorial,' a 'receiving of thoughts.' In this way his own thoughts are disturbed, 'drilled,' 'drawn off'; he cannot think when the voice speaks. A patient explained, 'They take my thoughts from me and nothing comes back but a ragamuffin.' What he thinks himself is distorted; his thoughts are 'plundered, organised and published.' 'The voices and my brain are one, I must think what the voice says,' said a patient, and a woman complained: 'The voices work on my thoughts from morning to evening, suggest dreams to me and torment me unceasingly.' Many of the patients must utter aloud their own thoughts or those that are given to them, 'low by movements of the lips,' 'say silly stuff to oneself.' 'It flows into the brain as a thought and expresses itself as words in the mouth,' said a patient. Another heard 'dead' and had to answer 'bread' (pp. 12–13).

The alien quality of delusional experience is, in our view, the key to understanding at least some of the delusions of schizophrenia and the nature of the irrationality of schizophrenic delusion.

That delusions *are* irrational we take to be obvious. Like Dutch book arguments and a desire for a saucer of mud, the delusions described above are *paradigms* of irrationality. Adopting a deficient betting strategy, as in the case of Dutch books, surely represents a misdemeanor of irrationality compared to the delusion that the FBI is controlling you by a radio surreptitiously sewn into your skull. We will assume, therefore, that a theory of rationality that does not explain why delusions such as these count as irrational is an inadequate theory. For the sake of simplicity we focus on the delusion of thought insertion which is widely thought to be an almost certain indication of schizophrenia (Torrey, 1995), but we suspect that other delusions will also be explained by this, or a similar, account.

3.2 The Etiology of Delusion

One of the central theories of the etiology of delusion in schizophrenia is that of Frith (1987, 1992), and we turn now to a consideration of his model.[6] Our proposal, however, does not depend on the adequacy of that model.[7] We take it that the constraint on rationality we identify by exploring this model is a genuine constraint whether or not it is actually violated in schizophrenia, or violated in the way Frith suggests. However, we accept that should it be discovered that there are *no* psychological conditions in which this constraint is in fact violated, it would cease to be relevant to the theory of rationality. Our view is thus susceptible of empirical refutation.

---

[6]   For a review of other accounts, see Garety and Freeman, 1999.
[7]   For some problems with Frith's model, see Currie, this volume.

Frith's account first distinguishes between two routes to the formation of an intention to act. The first is stimulus-driven; the second is driven by goals and plans. In the first case, a particular stimulus leads a subject to form the intention to act, as when, for example, one forms the intention to order chocolate cake after seeing chocolate cake on the menu. Frith calls these *stimulus-intentions*. In the second case, the formation of an intention to act does not follow upon a stimulus but upon a goal or plan. One might, for example, form the intention to get a French dictionary in order to pursue the goal of learning French. Frith calls these *willed intentions*. Frith further posits the existence of a cognitive monitor that keeps track of both kinds of intention as well as of the actions that are actually chosen by the subject. In effect, the monitor is a mechanism of *metarepresentation*: it represents the ordered pair of the intention (whether stimulus or willed) and the action chosen as a result of that intention (see Frith, 1992). Crucially, the effect of metarepresenting an intention is to bring that intention into the subject's consciousness.

Frith's hypothesis is that schizophrenic delusion is caused by *a failure of the monitor to represent willed intentions* (see also Feinberg, 1978; Feinberg and Guazzelli, 1999). Consider a simple example. It is one of my goals to learn French. At some stage, I form the willed intention to buy a French dictionary. The monitor metarepresents that intention and thereby brings it into consciousness. Having formed the intention to buy the dictionary, I initiate the action of buying it (all things being equal). The monitor metarepresents both my action and my intention and can thus verify that the action executed satisfies the relevant intention. Figure 1 gives a sketch of the view.

Now suppose that the process of self-monitoring is defective and the monitor fails to represent the intention to buy a dictionary. In this case, I would find myself buying a dictionary without any conscious awareness that I had formed the intention to do so, and I would therefore be faced with a puzzle: an action has been initiated, but I have no awareness of any intention to initiate it. I might, therefore, be tempted to look elsewhere for an explanation. One possibility is that some external force initiated the action for a reason of its own. This belief would of course be mistaken, indeed, delusional—a delusion of control.

Consider a different example from Frith (1987). I am in the tea-room talking to Tim, and I overhear John talking about wine. Since it is one of my goals to learn about wine, I form the intention to switch my attention from Tim to John. However, if I cannot monitor my intentions, I will find myself listening to John without any awareness of an intention to do so, and I might suppose that this happened because John was talking about me, and that is what got my attention—a delusion of reference.

If one now interprets 'action' in the model (see Figure 1) as including the thinking of a thought (as Frith intends), it is possible to account for other of the experiential symptoms of schizophrenia (Frith, 1987, 1992). Suppose one of my goals is to go to work on time each morning. On a particular morning,

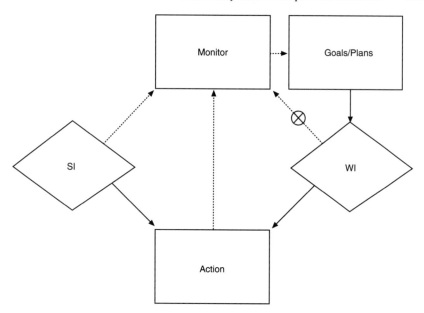

Figure 1 *Frith's model of the failure of self-monitoring. If the action is a thought, it may be (a) perceived in the form of a hallucination; (b) experienced as having been caused by an external agency as in the delusion of thought insertion or the delusion of passivity; or (c) the result of an unassociated stimulus as in the delusion of reference. WI = willed intention; SI = stimulus intention; ····· = feedback; ⊗ = lesion.*

I form the intention to catch the bus and then perform the action of thinking 'Catch the bus!' If I have not monitored the intention to catch the bus, I will find myself with a particular thought without any awareness of the intention that initiated it. As a result, I may experience the thought as having been put into my head by someone else—a delusion of thought insertion. If the thought 'Catch the bus!' occurs as inner speech, Frith claims, I will experience it in the form of a hallucination in which someone is *telling* me to catch the bus.

The examples above capture many of the significant features of Frith's model. The model provides parallel accounts of a number of schizophrenic symptoms, is testable, and has been supported by some recent data. For example, Malenka et al. (1982) and Frith and Done (1989) argue that self-monitoring in the domain of motor-behaviour allows subjects to make rapid corrections of motor errors. Schizophrenic subjects who suffer from delusions such as thought insertion fail to make such corrections, suggesting that their delusions may also reflect a failure of self-monitoring.

4. Egocentricity

Frith's model offers a functional explanation of the development of delusion. What does this account say about the nature of their irrationality? We propose that delusional irrationality consists in a failure of what we will call *egocentricity*, a property of thought closely related to the self-monitoring central to Frith's theory. Self-monitoring is the cognitive process of representing an intention; egocentricity is the property a thought gets in virtue of being so monitored. It is the property of the thought which allows the thinker of that thought to recognize it as having originated in his mind.

To illustrate egocentricity, consider the following case due to John Perry (1979).[8] Suppose I am pushing my cart down the aisle of a supermarket and notice that someone is producing a trail of sugar, presumably from a leaking bag. I move down the aisle and back up again in search of the person whose bag of sugar is leaking in order to tell him that he is making a mess. The trail gets thicker and thicker, but I am unable to catch up with this person. Eventually it dawns on me that *I* am the person whose bag of sugar is leaking, and, on realizing this, my behavior changes; I stop chasing the unknown person whose bag of sugar is leaking and close the bag of sugar in my own cart.

The central aspect of this case is the transition from my awareness that *someone* has a leaking bag of sugar to the awareness that I am that person. When I know that someone has a leaking bag of sugar, there is a sense in which I have a complete description of the situation in the supermarket aisle. What I fail to know is that *I* am the person whose bag of sugar is leaking. What I am missing is information about my role—my conceptual location, so to speak—in the situation.

Something analogous seems to be true of delusions in schizophrenia. If Frith's model is correct, then in thought insertion the subject has the thought 'Catch the bus!', but because there is no monitoring of willed intention, the subject does not have available to him an explanation of the source of that thought—an explanation of the form 'I have the intention to be on time which naturally led to the thought to catch the bus. The intention was mine and so, therefore, is the thought.'[9] While the subject is quite aware that the thought resides in his mind, he is not aware that it originated there. In effect, the subject is capable of thinking 'Someone has produced the thought "Catch the bus!"', but not 'I am that someone'. There is an awareness that a thought has been produced, as well as an awareness of the content of the thought, but no

---

[8]   We put Perry's case to a somewhat different use from that of Perry himself, however (see also Evans, 1982).

[9]   Notice, however, that questions remain about this aspect of the model. Why is it that an awareness of a thought is insufficient by itself to identify the thought as one's own but that the presence of an intention is sufficient? What enables the subject to identify the intention as his own? Why, in other words, is there no delusion of intention insertion?

awareness of one's own role as its producer.[10] As in Perry's case, the deluded subject has third-person, but not egocentric, information to the effect that the thought of which he is aware originated in his own mind. One way of conceiving of the failure of self-monitoring, therefore, is as a state of affairs in which the subject's thoughts fail to have the property that allows them to be identified as having originated in his mind. The thinker is thus in no doubt about who he is, or about the thoughts he is having. Rather, he fails to know that he produced those thoughts.[11] Because we have claimed that the delusions of schizophrenia are paradigm cases of irrationality and that a failure of egocentricity is the cause of those delusions, we take egocentricity to be a condition on rationality.

5. Does Egocentricity Belong in the Departments of Procedural or Content Rationality?

We turn now to the question of whether a failure of egocentricity belongs to procedural irrationality, content irrationality, or neither. On the face of it, egocentricity seems to bear no relation either to procedural or content conceptions of rationality. Nevertheless, the defender of the traditional departments will argue as follows. Even if one believes that egocentricity plays a causal role in the production of delusion, it does not follow that the violation of egocentricity is constitutive of delusional irrationality. One must distinguish between the causal sources of delusion and its psychological explanation on the one hand, and the conditions which are constitutive of the irrationality on the other. It is quite possible that a unique form of irrationality—supposing that that is what schizophrenic delusion is—may nevertheless belong with other forms of irrationality in one of the traditional departments.

We accept the distinction between causal factors in delusion and the correct classification of the irrationality so produced. We must show, therefore, that procedural and content accounts of delusion are not adequate to the phenomena. Since our approach is naturalistic, the correct description of schizophrenic delusion is the one that provides the best characterization of the phenomena overall. We argue that, however plausible procedural and content theories are, they fail to explain all of the features of the delusional state and hence that a different notion of irrationality is necessary to capture those features. Because

---

[10]   Notice the distinction between two potential mental confusions. I can be aware that someone has produced a thought, but be unaware that I am the person who has produced it. In contrast, I might be aware that John Perry has produced a thought, but be unaware that I am John Perry. The latter case may be relevant to explaining certain delusions of self-misidentification (see Breen et al., this volume).

[11]   See Peacocke, 1999, who also addresses Frith's conception of self-monitoring and its implications for self-knowledge: 'A conception of ownership which involves origination is crucial for rational thought and action' (p. 244).

it is the violation of egocentricity that leads to schizophrenic delusion, we conclude that the study of egocentricity belongs in that department as well.

5.1 Procedural and Content Accounts[12]

The classical accounts of rationality would characterize our central case of thought insertion as a failure of procedural rationality. On these accounts, a violation of a rule or a principle of reasoning is responsible for the deluded state. Content rationality, in contrast, locates delusion in the ineligibility of delusional belief. We consider a variety of such explanations below.

5.1.1 Reflective Equilibrium
Thought insertion may be caused by a violation of a principle of belief revision. Whatever the local plausibility of thought insertion as an explanation of a thought whose origin is unknown, it is wildly implausible against the background of our culture's common beliefs. If one assumes that the subject shares many of these beliefs, he violates a principle of *reflective equilibrium* (e.g. Harman, 1986), according to which one should aim for maximal coherence among one's beliefs. Reflective equilibrium would require rejecting thought insertion in favour of an explanation that cohered better with one's set of background beliefs, including those shared by the culture at large. In general, any account of rationality that requires coherence among beliefs will be violated by the hypothesis of thought insertion.[13]

5.1.2 Evidence
A closely related possibility is that thought insertion may violate a principle of relevant evidence. Stone and Young (1997; see also Young, this volume) have argued that subjects with Capgras delusion are susceptible to biases in explanation. That is, they are apt to ignore evidence—in Capgras delusion, for example, of how unlikely it is that a loved one has been replaced by a double—and to give undue weight to other kinds of evidence. Since the delusion fails to be supported by legitimate evidence, an evaluation of this evidence should lead the schizophrenic subject to reconsider the delusional belief.[14]

5.1.3 Methodology
A third procedural violation that might be invoked is a methodological one. The mere presence of a thought the origin of which is inaccessible to the subject is not itself sufficient for the production of a delusion. Suppose one were to think to oneself 'Catch the bus!' but be unable

---

[12] In psychiatry, psychosis is divided into two disorders: that of thought process and that of thought content (Kaplan and Sadock, 1995). Though related, these categories do not correspond to procedural and content rationality.

[13] Langdon and Coltheart, this volume, argue that a reasoning deficit in this area is one of the factors involved in producing delusions.

[14] Langdon and Coltheart, this volume, argue that the bias account is inadequate because biases can eventually be overcome. They therefore suggest a deficit account of delusion.

to explain the presence of that thought. One could choose to be puzzled by this occurrence without moving on to providing an explanation of it.[15] Such cases are commonplace. One wonders why a particular thought has popped into one's head; or one starts to daydream about something quite disconnected from the present conditions; or one gets an urge to go out into the sunshine; and so forth. In such cases, one rarely stops to wonder about the origins of these thoughts. Similarly, there are normal confusions, particularly of memory, in which one cannot remember, for example, whether a particular thought is originally one's own or was expressed by someone else, or whether a thought or image is a memory of a real event or of a dream. Further, illusions of memory occur just as perceptual illusions do: when an event is vividly imagined, the imagined event is often remembered as having occurred (Goff and Roediger, 1998), but one is not in general puzzled, or even aware, of these occurrences. One could, therefore, explain thought insertion as resulting from the violation of a methodological principle advocating a *suspension* of explanation when no reasonable explanation is available.[16]

There are cases more prosaic than delusion in which abstaining from explanation is the rational thing to do. Suppose, for example, that an experiment generates data that are inconsistent with the best relevant scientific theory. There are a number of things a scientist can do: she can reject the theory; doubt the correctness of the data; do further experiments; or do nothing. Suppose further that the scientist has great confidence in both the theory and in the data. In such a case it may be maximally rational to do nothing. Accepting inconsistency or inexplicability may often present the best choice under the circumstances,[17] and adopting a rule of reasoning according to which some explanation must be given in *all* circumstances would no doubt dispose one— and could dispose schizophrenics—to produce irrational explanations.

5.1.4 Content-ineligibility   Given the bizarre quality of thought insertion as a belief about one's experience, a content explanation looks promising. On a content account, a delusion will be said to be irrational because, as Lewis (1986) puts it, 'it assigns ineligible, unreasonable content when a more eligible assignment would have fit behavior equally well' (p. 39). Further, the schizophrenic subject manages to incorporate the implausible belief into his system of delusion in a way that is reminiscent of Lewis's description of the 'twisting'

---

[15] We thus differ from Langdon and Coltheart, this volume, in holding that the constraints of rationality do not *require* certain experiences to be explained.

[16] Notice that one can distinguish two senses of an explanation's being 'available' to a subject. On one sense of 'available', normal subjects in the same circumstances would be expected to have the cognitive ability to produce the relevant explanation. On a second sense, an explanation is available if a subject *ideally placed* would be able to appeal to it. Schizophrenic subjects are abnormal because certain explanations are not available to them in the first sense.

[17] This suggestion was explored by John Bigelow in an Australian Association of Philosophy presidential address: Armidale, Australia, 1995.

of belief and desire, namely, by a *system* of beliefs each of which is highly improbable or impossible on its own but which seems to acquire a veneer of plausibility from its coherence with the others.

Content irrationality may also offer a more parsimonious explanation of delusion than procedural accounts can. It is a familiar experience to reason oneself into a belief that seems plausible in the context of that reasoning but, subsequently, and in the absence of the reasoning context, seems quite implausible. The defender of procedural irrationality has to explain not only how delusion comes about but also why the delusion fails to be rejected upon review. If, however, the irrationality of delusion is located in the tendency of schizophrenic subjects to be insensitive to bizarre contents of thought, then there is no need to posit a procedural deficit in both the reasoning process and the subsequent process of evaluation but only a single deficit of 'bizarre content blindness'.

5.2 Problems with These Accounts

In our view, none of these accounts provides a satisfactory naturalistic explanation of schizophrenic delusion. We consider the difficulties with each account in turn.

5.2.1 Reflective Equilibrium   Reflective equilibrium offers an unsatisfactory explanation of the irrationality of thought insertion because if the schizophrenic agent has a global impairment in his ability to maintain coherence among his beliefs, one would expect this impairment to be domain-general. An inability to achieve reflective equilibrium among beliefs would infect the agent's whole system of beliefs, and one would expect the agent to experience delusions of every imaginable kind. But the delusions of schizophrenic subjects tend to be restricted to the social domain (Bentall et al., 1991; Frith, 1992).[18]

Even if the proceduralist were to hypothesize that the schizophrenic has an impairment of the ability to apply reflective equilibrium only in this restricted domain, delusional states tend to revolve around highly specific and predictable ideas and are therefore much rarer than delusion ought to be if schizophrenics have a deficiency of reflective equilibrium in the domain of the social. The classic Schneiderian taxonomy (Schneider, 1959) includes seven types of delusion as diagnostic of schizophrenia; a more recent classification identifies only five (Cutting, 1995). Given this small number of species of delusion, it is hard to see how one could identify a natural cognitive domain, social or otherwise, that would isolate all and only those topics that emerge in schizo-

---

[18]   One possible response to this argument, therefore, is that delusions all fall into a single category of *social reasoning* and, therefore, that the boundaries within which the errors of reasoning fall are natural ones (see Bentall et al., 1991). This claim could be developed in the context of a defence of the existence of a module for 'mentalizing', that is, for representing the mental states of others (see Currie, this volume).

phrenic delusion, and it would be quite ad hoc to posit a defect of reflective equilibrium that applies only to those topics by definition. No such hypothesis is likely to be supported by a scientific theory of schizophrenic pathology.

5.2.2 Evidence A principle of evidence evaluation suffers from the same problem as that of reflective equilibrium. A global problem within the web of belief should lead to innumerable false beliefs, delusions, and, indeed, to behavioural chaos, but this does not occur in schizophrenia. Schizophrenic subjects appear to be just as capable of using the presence of a sign saying 'Metro' as evidence that a metro is nearby. In addition, a hallmark of the ability to evaluate evidence is the capacity to *change* one's view based on the introduction of new evidence (see Langdon and Coltheart, this volume). This too is something that schizophrenic subjects do not seem to have trouble doing: new evidence to the effect that the Angrignon metro goes west and not east will lead the eastward-travelling schizophrenic to change lines. In contrast, delusional states are, by definition, highly stable and resistant to revision. Given that schizophrenics do not have a general difficulty with evidence, it is unlikely that this stability lies in an insusceptibility to evidence. And, again, the hypothesis of a *local* failure to be responsive to evidence suffers from the problem of identifying a cognitive domain that captures all and only the delusions of interest. If the hypothesized domain is too big, the hypothesis will fail to explain the specificity of delusion; if it is too small, it will fail to carve the cognitive domain at its joints.

5.2.3 Methodology This version of the procedural account is compelling because it appears at first blush to be based on a minimal norm of rationality and one that is very easy to obey: when no plausible explanations are available, suspend belief. But, in fact, this requirement on rationality is much more demanding than it first appears. We claimed that when a scientist is faced with data that conflict with theory, it may be maximally rational to do nothing. Is this a sensible course of action for the schizophrenic? It is natural to think of the schizophrenic subject's choice as one between believing that the CIA is inserting thoughts into his head and believing nothing, and the option of believing nothing seems far more appealing to the outside observer. But this is not a correct description of the options. The schizophrenic in fact faces the choice of having some account of what is happening to him—some account of the structure of his experience—and being utterly at a loss to understand that experience. In asking the schizophrenic subject to refrain from explaining his experience, we would be asking him to forgo any story about why his experience is so strange, and that seems to be a demand that no agent—at least no agent that approximates actual human agents—could meet. Such a demand would be little different from asking Joseph K., the central character of Kafka's (1925/1998) *Trial*, to stop wondering about why he's been arrested.

Given that our account is naturalistic, it should not posit a violation of a norm that no actual agent could meet.

Even in the scientific domain, it is not clear that such a constraint is plausible. The scientist in our case above is faced with a conflict between the data of an experiment and the theory that is relevant to that data. However, the scientific analogy to schizophrenia would rather be to giving up any account at all of a large and significant aspect of the world. Wilfrid Sellars (e.g. Sellars, 1963) conceived of science as a way of locating oneself in the world, and this requires having at least general working hypotheses. In addition, such hypotheses are also necessary to identify new lines of research. Thus, the schizophrenic subject might actually be *violating* a norm of scientific method by refraining from a working hypothesis with which to understand their experience.

There is a further virtue of adopting a delusional account of one's experience rather than no account at all. One assumes that delusional experience—at least in the case of thought insertion, paranoid delusions, and the like—is very unpleasant. A delusional account offers the subject the possibility not only of explaining his experience but of doing something about it, and that sort of motive is a powerful one for normal agents. It seems wrong-headed to claim that a widely shared motive among normal agents constitutes a form of irrationality in schizophrenics. Thus, faced with the strange experiences of schizophrenia, the hypothesis of thought insertion is perhaps one of the more *plausible* suppositions one might make.

Are there other grounds on which the schizophrenic is criticizable? If a suspension of explanation is too demanding a requirement on rationality, could we not demand of the schizophrenic subject that he opt for the hypothesis that he is mentally or neurologically ill? This may still be asking too much. The experience of non-egocentric thought may be so pervasive and compelling that any hypothesis that calls that experience into doubt is automatically ruled out of court. Again, it may be easier, and indeed more sensible, to adopt thought insertion as a hypothesis than to adopt the view that one's experience is systematically incorrect—that one is living in a sort of virtual reality. In addition, to posit mental illness in the face of the systematic strangeness of experience is to give up one's identity as an agent capable of understanding and interacting adaptively with the outside world. This is surely a core background assumption of the explanation of one's own behaviour and that of others. Thought insertion may seem a less radical option, therefore, than giving up that assumption.

5.2.4 Content-ineligibility   It is quite natural to characterize delusion as a pathology of belief and to assume that this pathology is responsible for the irrationality. However, the attempt to reduce the irrationality of delusion to the bizarre contents of delusional beliefs suffers from the same problem as the procedural accounts just evaluated: a content account does not explain why the bizarre beliefs of these subjects seem so narrowly restricted and predictable in content. If schizophrenic delusion were an instance of content irrationality, one would expect that bizarre beliefs would be shot through the system of belief, but this is not in fact the case. In general, schizophrenic subjects believe in eating food in order to satisfy hunger; in going inside to get warm; in taking the metro to get from place to place; and so on.

Further, even if we restrict our attention to the strange experience schizophrenics have and are, presumably, trying to explain, it remains the case that there are, in principle, an indefinite number of beliefs that could be generated on the basis of that experience, many of them less implausible than thought insertion. It is very surprising, therefore, that delusional subjects choose thought insertion as an explanation sufficiently frequently for it to be a hallmark of schizophrenia.[19]

There is a further difficulty with the content account. Not all delusional beliefs and desires will turn out to be beliefs or desires that are ineligible in Lewis's sense. What does 'ineligible' mean here? Lewis chooses as paradigms of ineligible contents the desire for a saucer of mud and the belief that emeralds are grue—green if examined before some time, *t*, in the future and blue otherwise. What unites both of these mental states is not that they are bizarre, but rather that they fall outside the network of mental states we take to be relevant to the description of the physical world and of human behaviour. In response to someone's expression of a bizarre desire—a desire to sing Pagliacci from the bottom of a herring barrel, for example—one might be inclined to question or dissuade. In response to the expression of a desire for a saucer of mud, one can only be incredulous. Where does one get a purchase on such a desire? Because it falls outside of the framework of human desires, as we understand it, one cannot. The same holds for the belief that emeralds are grue. One can argue with someone who believes that emeralds are pink, but one cannot negotiate with the grue-ascriber; emeralds *are* grue, after all. But grue is not a predicate that forms part of the apparatus we use to describe the physical world.

Are delusions ineligible in Lewis's sense? Clearly not. It is bizarre to think that the CIA is tapping your phone. In the light of the relevant evidence, this belief may be highly improbable, but it is not ineligible. The CIA may *indeed* be tapping your phone; just because you're paranoid, as they say, doesn't mean you don't have enemies. The same applies to our central case of thought insertion. The idea that the FBI has sewn a radio transmitter into your skull and is thereby inserting thoughts into your head is bizarre in the extreme, but it is not outside the bounds of explanations we are willing to consider. Even if the delusion is that thoughts are being inserted by telepathy or through some mysterious ether, we are willing to entertain it; science fiction is filled with scenarios of just this kind.

We conclude, therefore, that plausible procedural and content accounts of

---

[19]   Gerrans (this volume) assesses the extent to which Capgras delusion is related to, in our terms, procedural rationality. He also points to the confined nature of these delusions.

delusion are not successful explanations of the nature of the irrationality in schizophrenic delusion. A failure of egocentricity is not therefore either a procedural or a content failure. A different account of the location of the irrationality is required. We claim that the domain-specificity of schizophrenic delusion derives from the fact that the experience of schizophrenics has a content that makes their beliefs quite natural. Our proposal is that it is the *experience* of schizophrenic subjects that is defective, and, for this reason, delusions, and thus irrationality, are an inevitable outcome even if the reasoning procedures applied to those experiences are entirely normal. We will therefore suggest that a new kind of irrationality—experiential irrationality—must be posited to explain delusion in schizophrenia.

6. A New Department of Rationality: Experiential Rationality

Both procedural and content accounts of the irrationality of delusion assume that schizophrenics have strange experiences—on Frith's account, the experience of a thought whose origin is unknown—that are then explained by means of defective procedures of reasoning or with beliefs with ineligible contents (see Breen et al., Langdon and Coltheart, and Young, all in this volume). As we have seen, these accounts locate the irrationality of delusion in the defective reasoning procedures or the bizarre contents of belief. In our view, this is the wrong way to describe the phenomenology of delusion. Unexplained phenomena—such as the occurrence of a stray thought whose origin is unknown—are all around us. If schizophrenic subjects suffered from procedural or content irrationality, one would expect their mental life to be replete with delusions of every imaginable sort. But, as we have argued, this is not the case.

We suggested above that the central feature of the phenomenology of delusion is the alien nature of the subject's thoughts. This is entirely in keeping with Frith's account, according to which schizophrenic thoughts violate egocentricity and are experienced as originating outside of one's mind. We claim, therefore, that the source of thought insertion and related delusions is the experience itself of the schizophrenic subject, and, in particular, its alien quality. The elaboration of the delusion in hypotheses and ancillary beliefs should be understood to be derivative from, or secondary to, this experience. Thus the violation of egocentricity does not merely produce strange experiences that form the basis of delusional beliefs as the result of pathological processes of thought or reasoning. Rather, it is *the experience of non-egocentric thought as alien* that is the delusion itself. The alien quality of the delusional experience is part of its content, and it is the content of experience that is the locus of the delusion and thus of the irrationality. At least some delusions, therefore, are best explained as *disorders of experience* rather than disorders of belief, desire, or reasoning. Thus whereas Stone and Young (1997) and Langdon and Coltheart (this volume) locate the source of the delusion in the reasoning process that engages with the strange experiences of schizophrenic subjects, we claim that the source of the delusion is the strange experience itself. The verbal reports of patients express the *way* in which the experience is strange.[20]

Consider thought insertion again as an illustration. A thought appears in the mind of the subject. Because it is not tagged as originating from the subject's own mind, it is experienced as alien—an experience as of something alien having been introduced into one's consciousness. Recall the description given by Kraepelin (1919): '"My senses don't belong to me any more, they are being unlawfully taken from me." . . ."They take my thoughts from me and nothing comes back but a ragamuffin." . . . his thoughts are "plundered, organised and published." "The voices and my brain are one, I must think what the voice says".' The way in which a delusion—though not, in this case, the delusion of thought insertion—can be embedded in experience is brought out clearly in this quote from a schizophrenic subject (quoted in Torrey, 1995):

> At this point, I panicked and tried to run away, but the attendant in the parking lot seemed to be making a sign to motion me back. I thought I caught brief glimpses of a friend and my wife so I decided to go back into the hospital. A custodian's eyes attracted my attention; they were especially large and piercing. He looked very powerful. He had to be 'in on it,' maybe he was giving medicine in some way. Then I began to have the feeling that other people were watching me. And, as periodically happened throughout the early stages, I said to myself that the whole thing was absurd, but when I looked again the people really were watching me (p. 53).

It seems clear that the experiences of this subject do not lead him to a deluded hypothesis but rather that his experience misrepresents the world in a delusional way. Once we suppose that the origin of thought insertion is an experience of certain mental states as alien, the delusions of thought insertion, of control, and of persecution become much less surprising. The experience of an alien presence in one's consciousness is naturally expressed in these delusional states and in the system of beliefs that is built upon it. Once egocentricity is violated, the particular irrationality of these delusions is almost inevitable.

As we suggested above, in the light of schizophrenic experience, delusion can be seen as a sensible cognitive response. To refrain from explanation is,

---

[20]   Note that nothing we say is meant to suggest that the *only* kind of irrationality that presents itself in schizophrenic delusions of self-monitoring is the experiential irrationality brought about by a failure of egocentricity. For example, the fact that schizophrenic subjects do not subsequently revise their views about their delusions in the light of further evidence might require some reference to a form of procedural or content irrationality. Our claim is only that the best explanation of the original delusion itself is the irrationality of experience.

we have suggested, psychologically impossible, and the other options, such as hypothesizing that one is mentally ill, may require giving up beliefs that are more important to the agent—such as the belief that he *is* an agent; that he has some grip on the nature of his experience; or that he can affect his environment. Thought insertion, however bizarre, may be among the more adaptive hypotheses one could adopt. This seems particularly true if one supposes that delusional experience is pervasive in schizophrenia and that more 'rational' hypotheses than thought insertion would require dismissing the veridicality and relevance of one's experience. Certainly, normal subjects have a strong inclination to take most of their experience at face value, and one would expect the same of schizophrenic subjects. The subject quoted above, for example, resists the idea that people are watching him, but then his experience seems to overwhelm him: 'I said to myself that the whole thing was absurd, but when I looked again the people really were watching me.'

Further support for the experiential view derives from its continuity with the fact of perceptual abnormality that characterizes almost two-thirds of schizophrenic subjects (Torrey, 1995). Indeed, perceptual abnormality—such as heightened sensitivity to stimuli—is the most invariant feature of the early stages of schizophrenia (Cutting and Dunne, 1989). Given the pervasiveness of perceptual dysfunction, a theory of delusion that focuses on experience is more parsimonious than procedural or content accounts. It posits an abnormality in experience and is thus in the spirit of the proposal by Maher (1974), who locates the source of the delusion in abnormal perception.

The parsimony of the experiential view is enhanced when schizophrenic hallucination is considered because hallucinations are precisely perceptual experiences that are often intrinsically alien—such as when they are experiences of *other people's voices* commenting, giving a command, or whatever. A hallucination is an unusual form of experience, but no subsequent judgement is required on the part of the subject for the experience to become delusional. It has a delusional content, but that content is embedded in an experience rather than in a belief or desire. And, indeed, there is some evidence that hallucinations arise as a result of a violation of egocentricity in the domain of inner speech (Stein and Richardson, 1999), thus raising the possibility of a unification of delusion and hallucination in schizophrenia by means of the concept of egocentricity.

Finally, this account of delusion meshes well with a related symptom of schizophrenia, namely, the fact that schizophrenics sometimes experience their bodies, or body parts, as alien. One patient (quoted in Torrey, 1995) describes the experience this way:

> I get shaky in the knees and my chest is like a mountain in front of me, and my body actions are different. The arms and legs are apart and away from me and they go on their own. That's when I feel I am the other person and copy their movements, or else stop and stand

like a statue. I have to stop to find out whether my hand is in my pocket or not. I'm frightened to move or turn my head. Sometimes I let my arms roll to see whether they will land (p. 65).

The experience of body alienness also occurs in *anosognosia*, a lack of awareness of a sensory or neurological deficit (see Goetz and Pappert, 1999).[21]   An extreme version of this condition is the *alien hand syndrome*. Kaufman (1995) describes the condition as follows:

> In this disorder . . . a patient's left[22] hand retains some rudimentary motor and sensory functions, but they cannot be appreciated by the rest of the patient's brain. Without the patient's awareness, the hand moves semipurposefully, makes its own explorations, and performs simple tasks, such as scratching and moving bedclothes. In a unique, often quoted example, a patient reported that her hand was attempting to choke her. The alien hand syndrome rests on the patient having at least two misperceptions: (1) the patient does not possess the hand and (2) the hand's movements are independent or governed by another person (the alien). Most patients feel divorced from the hand or, at most, express a tenuous attachment to it (pp. 182–3).

The analogy with schizophrenic delusion is striking. In this case, however, it seems especially plausible that the idea that the hand is controlled by an alien stems from the subject's experience of the hand as disconnected from the subject's consciousness, both in the sensory and the motor domain, rather than from a belief or hypothesis formed on the basis of the fact that the hand is not under the subject's control. It is thus not surprising that a thought not identified as originating in one's own mind—like a limb not identified by sensation as belonging to one's own body—*feels* alien quite in the absence of any reasoning, or hypothesis-formation, about that thought.

A failure of egocentricity, therefore, leads to a mental state that is irrational even though there may be no irrational belief or desire content nor any explicit hypothesis (whether conscious or unconscious) that is invoked to explain the

---

[21]   Intriguingly, patients with damage to the left motor cortex are able to explain an inability to move a limb by appealing to their brain damage, but patients with right-cortical damage claim that they are unable to move a limb because it belongs to someone else. On our account, a possible explanation is the following. In left-hemisphere damage, motor commands are given to move the limb and are monitored. When the limb fails to move, the experience is of an inability to execute this command. In right-hemisphere damage, the motor command is not tagged as originating from the subject and so the experience of the limb is as of its belonging to someone else. After all, in normal circumstances a limb to which one cannot give commands *should* be experienced as belonging to someone else. (We are grateful to Max Coltheart for alerting us to this issue.)

[22]   The condition typically occurs in individuals with brain damage to a non-dominant right hemisphere. The incapacity is therefore to the left hand. (See note 21.)

experience. Although the form of irrationality produced by a violation of ego-centricity is not reducible to procedural or content irrationality, it is also a worthy deserver of the name 'irrational'. Because these irrational states do not fall within the traditional categories, we propose a new department of rationality called *experiential rationality*.

We note, finally, that if the present analysis is correct and there are experiential forms of irrationality, we expect that further investigation into the phenomena of psychopathology will reveal other constraints on rationality that do not fall within the departments of procedural or content irrationality.

References

American Psychiatric Association. 1994: *Diagnostic and Statistical Manual of Mental Disorders*, Fourth Edition (*DSM-IV*). Washington, DC: American Psychiatric Association.

Anscombe, G.E.M. 1957: *Intention*. Oxford: Blackwell.

Bentall, R.P., Kaney, S. and Dewey, M.E. 1991: Paranoia and social reasoning: An attribution theory analysis. *British Journal of Child Psychology*, 30, 13–23.

Brown, H.I. 1988: *Rationality*. London: Routledge.

Cherniak, C. 1986: *Minimal Rationality*. Cambridge, MA: MIT Press.

Cutting, J. 1990: *The Right Cerebral Hemisphere and Psychiatric Disorders*. Oxford University Press.

Cutting, J. 1995: Descriptive psychopathology. In S.R. Hirsch and D.R. Weinberger (eds), *Schizophrenia*. Oxford: Blackwell Scientific.

Cutting, J. and Dunne, F. 1989: Subjective experience of schizophrenia. *Schizophrenia Bulletin*, 15, 217–31.

Evans, G. 1982: *The Varieties of Reference*. Oxford University Press.

Feinberg, I. 1978: Efference copy and corollary discharge: Implications for thinking and its disorders. *Schizophrenia Bulletin*, 4, 636–40.

Feinberg, I. and Guazzelli, M. 1999: Schizophrenia: A disorder of the corollary discharge systems that integrate the motor systems of thought with the sensory systems of consciousness. *British Journal of Psychiatry*, 174, 196–204.

Frith, C.D. 1987: The positive and negative symptoms of schizophrenia reflect impairments in the perception and initiation of action. *Psychological Medicine*, 17, 631–48.

Frith, C.D. 1992: *The Cognitive Neuropsychology of Schizophrenia*. Hove, E. Sussex: Lawrence Erlbaum.

Frith, C.D. and Done, D.J. 1989: Experiences of alien control in schizophrenia reflect a disorder in the central monitoring of action. *Psychological Medicine*, 19, 359–63.

Garety, P.A., and Freeman, D. 1999: Cognitive approaches to delusions: A critical review of theories and evidence. *British Journal of Clinical Psychology*, 38, 113–54.

Goetz, C.G. and Pappert, E.J. 1999: *Textbook of Clinical Neurology*. Philadelphia: W.B. Saunders.

Goff, L.M. and Roediger, H.L. 1998: Imagination inflation for actions and events: Repeated imaginings lead to illusory recollections. *Memory and Cognition*, 26, 20–33.

Goodman, N. 1973: *Fact, Fiction, and Forecast*, 3rd edn. Indianapolis: Bobbs-Merrill.

Harman, G. 1986: *Change in View*. Cambridge, MA: MIT Press.

Hume, D. 1888/1978: *A Treatise of Human Nature*, 2nd edn, ed. L.A. Selby-Bigge and P.H. Nidditch. Oxford University Press.

Kafka, F. 1925/1998: *The Trial*, trans. B. Mitchell. New York: Schocken Books.

Kahneman D., Slovic P. and Tversky, A. 1982: *Judgement Under Uncertainty: Heuristics and Biases*. Cambridge University Press.

Kaplan, M. 1996: *Decision Theory as Philosophy*. Cambridge University Press.

Kaplan, H.I. and Sadock, B.J. (eds). 1995: *Comprehensive Textbook of Psychiatry*, 6th edn. Baltimore: Williams and Wilkins.

Kaufman, D.M. 1995: *Clinical Neurology for Psychiatrists*, 4th edn. Philadelphia: W.B. Saunders Company.

Kraepelin, E. 1919: *Dementia Praecox*, trans. R.M. Barclay, ed. G.M. Robertson. Edinburgh: E. & S. Livingstone.

Lewis, D. 1986: *On the Plurality of Worlds*. Oxford University Press.

Maher, B. 1974: Delusional thinking and perceptual disorder. *Journal of Individual Psychology*, 30, 98–113.

Malenka, R.C., Angel, R.W., Hampton, B. and Berger, P.A. 1982: Impaired central error correcting behaviour in schizophrenia. *Archives of General Psychiatry*, 39, 101–7.

Peacocke, C. 1999: *Being Known*. Oxford University Press.

Perry, J. 1979: The problem of the essential indexical. *Noûs*, 13, 3–21.

Rescher, N. 1988: *Rationality*. Oxford University Press.

Ryle. G. 1949: *The Concept of Mind*. London: Hutchison & Company.

Schneider, K. 1959: *Clinical Psychopathology*, trans. M.W. Hamilton. New York: Grune & Stratton.

Sellars, W. 1963: Science and the manifest image of man. In W. Sellars, *Science, Perception, and Reality*. New York: Routledge and Kegan Paul.

Skyrms, B. 1986: *Choice and Chance*, 3rd edn. Belmont: Wadsworth.

Stein, J. and Richardson, A. 1999: Cognitive disorders: A question of misattribution. *Current Biology*, 9(10), R374–6.

Stone, T. and Young, A.W. 1997: Delusions and brain injury: The philosophy and psychology of belief. *Mind and Language*, 12, 327–64.

Torrey, E.F. 1995: *Surviving Schizophrenia*, 3rd edn. New York: Harper Perennial Press.

7

Imagination, Delusion and Hallucinations

GREGORY CURRIE

Imagination is a cognitive tool of great power, but it is also potentially a rather dangerous one. Loss of the distinction between what is imagined and what is true, or seriously a candidate for truth, can be psychologically disastrous, and I shall suggest that this is what we see in the delusions and hallucinations that mark certain phases of schizophrenia. In addition, I want to display some connections between that claim and a hypothesis about schizophrenia developed by Chris Frith (1992). Frith's hypothesis is interpretable in two ways; in fact it would be better to say that what we have are two different theories. One of them provides a natural underpinning to my own proposal; it has other, perhaps more significant, merits as well. The other theory seems to me not very promising. So I shall take some trouble to distinguish these two theories. I also want to question some standard assumptions about the classification of delusions and of hallucinations in schizophrenia.

I am particularly interested here in the idea that a disordered imagination is a significant feature of schizophrenia, but I am not suggesting that schizophrenia is wholly a disorder of imagination. Nor am I claiming that the control of imagination is a significant factor in all kinds of delusions and hallucinations. For example, the various so-called 'delusional misidentification syndromes', such as Capgras syndrome, are likely to be explicable in other ways.[1]

I start by saying something about the kind of explanatory hypothesis I am offering.

1. Method

People with schizophrenia often have strange ideas which are not based on anything we would normally regard as evidence. The psychiatrist and philosopher Karl Jaspers (1963) said that the ideas of the person with schizophrenia are intrinsically non-understandable: they are simply the byproducts of a bio-

I am very grateful to Max Coltheart and Martin Davies for extensive comments on several earlier versions and for saving me more than once from serious error. Thanks also to Sandra Egege, Robyn Langdon and Andy Young.

[1]   On the relation between delusions in schizophrenia and in Capgras syndrome, see Stone and Young, 1997.

logical disorder, lacking all rational structure. Jaspers probably overestimated the extent to which these ideas are incoherent and resistant to revision; anyway, the choice is not between treating them as fully rational and treating them as devoid of cognitive significance. We need not think of rationality as a seamless whole; it may possess a complex inner structure not generally available to introspection or to a priori reflection. This complex inner structure may be vulnerable to damage, which, depending on its extent and location, can result in selective failures of rationality. So it may be possible to understand the peculiarities of schizophrenic thought as resulting from specific, functionally localizable damage to a system the proper function of which is to support reason. This functional picture would not be evident simply from inspection of the underlying biological stuff.

Of course this functional explanation must be answerable to facts about underlying biology; differences at the level of the functional organization of reason must, like differences of every other kind, be reflected in differences in physical constitution. Sometimes theorists do supplement their functional explanations with hypotheses about the underlying biology. Here is an example that will be relevant later on. Work in the mid eighties by Baron-Cohen and colleagues suggested that people with autism have an impaired capacity to infer the mental states of others. They sought to explain the impairment in terms of damage to a 'theory of mind module', the primary function of which is to provide the subject with the capacity to have thoughts about thoughts, or what is sometimes called the capacity for 'metarepresentation' (Baron-Cohen, Leslie and Frith, 1985; Leslie, 1987, 1988, 1992, 1994a, 1994b). And Baron-Cohen has suggested that this functionally defined mental structure is realized by a three-node brain circuit involving the superior temporal sulcus, the orbito-frontal cortex, and the amygdala; it is damage to this circuit that underlies the metarepresentational deficit (Baron-Cohen, 1995a, p. 88).

This final claim is a tentative one, and it remains difficult to find substantial evidence for such assertions about underlying brain pathology. Such evidence, where we can get it, is desirable because it adds, or may add, empirical support to our original hypothesis. Suppose that our hypothesis was that symptom-group S is due to the failure of functional component F, and that we have some independent reason to think that F is realized in a certain brain area B. Then our original hypothesis, together with the independently motivated claim that B realizes F, entails that people with S will show abnormality in B. If they do, then the original hypothesis gets additional support. Call that 'adding support vertically': the original hypothesis gets additional support by being linked to a hypothesis at the lower, implementation level. But there is also such a thing as adding support horizontally: a theory that postulates a deficit in the functional organization of some mental system in order to explain one disorder might then be recruited to the explanation of another disorder. If all goes well, the hypothesis gets more support simply because it itself explains more.

This point is important because one of Frith's theories—the one I am going to reject—displays something like this second pattern of development. It began life as a theory about autism, and was then applied to the case of schizophrenia. The theory is one I have already mentioned: that autism is centrally a deficiency in the capacity for metarepresentation. Frith suggests that while autistic children never develop a metarepresentational capacity, people with schizophrenia suffer damage to a previously intact and normally developed mentalizing capacity. And the hypothesis that I shall be arguing for here—the hypothesis that delusions and hallucinations in schizophrenia are due to a failure to identify imaginings—is itself closely related to a hypothesis about the causes of autism. This hypothesis about autism is that it involves a lack of imagination (Harris, 1988; Gordon and Barker, 1994; Currie, 1996), and the hypothesis about schizophrenia is that it involves a disorder—but not a lack—of imagination.

So Frith's theory and the one offered here differ in how they deal with the obvious and pressing fact that autism and schizophrenia are very different conditions. Schizophrenia is much more common than autism; it typically appears during a person's early twenties, while autism is usually identified in early childhood. While the prognosis for schizophrenia is generally poor, many people do make at least a partial recovery from it; autism is a life-long condition. Delusions and hallucinations, which are collectively described as 'reality distortions', are very common in schizophrenia but are not found in autism. On Frith's view the underlying cause is the same in both disorders and the differences between them are due to prior personal history and in particular to the age of onset. On my view, autism and schizophrenia both involve disorders of the imagination, but these are different disorders.

2. Is Metarepresentation Useful for Understanding Schizophrenia?

In his book *The Cognitive Neuropsychology of Schizophrenia*, Chris Frith (1992) argues that various symptoms of schizophrenia are the result of an underlying deficit of *metarepresentation*, the capacity to formulate thoughts about thoughts.[2] Frith suggests that poverty of action is due to an inability to produce self-willed (as opposed to stimulus-elicited) action, that this is in turn due to an inability to access one's goals and that it is failure of metarepresentation which is responsible for this lack of access to goals. For the same reason, delusions of persecution and of reference are due to a faulty awareness of other people's intentions, and delusions of control and thought insertion are due to faulty awareness of one's own intentions. Third-person hallucinations—the experience of hearing voices discussing one's actions—arise when what starts life as

---

[2]   Frith, 1992, p. 115. The taxonomy of symptoms given in the book is superseded by that in Johnstone and Frith, 1996, where hallucinations and delusions are treated as constituting a single dimension. I discuss hallucinations and delusions below.

a thought of the form S thinks that P turns, because of a metarepresentational incapacity, into a 'free-floating' thought, P (see especially Frith, 1992, p. 126).

So metarepresentational incompetence is supposed to lead to (i) inability to access one's goals, and hence to poverty of action; (ii) inability to access one's intentions, and hence to the impression that one's actions, including one's acts of thinking, are not under one's own control; (iii) inability to access the thoughts of others and hence to mistakes about what those thoughts are; (iv) inability to identify a thought as one's own, and hence to third-person hallucinations.

Some of these claims are doubtful. Take first the explanation of third-person (auditory) hallucinations (iv). Frith says that when I infer that Sally thinks that:

(1) Greg is boring,

I end up having *that* thought, (1), rather than the thought I should have, namely:

(2) Sally thinks Greg is boring.

This is because I have lost my capacity to metarepresent: I can represent a thought like (1), but not a thought about a thought, like (2). Frith's suggestion here does not cohere well with the idea that metarepresentational capacity is *lost* in schizophrenia. The proposal assumes, on the one hand, a metarepresentational deficit, and on the other, a capacity to formulate thoughts about others; the schizophrenic subject is supposed to formulate the thought that Sally thinks P, but to experience merely the thought that P. But if the subject genuinely lacked a metarepresentational capacity, he would not be able to formulate the thought that someone was thinking P in the first place. It would be better, from Frith's point of view, to suppose that schizophrenia is characterized by a *fragility* of metarepresentational capacity. If we suppose that the subject has a capacity to metarepresent which is unreliable, then we can suppose that he formulates the thought (2), but that the intentional operator 'thinks that' sometimes becomes detached, leaving him with the thought (1). But how, on Frith's view, does (1) come to be experienced as the thought of another? It will not do to say that defective metarepresentation attaches (1) to another operator, leaving the thought, say, that 'Fred thinks that Greg is boring'. For this is just another thought, and we have been given no explanation why this thought ('Fred thinks that Greg is boring') should be interpreted by the subject as the thought *of someone else*. Appeal to fragile metarepresentation alone cannot explain these delusions of thought-ownership.

Another difficulty for the metarepresentational hypothesis is that the thoughts that schizophrenic patients experience as third-person hallucinations tend to have peculiar content, referring to bizarre events and conspiracies. Recall: Frith's explanation for these hallucinations is that my thoughts about other people's thoughts have become 'disattributed': the thought that Sally thinks that P has become the thought that P. But then we must attribute to the patient, not merely a difficulty with maintaining thought attribution, but a tendency to attribute to others bizarre or threatening thoughts; such a tendency does not seem to be explicable solely in terms of a metarepresentational deficit, since the generation of the bizarre content must take place at a point prior to that at which the metarepresentational deficit takes effect.

At one point, Frith presents what purports to be an explanation of the strangeness of thoughts present in schizophrenia, suggesting that what starts as a perfectly reasonable thought ('I must go to work') becomes, through what he calls an 'impairment of content', a different and inappropriately grandiose thought, say, 'I must become the boss' (Frith, 1992, p. 127). But impairment of content, whatever it is, cannot be explained in metarepresentational terms; deficient metarepresentation might turn the thought 'A thinks I should go to work' into the thought 'I should go to work', but it cannot explain how the thought 'I should go to work' gets turned into the thought that 'I should become the boss'.

It is also doubtful whether metarepresentation is the right notion in terms of which to account for our normal ability to monitor our goals and intentions. Frith's view seems to be that we monitor goals and intentions by having thoughts of the form 'Such and such is my goal', and 'So and so is my intention'. But it is implausible that every time I perform an action on the basis of an intention, I formulate a thought which identifies that intention as mine, and that if I omitted to do so that action would seem to me to be something I had no control over. And there is a suspicion of a regress threatening: to identify the intention as mine I have to formulate the thought that it is mine, but what enables me to identify the thought that it is mine as my thought? Our sense that our actions are our own surely arises from the operation of more primitive, subpersonal mechanisms than those that are supposed to be operative in metarepresentation.

3. Agency

This brings us to the second of Frith's two theories, and it is a theory on which I shall draw heavily in what follows. While Frith sometimes treats metarepresentation as his central theoretical concept, there are places where he gives more emphasis to the notion of efference copying, which has been introduced to explain how organisms distinguish between changes in perception due to their own action and those due to changes in the environment. John Campbell explains the idea in this way:

> when a motor instruction is sent for bodily movement, a copy of that instruction—the 'efference copy'—is also sent to some other centre. . . . Held 1961 suggested that copies of the motor instruction are sent to a comparator, stored there, and compared to the proprioceptive or visual—'reafferent'—information about what movement was actually

made. . . . What explains the feeling that it is you who moved your arm is that at the comparator, an efferent copy was received of the instruction to move your arm which matches the movement you perceive. What explains the feeling that your arm was passively moved, perhaps by someone else, is that there is no efferent copy at the comparator of an instruction to move the arm in a way that matches the movement you perceive.[3]

Frith proposes that there is impairment of action monitoring in schizophrenia due to impaired efference copying, and that there is comparably based impairment to intention monitoring (Frith, 1987; Frith, 1992, especially pp. 80–83; Mlakar, Jensterle and Frith, 1994). Thus it becomes difficult for the schizophrenic person to detect her own actions, and also her own acts of will. We have here the postulation of a failure in a subpersonal mechanism, rather than the postulation of a difficulty with the personal-level mechanism of metarepresentation. For example, efference copying is assumed to take place in fruit flies, and it is fair to assume that these creatures lack personal-level psychological states altogether.[4]

There is a good deal of evidence to support Frith's idea. It is common for people with schizophrenia to say that their movements are controlled by another agent. Frith and colleagues have argued that this occurs when the subject performs an action but has no sense of having acted. They have also shown that people with schizophrenia do badly on tasks that require one to monitor one's own actions (Mlakar, Jensterle and Frith, 1994). On the other hand, people with schizophrenia sometimes say and do things which indicate that they greatly overestimate their powers of control; it seems difficult to reconcile this with an experienced loss of agency. However, these claims of control are often not based on anything like the ordinary experience of agency. One patient believed that he could release bombs over England by urinating. But he is reported as describing this as a God-like ability which was exercised 'without his willing it' (Bovet and Parnas, 1993, p. 590). Such claims seem to exemplify delusional ideas about the mysterious connectedness of things, rather than sensitivity to one's own actions.

Can we bring Frith's two theories together by supposing that the subpersonal-level theory which appeals to efference copying is a theory about how the person-level metarepresentational deficit is realized? That is unlikely. The two theories seem to be different in ways important to what they predict about

---

[3]   Campbell, 1999, pp. 611–12, which contains important discussions of Frith's theory and of its implications for the nature of thinking.

[4]   There are connections here with an approach to psychopathology due to Jim Russell, 1998; see also Pacherie, 1998. Frith goes beyond Russell in supposing that we can apply the idea of re-afference copying to explain the monitoring of intention as well as of action.

schizophrenia.[5] Thus the fragility of metarepresentation theory suggests that people will start by formulating the thought that Sally thinks that P but end up with the thought that P, while the fragility of efference copying theory suggests that people will formulate the thought that Sally thinks that P but end up by not recognizing this as a thought of their own.

From now on I am going to ignore Frith's metarepresentational theory, but I shall come back to his idea that schizophrenia involves damage to subpersonal mechanisms that results in a loss of the sense of agency. Before I do, I want to introduce the idea that hallucinations and delusions may result from a loss of the capacity to identify imaginings.

4. Misidentification of Imagination

Let us consider the idea that the schizophrenic patient is someone who has lost the distinction between what he or she imagines, and what he or she believes or experiences.[6] This theory is certainly different from the meta-representational theory: according to the disorder of imagination theory, the schizophrenic patient does not have a problem formulating thoughts of the form S thinks that P; he or she has a problem distinguishing between merely imagining some proposition and really believing it. The person with schizophrenia may imagine that there are Martians, but take herself to believe that there are. And she may imagine that Sally means her harm, but take herself to believe that Sally means her harm. She is capable of being confused about the cognitive status of her metarepresentational thoughts, and about her non-metarepresentational thoughts as well. Her incapacity is not one specifically of metarepresentation, but of attitude identification.

One point in favour of this proposal is that much of what exemplifies the strange and disordered thought of people with schizophrenia would not be remarkable if it were treated by the subject as belonging to the flow of her own imaginings. We often imagine things having a significance, or a connectedness, that we know they do not really have; we imagine connections between events, and we imagine those events as connected to ourselves. Normally these imaginings are fleeting, inconsequential and not much attended to. If they were not recognized as imaginings, their contents might dominate

---

5   Frith himself seems to regard the efference copy theory as a special case of the meta-representational theory. See Frith, 1992, p. 84.

6   There is certainly nothing original about this idea. Here, for example, is the psychiatrist Searles: 'the deeply schizophrenic individual has, subjectively, no imagination, The moment that something which we would call a new concoction of fantasy, a new product of his imagination, enters his awareness, *he* perceives this as being an actual and undisguised attribute of the world around him' (quoted in Sass, 1994, p. 19). Searles says that the schizophrenic person has no imagination, but as his other remarks indicate, he really means that the person takes what he imagines to be real. Searles might have said that the person with schizophrenia has no normally functioning imagination.

our thoughts, and lead to the sorts of behaviours we see in schizophrenia, which often begins with a heightened and unjustifiable sense of the significance of events. The psychiatrist Klaus Conrad noted an incident that followed a soldier's being taken to hospital because he was behaving oddly: 'He noticed that there were some cows lowing outside the building, and he suddenly was convinced that he was to be exterminated, that he had to be slaughtered like cattle.' Later, the patient was overwhelmed by the thought that 'he would be converted into an animal through hypnosis' (quoted in Bovet and Parnas, 1993, p. 587). Many of us, especially in a situation we could not fully account for and which we found worrying, might see cows and be prompted to imagine ourselves being 'slaughtered like cattle', or becoming a cow. If we could not identify these thoughts as imagining, we might treat them as among the contents of our beliefs, or at least attend to them and give them consideration that we would not give to what we knew to be imagination.

5. Imagination and Delusion

It is one thing to fail to recognize that an idea is part of one's imaginings; it is another to come to believe that idea. It seems that we have only told part of the story about delusional belief in schizophrenia. There may be a number of ways an agent comes to assimilate the unrecognized contents of imagining, and it is important to see that not all of them result in straightforward belief. The agent may maintain an ambiguous relationship with the thought content; it exerts a powerful psychological force, absorbing inner mental resources, but it fails to engage behaviour in the way that genuine belief would. Bovet and Parnas describe a patient, 'a 50-year-old female with paranoid schizophrenia and delusional ideas, which she in no way enacted, [who] lived peacefully with her mother in a small Swiss town. . . . She expressed her paranoid ideas about her sister, which she maintained for years quietly and without anger' (Bovet and Parnas, 1993, p. 588). And Bleuler wrote of his own patients: 'None of our generals has ever attempted to act in accordance with his imaginary rank and station'.[7] Perhaps in cases like these the agent believes that she believes a certain thought, but actually does not believe it.[8]

The claim that many of a schizophrenic person's 'ideas' (a term I intend as neutral between belief and some weaker mode of possession) are not really beliefs but are instead assumed by the subject to be her beliefs, has implications for the classification of symptoms. Hallucinations standardly occur when an experience which is of one kind—it is nonveridical—presents itself as of a

---

[7]   Quoted in Sass, 1994, p. 3. I am in agreement with Sass in emphasizing that belief is often not the right category within which to place the thoughts of the person with schizophrenia, but we disagree about the positive characterization.

[8]   So, on this hypothesis, certain 'first rank' symptoms of schizophrenia actually require a meta-representational capacity.

quite different kind—as veridical. And hallucinations sometimes give rise to delusional beliefs; I have an experience as of P, and I come to believe that P. Let us broaden the notion of hallucination somewhat so as to include what we might call 'cognitive hallucinations', which occur when a mental state of one kind (an imagining) presents itself to the subject as a mental state of another kind (a belief). We can now say that what we normally describe as the delusional belief that P ought sometimes to be redescribed as the delusional belief that I believe that P,[9] attendant on the cognitive hallucination that this is a belief that P, when in fact it is an imagining that P.

How are such cognitive hallucinations possible? How is it that what is in fact a case of imagining that P presents itself as a case of believing it? The answer is partly that imaginings are essentially simulative states—states which mirror some of the features of other mental states, of which they can be regarded as counterparts. For example, we know that even very young children, when asked to imagine events in a pretend scenario, will also imagine simple consequences of those events just as they would if they really believed what was going on in the story; they will, for example, spontaneously imagine that an animal (actually a stuffed toy) is wet as a result of having a cup (actually empty) of pretend water inverted over it (Harris and Kavanaugh, 1993). And adults clearly make belief-like inferences of quite complex kinds from what they imagine in a fictional story. So imaginings are hard to distinguish from beliefs at the level of inference.

How, then, do we normally distinguish between what we imagine and what we believe? We might suppose that we examine other aspects of the functional roles of these two states, such as their connections with actions, concluding that our thought is an imagining when we find that we do not act on it. But this is very unlikely; the connections between beliefs and actions are notoriously complex, and anyway most of the time we are confident that our thought is an imagining well in advance of doing any checks on our behaviour.[10]

It is at this point that I return to Frith's suggestion that schizophrenia involves a loss of the sense of agency. Suppose that the subject loses, perhaps intermittently, the capacity to monitor her own actions, or suffers a reduction in this capacity so that the threshold of what she can detect among her own actions is substantially raised. How might this impair her capacity to distinguish between what she imagines and what she believes? Wittgenstein said that we distinguish between what we imagine and what we really experience via our

---

[9]   It is not clear that such beliefs would count as delusional according to the strict letter of standard definitions of delusion, but that is true of many things that are widely and non-collusively agreed to be delusions. See Fulford, 1994.

[10]   For a somewhat fuller discussion of this issue, see Currie, 1998.

awareness of our own agency.[11] He seems to have been thinking about this in terms of imagery, particularly visual imagery; on his view, we distinguish between merely imagined sensory experiences and genuine perceptions not, as is sometimes said, by noticing that imagery is less 'vivid' than perception, but by our sense that having a mental image is an act, while perceiving something is not, though there are acts that go with perceiving which are intimately connected with what we perceive, like acts of looking. It is true, of course, that we sometimes have the sense of not being able to control our imagery, but that is also true of things that certainly are actions, as when people act out of a compulsion. So the sense that imagery is not always under voluntary control does not tell against the view that having a mental image is an action.[12]

Suppose this is right: that our primary ground for identifying something as an imagined thought is our identification of it as the outcome of our will or agency. And suppose that imaginings are significantly similar to beliefs in their inferential role. And suppose, finally, that Frith is right that schizophrenia involves a loss of the sense of agency. We have here the makings of an explanation of why someone with schizophrenia would take an imagined thought to be a belief.

I have suggested that what is often described as a delusion—a belief that is irrationally formed and irrationally held—would sometimes be better described as a delusional metabelief based on a cognitive hallucination. We now have an explanation of such cognitive hallucinations. But it would be unwise to suppose that everything commonly described as delusion in schizophrenia could adequately be redescribed in this way.[13] People with schizophrenia sometimes do act on their thoughts, occasionally with tragic results; perhaps at this point their thoughts have arrived at the status of beliefs, though they will often not retain this status indefinitely.[14] The theory I am proposing cannot, on its own, explain this. At the least, it needs supplementation from a theory about how believing that we believe something makes us prone actually to believe it. We might appeal to the hypothesis that genuine delusional belief is formed in response to, and by way of explanation of, hallucination. This view is most commonly held with respect to perceptual hallucinations: a strange belief results from an aberrant perception.[15] But if we treat the belief

---

[11]   See Budd, 1989, ch. 5, and Hacker, 1990, especially p. 420, for careful exposition and commentary.

[12]   There are some indications that people with schizophrenia can occasionally retain some sense that these ideas are, after all, imaginings. They may also occasionally be tempted to think that the real is imaginary. See Sass, 1994, pp. 26–7 and p. 33.

[13]   See Buchanan and Wessely, 1997. The authors argue that 'actions based on delusional beliefs are more common than had previously been recognized' (p. 260).

[14]   Another possibility, akin to a suggestion of Bleuler, 1924, is that imaginings which are misperceived as beliefs can motivate action via their effects on emotion. Buchanan and Wesseley, 1997, found that delusional ideas are more likely to be acted on if they have strong emotional consequences.

[15]   This view is discussed in Langdon and Coltheart, this volume.

that I believe P as a misperception of something as a belief when in fact it is only an imagining, then it is easy to see how this might result in the belief that P. I believe that I believe that P; there is a general presumption that one's beliefs are true, so I conclude that P is true.[16]

6. Thought Insertion and Withdrawal

In the territory between that which is acknowledged as imagination and that which is genuinely believed lies one of the most puzzling symptoms of schizophrenia, 'thought insertion', where a patient claims that the thoughts of another are inserted into his mind. John Campbell (1999) again:

> The thought inserted into the subject's mind is indeed in some sense his, just because it has been successfully inserted into his mind; it has some special relation to him. He has, for example, some especially direct knowledge of it. On the other hand, there is, the patient insists, a sense in which the thought is not his, a sense in which the thought is someone else's, and not just in that someone else originated the thought and communicated it to the subject; there is a sense in which the thought, as it were, remains the property of someone else. It is not really enough to say that we can make no sense of them; these are compelling reports of experience which many people agree in giving; at the very least we should want to understand why it is so natural, so compelling, to describe experience in this way (p. 610).

I agree with Campbell that we should take these reports seriously—not as literal and veridical reports of thought insertion, but as reports prompted by experiences which either seem to be experiences of thought insertion, or are experiences which seem, to the subject, to make some sense in the light of the hypothesis that they are experiences of thought insertion. We have seen how someone with an impaired capacity to monitor action might fail to recognize her imaginings *as* imaginings. What needs to be explained here is how this failure of recognition might lead the subject to believe that she is subject to thought insertion.

When we come to believe something, we normally do so on the basis of perception or on the basis of what we already believe; we do not choose what to believe, though it may be true that what we believe is influenced by what we want to be the case. But if, as Wittgenstein suggests, imagining is a (mental)

---

[16] We can ask at this point, in the spirit of Langdon and Coltheart's contribution to this issue, why it is that people with schizophrenia do not reason contrapositively: P is obviously not true; so, despite appearances, I don't believe P. As Langdon and Coltheart make clear, this is a general problem with theories of delusional belief. Their own proposal, in terms of reasoning biases, might be invoked here.

act, there is a sense in which we really are 'inserting' the imagined thought into our own mind. Earlier I said that imaginings are simulative states. Current work in cognition has made much of this idea; simulation theorists say that we project ourselves imaginatively into another's situation by 'giving ourselves pretend versions of her beliefs and desires, running these pretend beliefs and desires "off line" so as to mirror the target subject's practical and theoretical reasoning'.[17] On this view, imagining literally involves a kind of thought insertion—only it is you that is doing the inserting. Suppose, then, that a person with an impaired capacity to monitor action engages in some imagining of this kind. She may retain a sense that the thought emerges in some way different from the way in which her beliefs standardly do, but be unable to identify the thought as a piece of imagining. The thought, particularly in the case where it has bizarre content that does not cohere at all with her beliefs, may seem to be inserted, but she does not recognize herself as the agent who inserts it. She might then be tempted to make sense of the experience in terms of this being a thought which is inserted *by someone else*.[18]

A phenomenon which is, if anything, stranger than thought insertion is 'thought withdrawal'. This sense of having a thought removed from one's mind is certainly difficult to make sense of, partly because the subject's awareness that the thought is gone must surely be an awareness of that very thought. But suppose the subject engages in a piece of otherwise perfectly ordinary mental simulation which, through loss of a sense of agency, she does not recognize as such. Once an episode of imagining has run its course, the thought that is being run 'off line' must be removed from the subject's inferential machinery. This does not mean that the subject is thereafter unable to access the propositional content of that thought; that content is thinkable by the subject just as any other is. It is just that the thought has ceased to play a belief-like role in the subject's mental economy. This might be experienced as the removal of a thought.

7. Hallucination and Agency

Other positive symptoms of schizophrenia are predictable on the assumption that the disease involves misidentification of imaginings. So far we have been discussing the kind of imagining where I imagine that such and such is the case: factive imagining, we might call it. But there are other kinds of imaginings, and, like factive imaginings, they are simulative in form. Thus the various

---

[17]   This is the formulation originally suggested by Robert Gordon and favoured by Alvin Goldman; other simulation theorists put the matter differently. See the essays in Davies and Stone, 1995a; Davies and Stone, 1995b.

[18]   But note aspects of the experience of thought insertion that are not accounted for here. Cahill and Frith, 1996, report a patient who claims to be able to identify the exact point of entry into his head of the inserted thought.

modes of perceptual imaginings such as visual and auditory imagery share important features in common with the corresponding kinds of perception. The subjective experience of visual imagery is strikingly similar to that of vision. That is presumably why we spontaneously and noncollusively describe visual imagery in visual terms.[19] Indeed, our ordinary ways of identifying both imagery and perceptual experience are similar enough for us sometimes to mistake perception for imagery. In a classic experiment which has been reproduced with better methodology, the American psychologist Perky asked people to visualize a banana. These people did not know that there was in fact a just visible image of a banana on the screen they were looking at. It was clear from their own descriptions that what they took to be mental images were in fact percepts of a banana depiction (see Brown and Herrnstein, 1981, for details and references). People can also find it difficult to remember whether they have seen something or merely formed a visual image of it (Kosslyn, 1994, p. 55; Reisberg and Leak, 1987). And there have been reports of patients who, though they are blind, mistake their imagery for intact perception (Goldenberg, Muellbacher and Nowak, 1995).

It is estimated that 50% of people with schizophrenia suffer auditory hallucinations, which often involve the experience of someone speaking to or about the subject, while 15% have visual hallucinations and 5% tactile hallucinations (Cutting, 1995). To explain hallucinations in terms of the misidentification of imagining, we may assume that a loss of a sense of agency robs the subject of the capacity to distinguish between genuinely perceptual experience and mental imagery in its various modes. Just as with belief-like imaginings, imaginings that have visual, auditory or other modes of imagery as their counterparts would be apt to be confused with experiences in those modes, were it not for our sense that they are willed by us.[20]

That there might be a connection between hallucinations and imagery has occurred to people before of course, but research in this area has tended to concentrate on the question whether hallucinations are correlated with vividness of imagery—a question concerning which the evidence is equivocal (Bentall, 1990; Nayani and David, 1996). If the suggestion above about the reason why imagery and perception are confused is correct, there would be no reason to expect such a correlation.

---

[19]   This is true even when people describe the difference between imagery and vision. Here is a response to Galton's survey of imagery: 'Dim and not comparable in brightness to the real scene. Badly defined, with blotches of light; very incomplete; very little of one object is seen at one time' (quoted in Richardson, 1999, p. 12).

[20]   It is sometimes claimed that an hallucination must not be under voluntary control (Slade and Bentall, 1988, p. 23). It might be better to say 'not perceived by the subject as being under voluntary control'.

8. Conclusion

I have argued that some symptoms of schizophrenia, such as delusions and hallucinations, involve a loss of the capacity to identify imaginings. This is consequent on a general loss of the sense of agency, which Frith has suggested is a significant characteristic of the disease. So the explanatory picture looks something like this: a loss of the sense of agency leads directly to such symptoms of schizophrenia as a sense that aliens are in control of one's body. And indirectly, via a loss of the capacity to identify one's imaginings, loss of the sense of agency leads to delusions and hallucinations. But, as I have indicated above and will be evident to those with knowledge of schizophrenia, this can be only the roughest sketch of some aspects of a bewildering condition.

References

Baron-Cohen, S. 1995: *Mindblindness: An Essay on Autism and Theory of Mind*. Cambridge, MA: MIT Press.

Baron-Cohen, S., Leslie, A.M. and Frith, U. 1985: Does the autistic child have a 'theory of mind'? *Cognition*, 21, 37–46.

Bentall, R.P. 1990: The illusion of reality: A review and integration of psychological research on hallucinations. *Psychological Bulletin*, 107, 82–95.

Bleuler, E. 1924: *Textbook of Psychiatry*, trans. A.A. Brill. New York: Macmillan.

Bovet, P. and Parnas, J. 1993: Schizophrenic delusions: A phenomenological approach. *Schizophrenia Bulletin*, 19, 579–97.

Brown, R. and Herrnstein, R. 1981: Icons and images. In N. Block (ed.), *Imagery*. Cambridge, MA: MIT Press.

Buchanan, A. and Wessely, S. 1997: Delusions, action, and insight. In X.F. Amador and A.S. David (eds), *Insight and Psychosis*. Oxford University Press.

Budd, M. 1989: *Wittgenstein's Philosophical Psychology*. London: Routledge.

Cahill, C. and Frith, C.D. 1996: False perceptions or false beliefs? Hallucinations and delusions in schizophrenia. In P. Halligan and J. Marshall (eds), *Method in Madness*. Brighton: Lawrence Erlbaum Associates.

Campbell, J. 1999: Schizophrenia, the space of reasons, and thinking as a motor process. *The Monist*, 82, 609–25.

Currie, G. 1996: Simulation-theory, theory-theory and the evidence from autism. In P. Carruthers and P.K. Smith (eds), *Theories of Theories of Mind*. Cambridge University Press.

Currie, G. 1998: Pretence, pretending and metarepresentation. *Mind and Language*, 13, 35–55.

Cutting, J. 1995: Descriptive psychopathology. In S. Hirsch and D. Weinberger (eds), *Schizophrenia*. Oxford: Blackwell.

Davies, M. and Stone, T. 1995a: *Folk Psychology*. Oxford: Blackwell Publishers.

Davies, M. and Stone, T. 1995b: *Mental Simulation*. Oxford: Blackwell Publishers.

Frith, C.D. 1987: The positive and negative symptoms of schizophrenia reflect impairments in the perception and initiation of action. *Psychological Medicine*, 17, 631–48.

Frith, C.D. 1992: *The Cognitive Neuropsychology of Schizophrenia*. Hove, E. Sussex: Lawrence Erlbaum Associates.

Fulford, K.W.M. 1994: Value, illness and failure of action: Framework for a philosophical psychopathology of delusion. In G. Graham and L. Stephens (eds), *Philosophical Psychopathology*. Cambridge, MA: MIT Press.

Goldenberg, G., Muellbacher, W. and Nowak, A. 1995: Imagery without perception: A case study of anosognosia for cortical blindness. *Neuropsychologia*, 33, 1373–82.

Gordon, R. and Barker, J. 1994: Autism and the theory of mind debate. In G. Graham and L. Stephens (eds), *Philosophical Psychopathology*. Cambridge, MA: MIT Press.

Hacker, P.M.S. 1990: *Wittgenstein: Meaning and Mind*, vol. 3 of *An Analytical Commentary on the Philosophical Investigations*. Oxford: Basil Blackwell.

Harris, P.L. 1988: *Children and Emotion: The Development of Psychological Understanding*. Oxford: Blackwell.

Harris, P.L. and Kavanaugh, R.D. 1993: Young children's understanding of pretense. *Monographs of the Society for Research in Child Development*, 231.

Held, R. 1961: Exposure history as a factor in maintaining stability of perception and distance information. *Journal of Nervous and Mental Diseases*, 132, 26–32.

Jaspers, K. 1963: *General Psychopathology*, trans. J. Hoenig and M.W. Hamilton. Manchester: Manchester University Press.

Johnstone, E.C. and Frith, C.D. 1996: Validation of three dimensions of schizophrenic symptoms in a large unselected sample of patients. *Psychological Medicine*, 26, 669–79.

Kosslyn, S.M. 1994: *Image and Brain: The Resolution of the Imagery Debate*. Cambridge, MA: MIT Press.

Leslie, A.M. 1987: Pretense and representation: the origins of 'theory of mind'. *Psychological Review*, 94, 412–26.

Leslie, A.M. 1988: Some implications of pretense for mechanisms underlying the child's theory of mind. In J. Astington, P. Harris and D. Olson (eds), *Developing Theories of Mind*. Cambridge University Press.

Leslie, A.M. 1992: Pretense, autism, and the theory-of-mind module. *Current Directions in Psychological Science*, 1, 18–21.

Leslie, A.M. 1994a: Pretending and believing: Issues in the theory of ToMM. *Cognition*, 50, 211–38.

Leslie, A.M. 1994b: ToMM, ToBy, and agency: Core architecture and domain specificity. In L. Hirschfeld and S. Gelman (eds), *Mapping the Mind*. Cambridge University Press.

Mlakar, J., Jensterle, J. and Frith, C.D. 1994: Central monitoring deficiency and schizophrenic symptoms. *Psychological Medicine*, 24, 557–64.

Nayani, T. and David, A. 1996: The neuropsychology and neurophenomenology of auditory hallucination. In C. Pantelis, H. Nelson and T. Barnes (eds), *Schizophrenia: A Neurophysiological Approach*. Chichester: Wiley.

Pacherie, E. 1998: Motor-images, self-consciousness, and autism. In J. Russell (ed.), *Autism as an Executive Disorder*. Oxford University Press.

Reisberg, D. and Leak, S. 1987: Visual imagery and memory for appearance: Does Clark Gable or George C. Scott have bushier eyebrows? *Canadian Journal of Psychology*, 41, 521–6.

Richardson, J.T.E. 1999: *Imagery*. Hove, E. Sussex: Psychology Press.

Russell, J. 1998: How executive disorders can bring about an inadequate 'theory of mind'. In J. Russell (ed.), *Autism as an Executive Disorder*. Oxford University Press.

Sass, L.A. 1994: *The Paradoxes of Delusion: Wittgenstein, Schreber, and the Schizophrenic Mind*. Ithaca, NY: Cornell University Press.

Slade, P.D. and Bentall, R.P. 1988: *Sensory Deception: A Scientific Analysis of Hallucination*. London: Croom Helm.

Stone, T. and Young, A. 1997: Delusions and brain injury: The philosophy and psychology of belief. *Mind and Language*, 12, 327–64.

8

The Cognitive Neuropsychology of Delusions

ROBYN LANGDON AND MAX COLTHEART

1. Introduction

Delusions are a key feature of psychosis. Together with hallucinations—the other so-called 'reality distortion' symptom—these symptoms mark what we commonly conceive of as 'madness'. In its *Diagnostic and Statistical Manual of Mental Disorders*, Fourth Edition (*DSM-IV*), the American Psychiatric Association (1994) defines a delusion as:

> A false belief based on incorrect inference about external reality that is firmly sustained despite what almost everyone else believes and despite what constitutes incontrovertible and obvious proof or evidence to the contrary. The belief is not one ordinarily accepted by other members of the person's culture or subculture (e.g. it is not an article of religious faith) (p. 765).

Despite concern about how such a definition should be operationalized by clinicians, and despite debate about whether delusions should be distinguished from normal beliefs in terms of dichotomy or continuum (see, for example, Garety and Hemsley, 1994), there is some consensus that the characteristic features of delusions are:

- that they run counter to the beliefs held by others within the same socio-cultural environment;
- that they defy rational counter-argument;
- that they are maintained despite overwhelming counter-evidence.

Deluded individuals can also be found to espouse their beliefs with a note of absolute conviction—as if the delusional beliefs are self-evident incontrovert-

We would like to thank participants in the workshop held at Macquarie University in July/August 1998 for helpful discussion of many issues discussed in this chapter, especially Andy Young. Special thanks must also go to Martin Davies and Greg Currie for invaluable advice on an earlier draft of this chapter.

ible truths—despite the fact that others clearly find the deluded individuals' ideas to be patently absurd (Cutting, 1985; Sims, 1988).

Delusions come in a myriad of forms. In psychiatric textbooks and in clinical rating scales, delusions are usually classified by thematic content; for example, there are bizarre delusions, grandiose delusions, persecutory delusions, and somatic delusions. Delusions can also vary in scope: some deluded individuals present with tightly circumscribed delusions, whereas other individuals present with a propensity to be delusional about anything that grabs attention. For example, Stone and Young (1997) have noted the contrast between monothematic delusions that can arise after right-hemisphere brain damage—such as the belief that your arm is someone else's (Halligan, Marshall and Wade, 1995) or the belief that people in disguise are following you (de Pauw, Szulecka and Poltock, 1987)—and some cases of schizophrenia where the deluded individual inhabits a separate 'reality' peopled by imaginary beings and filled with delusional events. Here the delusions are polythematic.

The aim of this chapter is to review research investigating the factors that may contribute towards delusion formation in order to develop a theory of the processes which underpin normal belief generation and belief evaluation; a theory which can then be used to explain delusions of *all* types. As such, our aim here is to advance the field of cognitive neuropsychiatry by applying the logic of cognitive neuropsychology in order to explain delusions—a symptom which is generally described as psychiatric. The approach of cognitive neuropsychology has two main aims (Coltheart, 1984; Ellis and Young, 1988). The first is to explain aberrant behaviours and symptoms seen in patients after brain damage in terms of what has been lost (damaged or disconnected) and what remains intact in a model (or theory) of normal cognitive functioning. The second is to evaluate models of normal cognition in terms of how well they explain the various patterns of spared and dysfunctional cognitive capacities observed in neurological patients. Since our aim here is to develop a model of the normal cognitive system of belief generation and belief evaluation which can then explain *all* types of delusions in terms of damage to one or more components of that cognitive system, we will use as our primary examples cases of 'organic' delusions and cases of 'psychotic' delusions. The former refer to delusions which occur after known organic brain damage and the latter refer to delusions found in psychiatric disorders where the nature of the neuropathology remains unspecified. Historically, this distinction has also been described in terms of the 'organic' versus 'functional' psychoses (Frith, 1992). In particular, we will focus on cases of misidentification delusion which can occur after known right-hemisphere brain damage (primarily, Capgras delusion—the belief that an impostor has replaced a loved one) and various types of psychotic delusions found in cases of schizophrenia. The contrast between 'organic' misidentification delusions and 'psychotic' schizophrenic delusions also highlights another relevant contrast in the study of delusions, and that is the distinction between circumscribed monothematic delusions and widespread polythematic delusions, as noted earlier. That is, whereas Capgras patients will often present with a tightly circumscribed delusion—they may only be delusional about the impostor who is impersonating their loved one— patients with schizophrenia will often present with a florid widespread delusional system. However, it is worth noting here that this need not be the case—that is, the circumscribed versus polythematic distinction does not always map neatly onto the organic versus psychotic distinction. Some Capgras patients do build a more extensive network of delusional beliefs stemming from that first deluded belief about an impostor, and some schizophrenic patients do present with tightly circumscribed delusions—for example, there are patients with schizophrenia who have auditory hallucinations, specifically of the voices commenting[1] type, and who only develop delusional beliefs about the source of their auditory hallucinatory experiences.

A useful distinction to bear in mind when considering the factors which may contribute towards delusion formation is that between factors which play a role in shaping the *thematic* content of different delusional beliefs and factors which explain the *presence* of a delusional belief. In other words, there is a difference between explaining what it is that a person comes to be deluded about and explaining why that person is deluded in their thinking about those ideas.

We begin by reviewing research investigating the role that perceptual aberrations and attributional biases may play in the explanation of delusions. Our line of argument will be to question whether either of these factors or both in combination is sufficient to explain the presence of a delusional belief. We will conclude that, whilst the presence of a perceptual aberration when coupled with a particular type of attributional bias may be necessary to explain the thematic *content* of a particular bizarre delusion, neither of these factors, whether in isolation or in combination, is sufficient to explain the *presence* of a delusional belief. We then consider research investigating whether deluded individuals show deficits of reasoning in order to derive a model of normal belief generation and belief evaluation which we then use to explain a variety of delusions.

2. The Role of Perceptual Aberrations

One prominent and influential approach to explaining delusion formation has come from Maher and colleagues (Maher, 1974, 1988, 1992; Maher and Ross, 1984; Maher and Spitzer, 1993) who proposed that delusions are meaningful hypotheses which have been generated by *normal* reasoning processes to explain

---

[1]   Auditory hallucinations of the voices commenting type are experiences where patients hear another voice commenting on their behaviour in the second person, as distinct from third-person auditory hallucinations where patients hear two or more voices discussing them in the third person, and auditory hallucinations where patients hear non-vocal sounds.

aberrant perceptual experiences, such as hallucinations. In other words, Maher takes the view that the presence of an aberrant perceptual experience is necessary and sufficient to explain the presence of a delusional belief. Whereas Maher was primarily interested in understanding the role of perceptual aberrations in explaining the generation of schizophrenic symptoms, Young and colleagues (Ellis and Young, 1990; Wright, Young and Hellawell, 1993; Young, 1994; Young, Leafhead and Szulecka, 1994; Young, Reid, Wright and Hellawell, 1993) have, more recently, been interested in investigating the possible role that perceptual aberrations may play in the generation of misidentification delusions, in particular Capgras delusion—the belief that a loved one has been replaced by an impostor. In this section, we review empirical research investigating the nature of perceptual aberrations implicated in both Capgras delusion and delusions of alien control, the latter being among the first-rank symptoms of schizophrenia.

Individuals with Capgras delusion believe that a loved one, usually their spouse, has been replaced by an impostor who looks identical to the real loved one. Researchers investigating the factors that may be implicated in the generation of Capgras delusion have proposed that this delusional belief arises when an individual loses the sense of affective responsiveness which normally co-occurs with explicit recognition of a familiar face (Ellis and Young, 1990). The resultant discordance between 'he looks right' and 'he doesn't feel right' is then resolved by the individual adopting the belief that the loved one has been replaced by an impostor—an idea which, plausible or no, does have explanatory sufficiency, given the nature of the perceptual aberration. The suggestion that lessened autonomic responsiveness to a loved one's face does have some role to play in the generation of Capgras delusion has been investigated by Ellis, Young, Quayle and de Pauw (1997a). In their study, Ellis et al. (1997a) predicted that, if people with Capgras delusion are under-responsive to familiar faces, then they should fail to show a pattern of autonomic discrimination[2] between familiar and unfamiliar faces when compared to both non-clinical control subjects and psychiatric patients who were taking similar anti-psychotic medications but who were experiencing different types of delusions (e.g. delusions of persecution). Furthermore, these researchers predicted that, since Capgras patients are deluded about a loved one's face but may be able to recognize that loved one's voice when encountered on the telephone (see Ellis, Young, Quayle and de Pauw, 1997b), the autonomic under-responsiveness observed in these patients should be circumscribed—that is, specific to face recognition. Both hypotheses were supported by the data. Familiar and unfamiliar faces produced equal degrees of affective response in Capgras

---

[2]   In this study, skin conductance responses (SCRs) were recorded while subjects were shown a series of predominantly unfamiliar faces, with occasional familiar (famous) faces interspersed. The difference in mean SCR to familiar and unfamiliar faces was then used to index autonomic discrimination of familiar and unfamiliar faces.

patients, in contrast to both control groups who showed significantly greater autonomic responsiveness to familiar faces. Furthermore, this was not due to some general under-responsiveness of the Capgras patients, since these patients showed normal autonomic orienting to a novel auditory tone and a normal pattern of autonomic habituation to repetitions of that tone.

In the case of delusions of alien control in schizophrenia, patients who experience these delusions express the belief that their actions are being controlled by an external agent—sometimes an alien being, sometimes a spiritual power. Note here that a delusion of alien control is not the same thing as believing that one's chosen course of action has been strongly influenced by the views of significant others, as is the case, for example, in missionaries who believe that they are acting out the word of God. Instead, patients with delusions of alien control describe experiences of disembodied or depersonalized agency—for them, there is no sense of personal choice. They are performing the actions, but someone else is pulling the strings. Researchers investigating the factors which may contribute towards the generation of delusions of alien control have proposed that these patients experience a discordant sense of passivity which arises when normal on-line self-monitoring is disrupted, resulting in loss of the sense of self-generation which normally co-occurs with self-initiated action (Frith and Done, 1986, 1989; Frith, 1992). In more detail, the idea here is that normal self-initiation of action involves the coordination of two matching signals: (1) a motor instruction to initiate bodily movement; and (2) a record of that instruction (a reafference copy of the intended act) which is registered with a central monitor. In the case of delusions of alien control, it is argued, registration of this second signal is disrupted. Consequently, these individuals see and feel themselves acting in ways which are appropriate and meaningful in the circumstances in which they find themselves, but with no associated sense of self-agency—from which they conclude that they are robots or puppets being manipulated by an external power.

One way of testing the hypothesis that defective self-monitoring plays a role in the generation of delusions of alien control derives from the idea that central monitoring underpins our normal ability to make rapid corrections of inappropriate responses before needing to wait to see the consequences of an error (Angel, 1976; Frith and Done, 1986). That is, by on-line monitoring an intended act (via monitoring of a reafference copy) and matching that against the overall goal, we can quickly identify errors and sometimes short-circuit mistakes before they are fully acted out, as when interrupting speech mid-word in order to correct an error (Leudar, Thomas and Johnston, 1994). Frith (1992) describes the capacity as follows:

> we can be aware that an intended response was wrong after we have initiated that response, but before the consequences of that response are visible (p. 83).

If we accept such a model of normal action control which involves two processes, one being based on internal monitoring of intentions and the other being based on external monitoring of the consequences of action (Frith and Done, 1986), and if it is the case that patients with delusions of alien control do have defective internal monitoring, then these patients should perform poorly on error-prone motor response tasks when access to visual feedback is denied. Frith and Done (1989) have tested this hypothesis by investigating patterns of error correction in schizophrenic patients with alien control experiences,[3] schizophrenic patients without such experiences, non-schizophrenic psychiatric controls and normal controls. In their study, presented as a video game, subjects moved a joystick in order to shoot a target which could appear at different locations. The difficulty of making correct moves was manipulated in order to induce a high error rate. In one version of the task, subjects moved their joystick and saw the trajectory of their shot being tracked across the computer screen (a shot took 2800 msecs to reach a target). Under these circumstances, all subject groups corrected 100% of their errors within 2000 msecs. In the second version of the task, the trajectory of a shot was hidden (behind a wall depicted on the screen) for the first 2000 msecs after making a response. Under these circumstances—with no visual feedback as to whether a mistake had been made for the first 2000 msecs—only 8% of patients with alien control experiences corrected their errors within 2000 msecs, compared to 80% of schizophrenic patients without alien control experiences, 40% of psychiatric controls and 67% of normal controls.

However, although empirical findings such as those cited above clearly support the view that perceptual aberrations play some role in the generation of bizarre delusions, such as Capgras delusion and delusions of alien control, it cannot simply be the case that a perceptual aberration is sufficient to explain the presence of a delusional belief. Consider, for example, why it is that the deluded Capgras patient and the schizophrenic patient with delusions of alien control fail to accept the perfectly plausible hypothesis that brain damage or dysfunctional neurochemistry has caused their senses to provide unreliable information about the environment or themselves. Even more puzzling, why do these individuals fail to reach the simple conclusion that 'something strange must be going on, but I don't know what' (Stone and Young, 1997)?

If the presence of a perceptual aberration were a sufficient condition for the presence of a delusional belief, then any individual who experienced an aberrant perceptual experience should develop a delusional belief. But that is not so. Take, for example, the case of phantom limb experiences. Many individuals who have had a limb amputated have the vivid experience that their

---

[3]   Alien control experiences, as operationalized by Frith and colleagues (Frith, 1992; Frith and Done, 1989), include delusions of alien control and also auditory hallucinations of the voices commenting type which are interpreted as a patient 'hearing' his or her internal commentary, disconnected from any sense of self-generation.

lost limb is still present, and in many cases also painful. Recent studies using microelectrode recording, microstimulation, and various imaging techniques, have provided evidence that part of the thalamus which originally responded to nerve inputs from a limb which has been amputated can remain functional and can mislocalize sensory stimulation from other sources after cortical reorganization of connections to the thalamic 'limb' neurons (Davis et al., 1998; Flor et al., 1998; Ramachandran and Hirstein, 1998).

The critical point here is that although something is dysfunctional in the brains of amputees with phantom limb experiences, and although these individuals have no direct access to the nature of the dysfunction which causes their aberrant experience—feeling a limb which cannot be seen and which doctors say has been removed—these individuals do not become delusional. They do not develop the belief that their arm is still intact and that 'evil' doctors have made it invisible; instead they readily accept that something has gone wrong (in their brain) which makes it feel to them as if their limb is still present, when in fact they know that their limb has been removed.

Even more compelling grounds for rejecting the view that the presence of a perceptual aberration is sufficient to explain the presence of a delusional belief comes from evidence that some non-deluded individuals may be experiencing the same, or at least very similar, perceptual anomalies to those found in patients with Capgras delusion and delusions of alien control. To begin, recall that, in the case of Capgras delusion, it was argued that intact explicit recognition of a loved one's face coupled with the loss of affective response to that loved one's face generates a discordant perceptual experience which is then resolved by the individual adopting the belief that the loved one has been replaced by an impostor. Empirical support for that view came from evidence that Capgras patients fail to show a normal pattern of autonomic discrimination between familiar and unfamiliar faces. However, Tranel, Damasio and Damasio (1995) have found that patients with damage to bilateral ventromedial frontal regions of the brain also fail to autonomically discriminate between familiar faces (which they recognize explicitly) and unfamiliar faces; yet these patients were not delusional. If we assume that the dissociation between intact explicit recognition of a familiar face and the loss of autonomic responsiveness to that face generates the same perceptual aberration in both Capgras patients and Tranel et al.'s (1995) frontal patients, then what makes for the formation of a delusional belief in Capgras patients or, instead, what is it that protects the frontal patients from becoming delusional?

But perhaps assuming that a similar pattern of empirical data indexes a similar perceptual anomaly in Tranel at al.'s (1995) frontal patients and Ellis et al.'s (1997a) Capgras patients is unjustified. It is possible that inability to generate discriminatory autonomic responses to familiar and unfamiliar faces occurs for different reasons in non-deluded patients with bilateral ventromedial frontal lesions and Capgras patients, some of whom are known to have different sites of brain damage—in particular, occipito-temporal or temporal-parietal lesions

(Stone and Young, 1997). And perhaps these different reasons lead to qualitatively distinct phenomenal experiences. It is worth noting, in this context, that the Tranel et al. (1995) study and the Ellis et al. (1997a) study differ in that the former did not demonstrate that the under-responsiveness of their patients was circumscribed. Indeed, Damasio, Tranel and Damasio (1991) have reported elsewhere that patients with bilateral ventromedial frontal lesions fail to show normal autonomic responses to emotionally charged visual stimuli such as pictures of mutilations and social disasters. It is therefore possible, that, even though Tranel et al.'s (1995) frontal patients show empirical evidence of a discordant mismatch between intact explicit face recognition and loss of autonomic face recognition, if that mismatch occurs in the context of general affective flatness (which may well be the case in these patients), then the resultant perceptual experience (when encountering a familiar face) may differ from that of Capgras patients and may indeed not even register as aberrant.

Let us then consider two distinct clinical disorders where patients present with very similar phenomenological self-reports of their experiences. The first of these is depersonalization disorder, classified in *DSM-IV* as a dissociative disorder which is characterized by altered perceptions and experiences of self. These individuals describe their experiences in very much the same way that schizophrenic patients with delusions of alien control do—that is, they describe experiences of being outside of their bodies, of feeling like mechanical robots, and of having no sense of being in control of their own actions (Davison and Neale, 1998). Indeed, the similarity is so striking that patients with depersonalization disorder have been misdiagnosed as having schizophrenia. However, there is a critical feature which distinguishes the two clinical disorders: whilst the insightful patient with depersonalization disorder describes his or her experience in 'as if' terms (it is *as if* an alien is controlling my actions), the deluded schizophrenic patient with passivity experiences lives the concrete reality (an alien *is* controlling my actions). In other words, what distinguishes these two disorders is precisely whether or not some critical faculty which underpins normal reality testing, or belief evaluation, is operating.

Sno (1994) has presented a somewhat similar argument when contrasting non-pathological *déjà vu* experiences and some cases of reduplicative paramnesia. Non-pathological *déjà vu* experiences occur when an individual experiences an inappropriate subjective impression of familiarity about the present situation (as if one's present surroundings are identical to some unspecified place that one has visited in the past), whilst at the same time being aware that this is an impossibility. In contrast, reduplicative paramnesia is the deluded belief that a familiar place (or person) from the past has been duplicated in the present (Breen, Caine, Coltheart, Hendy and Roberts, this volume; Hakim, Verma and Greiffenstein, 1988). To illustrate, reduplicative paramnesia often takes the form of patients believing that they are in a hospital which they have been in before, usually in their home-town, when in fact the hospital in which they are currently a patient is located in a completely different city; a belief which is persistently sustained despite compelling counter-evidence (Benson, Gardiner and Meadows, 1976; Filley and Jarvis, 1987; Roehrenbach and Landis, 1995). The implication here is that both non-deluded individuals with *déjà vu* experiences and deluded patients with some forms of reduplicative paramnesia may be experiencing a common perceptual aberration (most likely caused by inappropriate activation of memorial familiarity) which is then interpreted differently depending upon the presence or absence of some critical faculty involved in normal belief evaluation.

In sum, the empirical findings reviewed in this section support the view that, although perceptual aberrations contribute towards the generation of bizarre delusions, such as Capgras delusion and delusions of alien control, the presence of a perceptual aberration is not sufficient to explain the *presence* of a delusional belief, since there exist individuals who experience very bizarre perceptual experiences—for example, the feeling that an amputated limb is still present and indeed painful—who are not delusional. Furthermore, there are grounds for thinking that the same perceptual aberration can be found in both non-deluded individuals and deluded patients.

In the following section, we consider whether the presence of a perceptual aberration when coupled with a particular type of attributional bias, or a statistically deviant attributional bias, is sufficient to explain the presence of a delusional belief.

3. The Role of Attributional Biases

Attribution theory is that area of social psychology concerned with understanding how ordinary people explain why things happen (Hewstone, 1983, 1989). One of the historical forerunners of attribution theory is the 'naïve psychology' of Heider (1944, 1958) who, for example, conceptualized potential causal factors as being either internal to an actor (ability, effort) or external (task-difficulty, luck). In terms of that dichotomy, 'person' attributions were seen to be more likely than 'situational' attributions since a person, it was argued, fits the prototype of causal origin—an attributional bias which can have nasty consequences since a particular person in a group may be punished for something bad that has happened in order for the rest of the group to effect some sense of control over frightening circumstances. Another important contribution from Heider is the idea that perceived similarity between an 'actor' and an 'act' can determine the likelihood of a causal attribution. For example, a 'bad' action is more likely to be attributed to a 'bad' person than a 'good' person. Now there are plenty of examples of this type of attributional bias operating—just think about our jail populations and how 'badness', when defined along racial lines, might be operating here.

In more recent times, Weiner (1988, 1990) has had a major impact on attribution theory by extending the properties, or dimensions, of cause beyond internal/external locus. According to Weiner, causal biases can be theoretically classified along three dimensions: locus (internal/external); stability (stable/unstable); and controllability (controllable/uncontrollable). For other researchers, the degree of globalness is also seen to be an important dimension of causality (Seligman et al., 1979). Much of the present-day research investigating the influence of attributional biases uses self-report questionnaires which incorporate these various dimensions of causality. For example, in the Attributional Style Questionnaire (ASQ) (Peterson et al., 1982; Seligman et al., 1979), subjects are asked to generate likely causes for six positive events, and six negative events, and they are then asked to self-rate those causes on dimensions of internality (that is, the degree to which events are attributed to self or to external causes), stability (that is, whether causes will persist into the future), and globalness (that is, the degree to which causes can influence a range of events beyond the original event being considered). To illustrate, people might be asked to imagine the positive event of meeting a friend who then compliments them on their appearance, or they might be asked to imagine the negative event of looking for a job and not being able to find one. For each imagined positive and negative event, subjects must then write down the one major cause for that event and they must then make three separate ratings on a linear scale: (1) how much do they think that cause is due to other people/circumstances or due to themselves; (2) whether they think that cause will always be present or is unlikely to happen again; and (3) whether that cause influences just this particular situation or influences all situations in their life.

In clinical contexts, the ASQ has been used traditionally with depressive patients in order to reformulate the learned helplessness model of depression in terms of personality dispositions (Abramson, Seligman and Teasdale, 1978). For example, Sweeney, Anderson and Bailey (1986) have conducted a meta-analysis of studies investigating attributional style in depressed individuals and found that as attributions for negative events became more internal, stable and global, depression increased. More recently, Bentall and colleagues (Bentall, Kaney and Dewey, 1991; Kaney and Bentall, 1989; Lyon, Kaney and Bentall, 1994) have adopted attribution theory in order to investigate whether a particular type of attributional bias is implicated in the generation of delusional beliefs. For example, Kaney and Bentall (1989) first used the ASQ with delusional paranoid patients, depressive patients and normal controls and found that both deluded patients and depressed patients were more likely to make excessive global and stable attributions for negative events. Of more interest, however, was evidence that patients with persecutory delusions were more likely to make excessive external attributions for negative events and excessive internal attributions for positive events, when compared to normal controls—the exact reverse of the pattern found in depressed patients. These results have since been replicated by Candido and Romney (1990) and extended in various other studies which have also investigated the role of self-esteem and self-concept (Bentall et al., 1991; Bentall and Kaney, 1996; Kinderman et al., 1992;

Kinderman and Bentall, 1996a, 1996b, 1997; Lyon et al., 1994). Based on this work, Bentall, Kinderman and Kaney (1994) have developed a general theory of persecutory delusions wherein threat-related information in the environment activates self/ideal discrepancies which then promote a self-defensive attributional bias towards locating the cause for negative events in external sources. To try to put it more simply, the idea here is that deluded patients with persecutory delusions try to maintain self-esteem by avoiding discrepancies between their 'ideal' self (who they want to be) and their 'actual' self (as indicated by information in the world) by externalizing the cause for negative events and internalizing the cause for positive events. For a more detailed account of this position and a review of empirical research investigating the role of self/ideal discrepancies in some deluded subjects, readers are referred to Garety and Freeman (1999).

For the purposes of the present chapter, we mention the Bentall model because it raises the possibility that a perceptual aberration when coupled with an attributional bias to externalize the cause for negative events—a bias which, evidence suggests, is present in deluded paranoid patients—may be sufficient to explain the presence of a delusional belief. At first sight, that sounds a perfectly plausible notion. Consider, for example, the case of Capgras delusion. It has been proposed that Capgras delusion arises when the loss of affective responsiveness to a loved one's face generates an aberrant, perhaps frightening, negative experience ('he looks right but doesn't feel right') which is then mis-attributed to something going wrong in the world (an impostor has replaced my loved one) rather than something going wrong internally (brain damage has caused me to lose affective responsiveness to familiar faces) (Wright et al., 1993; Young et al., 1993). Further support for this view comes from evidence that Capgras patients often present with a pervasive mood of suspiciousness/paranoia (Fleminger and Burns, 1993) which, as noted earlier, is known to be associated with an externalizing bias for negative events.

However, not every deluded subject has an external bias for negative events. Indeed, rather than one particular type of attributional bias—that is, an externalizing bias for negative events—being associated, in general, with the presence of delusional beliefs, it appears that different types of attributional bias can account for different delusional misinterpretations of the same perceptual aberration. For example, the two distinct delusions of Capgras delusion (the belief that an impostor has replaced a loved one) and Cotard delusion (the belief that you are dead) are said to arise when the same perceptual aberration (lack of affective response to personally significant faces) interacts with different attributional styles; a suspicious externalizing bias for negative events in the case of Capgras delusion and a depressive internalizing bias for negative events in the case of Cotard delusion (Young et al., 1992, 1994; Wright et al., 1993). To clarify, whereas the suspicious Capgras patient resolves the discordant perception—'he looks right but doesn't feel right'—by externalizing blame in the world (an impostor is impersonating my loved one), the Cotard patient, who typically presents in the context of a general depressive state, internalizes blame and concludes that something must be drastically wrong with themselves and not with others—hence they must be dead. Indeed, Wright et al. (1993) have reported the case of a patient who shifted from having Cotard delusion to Capgras delusion as his mood changed from depression to suspiciousness and paranoia.

And it is not only among misidentification delusions that we can find examples of the same perceptual aberration being delusionally misinterpreted in different ways, depending upon an individual's particular style of attributional bias. Consider here schizophrenic patients who experience the sensation that their thoughts are transparent to others. Let us for the moment assume that this is a perceptual aberration in the same way that loss of the sense of self-generation normally associated with self-initiated action is a perceptual aberration. However, in this case the idea would be that there is loss of the sense of subjective privacy associated with 'hearing in mind' one's own thoughts (David, 1994). We say more about this perceptual anomaly later. For now, the point here is that this same perceptual aberration may give rise to different types of 'loss of boundary' delusions, depending upon an individual's particular attributional bias. That is, for individuals who tend to internalize blame for negative events, that aberrant perceptual experience may give rise to thought broadcast delusions—that is, the belief that you are broadcasting or transmitting your thoughts to others; whereas individuals who tend to externalize blame for negative events may develop mind-reading delusions or thought insertion delusions—that is, the belief that others have the power to read your mind or the belief that others can insert thoughts into your mind.

A perceptual aberration and a particular type of attributional bias—an externalizing bias for negative events—cannot be jointly sufficient to explain the presence of a delusional belief since there are some deluded individuals who have the opposite attributional bias—that is, an internalizing bias for negative events. However, perhaps what is critical here is not the direction of the bias but the degree of bias. All of the examples of delusions which we have described thus far are consistent with the notion that a perceptual aberration when coupled with a statistically deviant degree of attributional bias, in whichever direction—whether a tendency to internalize blame or externalize blame for negative events—may be sufficient to explain not only the thematic content of a particular delusion but also why that individual becomes deluded about that content.[4] However, even that cannot be so, since not all deluded individuals show evidence of a statistically deviant degree of attributional bias. Here we refer to work by Sharp, Fear and Healy (1997) who investigated the attributional styles of paranoid and/or grandiose patients and non-paranoid/non-

---

[4]   Up until now we have only discussed internalizing biases for negative events in connection with depression. But having depression need not preclude being delusional—that is, delusions can be found in cases of major depression.

grandiose patients with somatic delusions or delusions of morbid jealousy. In their study, Sharp et al. (1997) found that paranoid/grandiose patients did make excessive external attributions for negative events when compared to normal controls—thus replicating the pattern of results found by Bentall and colleagues; however, these researchers also found that their non-paranoid/non-grandiose patients, who were just as deluded as the paranoid/grandiose group, did not differ statistically from normal controls in their tendency to internalize or externalize the blame for negative events.

At this point, there is one other type of attributional bias which we will mention before moving on to present an interim summary of the discussion thus far. In contrast to individual attributional biases, we think it likely that there is a specific attributional bias which all people have, and that is the bias to favour personal-level causal explanations over subpersonal-level causal explanations. The Capgras patient's belief that an impostor has replaced a loved one and the Cotard patient's belief that he or she is dead are both examples of personal-level causal explanations. That is, these beliefs locate cause somewhere in the interaction between self and the environment. In contrast, subpersonal causal explanations locate cause in the subpersonal mechanisms which underpin 'my being me in the world'. The belief that dysfunctional neurochemistry has caused me to fail to experience the feeling that I should have when I see a loved one's face is a subpersonal causal explanation. Our suggestion here is that subpersonal causal explanations which may require us to question the integrity of the subpersonal processes which provide us with information about the world are intrinsically difficult for any of us to entertain. In other words, it is part of the normal human condition, we think, to have an attributional bias which favours personal-level causal explanations over subpersonal-level causal explanations.

4. Interim Summary

We began this chapter with a working definition of delusions: delusions are beliefs which run counter to the general beliefs held by others within an individual's socio-cultural environment and which an individual maintains despite rational counter-argument and overwhelming counter-evidence. Before reviewing research investigating the factors which may contribute towards delusion formation, we alerted readers to a useful distinction to bear in mind when evaluating relevant empirical evidence. That is, there is a difference between explaining delusional *content*—what it is that a person comes to be deluded about; and explaining the *presence* of a delusional belief—why that person is deluded in their thinking about those ideas.

Empirical evidence was reviewed which supported the existence of different types of perceptual aberrations in different groups of deluded individuals, such as those with Capgras delusion and those with delusions of alien control. Such evidence leads us to conclude that the presence of a perceptual aberration is necessary to explain why a delusion is *bizarre*, by which we mean having aberrant thematic content which runs counter to the everyday commonsense beliefs of others. The contrast here is with *ordinary* delusions—that is, delusions which are about everyday things, such as believing that a loved one is having an affair. We will say more about ordinary delusions later. For now, the point to be noted here is that the presence of a perceptual aberration explains why it is that such affected individuals generate bizarre delusions with aberrant content since, in these cases, the deluded individuals with perceptual aberrations are not experiencing themselves or the world in the same way that normal individuals are. It is therefore not surprising that they will generate bizarre ideas which run counter to the everyday commonsense beliefs of others. Furthermore, the existence of different types of perceptual aberrations (e.g. loss of affective responsiveness to faces and loss of the sense of self-generation associated with self-initiated action) helps us to explain why deluded individuals can differ so widely with respect to the thematic content of their bizarre delusions and may explain why deluded individuals differ so widely with respect to the scope of their delusions. That is, some delusions may be mono-thematic because only one perceptual aberration is present (e.g. the Capgras delusion is solely about spouse replacement) whereas other delusions may be polythematic because the deluded individual is bombarded with more than one perceptual aberration (e.g. this may be the case in the classic example of Dr Daniel Schreber, a German judge, whose highly complex delusional system included beliefs about his being transformed into a female to be fertilized by God and beliefs that doctors were committing soul-murder upon him (Freud, 1963)).

However, the presence of a perceptual aberration, although necessary to explain the *content* of a bizarre delusion, is not sufficient to explain the *presence* of a delusional belief, since, as we have already stated, some individuals with bizarre perceptual experiences do not have delusions and since there are grounds for thinking that both non-deluded and deluded individuals can be experiencing the same perceptual aberration.

We then considered the possibility that a perceptual aberration when coupled with a particular type of attributional bias, or a statistically deviant degree of bias, might be jointly sufficient to explain the presence of a delusional belief. However, although an externalizing bias for negative events was found to be associated with persecutory delusions, in general, and the Capgras delusion, in particular, the presence of an externalizing bias for negative events is not characteristic of all delusions. In particular, Cotard delusion, it was noted, is said to arise when the loss of affective responsiveness to a loved one's face is delusionally misattributed to oneself being dead in the context of a disposition to internalize blame for negative events. Furthermore, not even the presence of a statistically deviant degree of bias—in whichever direction—is sufficient to explain the presence of a delusional belief since groups of deluded individuals can be found who do not differ significantly from normal subjects in the extent to which they internalize or externalize the blame for negative events.

In sum, perceptual aberrations may be necessary but are not sufficient to explain the generation of bizarre delusions. Attributional biases, of any particular type or any particular strength, we think neither necessary nor sufficient to explain the presence of a delusional belief. Deluded individuals are found with all styles of attributional bias and without an abnormal degree of bias. Furthermore, it is not pathological to have an attributional bias—whatever the direction and whatever the strength. Differences in attributional bias play a role in many non-clinical aspects of everyday life: determining drive for success in the classroom, influencing ability to cope with stress, shaping responses to marital conflict, and influencing worker attitudes in big organizations (Graham and Folkes, 1990). We all differ to varying degrees in our disposition to allocate blame internally or externally and we are all influenced by a universal bias to favour personal-level causal explanations over subpersonal-level causal explanations. The existence of such normal attributional biases can help us to explain some of the individual variation in delusional content (e.g. Capgras delusion versus Cotard delusion) and may help us to explain why deluded individuals are not swayed by medical evidence of subpersonal causality; however, we still need something more for a full causal account of delusions since non-deluded individuals with phantom limb experiences and depersonalization disorder can reason against their natural biases and accept a rational subpersonal explanation. Why can't deluded individuals? In the following section, we review research investigating whether deluded individuals show deficits of reasoning and/or logical thinking.

5. Studies of Reasoning in Deluded Individuals

Recall that Maher (1974, 1988, 1992) takes the view that a delusional belief is a rational attempt to make sense of an aberrant perceptual experience. Now, although we do not consider that the presence of a delusional belief is completely explained by the abnormality of a perceptual experience—for all of the reasons listed above—there are some grounds for accepting Maher's view that reasoning processes in deluded individuals are not markedly abnormal. Delusions do not require the presence of general intellectual deterioration. Circumscribed delusions are found in non-demented individuals (Stone and Young, 1997) and, despite evidence of poor performance on IQ tasks by chronic schizophrenic patients, IQ deteriorates in only some schizophrenic individuals, and that only after the onset of the disorder (Elliott and Sahakian, 1995). As for the possibility of other types of abnormal reasoning in deluded individuals, much early interest in this issue focused more specifically on the question of whether communicative deficits in schizophrenia are better understood as abnormalities of communication or as abnormalities of thinking (Kasinin, 1944). Some ideas proposed at that time were that schizophrenic patients show poor abstract thinking (that is, patients are concrete thinkers who interpret proverbs literally), poor concept formation (for example, on object sorting tasks and categorisation tasks) and impaired syllogistic reasoning (that is, patients are prone to make errors of the type 'Diana is a princess, my initial is D, therefore I am a princess'). Much of that research continues to the present day, although the primary focus now is on executive function deficits in schizophrenia. There is no scope to review this line of research in any detail here. It will suffice to point out that concrete thinking and poor abstraction can be found in non-deluded patients with frontal lesions or depression. Furthermore, recent studies of syllogistic reasoning report little evidence of differences between deluded patients and normal controls (Kemp et al., 1997). So, although these abnormalities of thinking may be characteristic of at least some schizophrenic patients, it is not likely that such abnormalities of thinking will provide an explanation of delusions in general.

Overall, deluded patients appear to reason just as ably as normal subjects on tests of logical deductive reasoning (conditional reasoning and syllogistic reasoning) (Kemp et al., 1997). When differences are found, these appear to be specific to inductive reasoning tasks involving probability judgements. For example, Huq, Garety and Hemsley (1988) used an inferential reasoning task in which subjects are shown two containers of coloured beads. One container has pink and green beads in the proportion of 85 to 15, whereas the other container has beads in the reverse proportion. The containers are placed out of sight and the experimenter draws a sequence of beads from one container. Subjects must indicate when they believe that they can make a judgement about which container the beads are being drawn from and how confident they are about their decision. Deluded schizophrenic patients, when compared to non-deluded non-schizophrenic psychiatric controls and normal controls, were found to gather less information before making a judgement (that is, waited for fewer beads to be drawn) and they were found to be overconfident in rating the correctness of their decisions. Subsequent to that initial study, the performances of schizophrenic deluded patients, non-schizophrenic deluded patients (with diagnoses of delusional disorder), anxious controls and normal controls have been compared on a similar task (Garety, Hemsley and Wesseley, 1991). Both groups of deluded subjects (whether schizophrenic or not) were found to show the same general pattern of an overconfident jumping-to-conclusions style of belief formation when compared to the two control groups. Of further note, the Garey et al. (1991) study also found that their deluded patients were more likely than controls to change their hypotheses when shown disconfirmatory evidence—that is, after having stated their hypothesis about which jar the beads were being drawn from, deluded patients were more likely and quicker to switch to saying that it must be the other jar when shown a new draw of a coloured bead which went against their stated hypothesis. Similar patterns of performance have also been found in non-clinical delusion-prone individuals (Linney, Peters and Ayton, 1998).

Garety and Freeman (1999) have recently carried out an extensive review of probabilistic reasoning and other forms of reasoning in deluded subjects, in particular patients with diagnoses of schizophrenia and delusional disorder, and delusion-prone non-clinical individuals. These authors conclude that deluded, or delusion-prone, individuals show a jumping-to-conclusions style of belief formation when allowed to decide how much information is needed before reaching a decision (e.g. number of draws of a bead). In contrast, when subjects are given a fixed number of trials and asked to make probability estimates, deluded subjects do not differ, in general, from control subjects. In other words, Garety and Freeman (1999) suggest that deluded subjects have a data-gathering bias rather than a probabilistic reasoning deficit. Furthermore, a number of studies have found evidence of a disconfirmatory bias in deluded individuals—that is, people with delusions not only appear more ready to jump to conclusions on the basis of little data, they also appear more ready to abandon an existing hypothesis and form a new one on the basis of less first-hand evidence which runs counter to their current belief. This last set of results is of some note since our working definition of delusions is that these are false beliefs which are resistant to counter-evidence. Perhaps what counts for deluded subjects is the nature of that counter-evidence. We will come back to that point later.

In sum, delusions are found in the absence of marked intellectual deterioration. Furthermore, deluded individuals show relatively intact logical deductive reasoning—a finding which is compatible with clinical observations of schizophrenic patients who have highly systematized delusional systems with their own idiosyncratic internal logic—and they are perfectly capable of making accurate judgements of probability when given all of the relevant information. Overall then it seems that Maher is right in saying that a failure of rational and/or logical thinking is not characteristic of deluded patients. Rather than an abnormality of reasoning, it seems that what is characteristic of deluded individuals is an abnormality in the way that they treat hypothesis-generating evidence.

6. Cognitive Accounts of the Presence of Delusional Beliefs

Based on the empirical evidence reviewed above, Garety and Hemsley (1994) have proposed that what is critical for explaining the *presence* of a delusional belief (rather than the thematic *content* of a particular delusional belief) is that deluded individuals have a bias towards focusing on current stimuli when forming beliefs, rather than being influenced by past regularities of experience. In other words, the notion here is that what sways judgement, or belief, in the deluded individual is what is happening here and now, rather than what might have happened in the past, or indeed what might happen in the future. Stone and Young (1997) have come to a somewhat similar conclusion in their account of circumscribed delusions, in particular Capgras delusion. More specifically, these latter authors propose that normal belief formation involves weighing up hypotheses that are observationally adequate—that is, which equate with the evidence of our own senses—against hypotheses which fit conservatively within our current web of beliefs about how the world should be. These two need not pull against each other in the normal run of things, but in the case of Capgras patients they do. And so, it is argued, Capgras delusion arises when a perceptual aberration (loss of affective responsiveness to a loved one's face) is misattributed in the context of an externalizing bias for negative events—these two factors explain the specific content of the delusion—and then an additional reasoning bias is needed to explain why these individuals become deluded. The nature of that reasoning bias is that these individuals tend to put more weight on forming a belief which satisfies the evidence of their own senses rather than forming a belief which fits more conservatively within their current stock of beliefs about the world, but which is not as observationally adequate.

Thus, both Garety and Hemsley (1994) and Stone and Young (1997) have proposed bias accounts of delusion formation—that is, the *presence* of a delusional belief is explained by the presence of a particular reasoning bias. For Garety and Hemsley (1994), that bias is conceptualized primarily in terms of a conflict between different sources of information (current information versus past and/or future information), whereas Stone and Young (1997) conceptualize bias more in terms of a conflict between the different 'purposes' that beliefs play in our lives. That is, on their view, the conflict is between beliefs that adequately address the evidence of our own senses versus beliefs that fit within our current web of beliefs about how the world should be without the need for major internal reorganization.

Although there is much to be said for bias accounts of delusion formation (see Stone and Young, 1997), it is our opinion that a deficit model will offer a more plausible account of delusions, in particular bizarre delusions which defy commonsense and appear impervious to rational counter-argument. Bentall (1995) has defined a cognitive deficit as an inability (which might occur to varying degrees) to perform a certain kind of information-processing operation, whereas a cognitive bias is a tendency to use information in one way rather than another way. If the formation of a delusional belief were just a question of bias, then surely the weight of counter-arguments would eventually tip the scales in favour of rationality. But, if, instead, normal belief evaluation is impaired in deluded individuals because of an inability to critically evaluate competing causal explanations in the light of general knowledge and our broader web of beliefs, then no amount of rational counter-arguments coming from others, including respected doctors, will dislodge a belief once it has been adopted. In this case, deluded individuals might find themselves holding quite absurd beliefs, given their web of general knowledge, and feeling just as confused as everyone else as to why in all good sense they should believe such things—as appears to be the case in some deluded patients (Alexander, Stuss and Benson, 1979).[5]

If, as Garety and Hemsley (1994) and Stone and Young (1997) argue, deluded individuals are prone to explanations of one type (explanations that derive from the immediate evidence of our own senses) over explanations of another type (explanations that conform to past regularities of experience, general knowledge and our broader web of beliefs), then that implies, if we think in terms of deficit rather than bias, that normal belief evaluation may depend upon the suspension of automatically prioritized explanatory biases, which reflect, in part, the relative salience of different sources of information:

(1) first-person information which we access directly via our senses;
(2) second-person information which others tell us about or that we infer from others' actions;
(3) third-person information about the world that we have acquired through learning and past experience.

On this view, normal rational evaluation of the plausibility and probability of competing explanations is sustained by a more fundamental ability to 're-initialize' explanations that derive from different sources of information in order to give equal priority to hypotheses based on first-person, second-person and third-person evidence. Given this, then we would also need to argue that it is a normal human bias to favour explanations that derive from first-person sensory information over explanations that derive from indirect second-person and third-person information. But that sounds quite reasonable. It would be surprising if we did not default to first believing the evidence of our own senses. After all, there would be little evolutionary advantage in doubting the evidence of our own senses—much safer to act first on the basis of directly perceived danger and then evaluate whether or not we were misguided if prompted to do so later by conflicting second-person and/or third-person information. Furthermore, subsumed within this natural human bias to favour hypotheses based on first-person evidence would be that other universal bias, referred to earlier, to favour personal-level causal explanations over subpersonal-level causal explanations. Since we do not have direct sensory access to subpersonal states, subpersonal causal explanations will always depend upon second-person and/or third-person information and hence will always be low on our priority listing of possible explanations, if they make the list at all. And

---

[5]   Note here that we are not suggesting that all delusions are fixed and stable. Delusions can come and go and may respond to anti-psychotics. Rather, what we are suggesting is that the presence of a delusional belief reflects a failure of normal belief evaluation which is more fundamentally caused by some neuropathy and that neuropathy may or may not be part of an unstable 'disease process' which is responsive to medication.

finally, individual biases of attributional style would also serve to prioritize certain types of causal explanations for a particular individual.

In sum, Maher is right, we think, in arguing that it is not irrational to generate a bizarre causal hypothesis, relative to what others believe, when confronted by a bizarre perceptual experience which does not accord with the way that the rest of society experiences reality. The nature of the perceptual aberration, nuanced by an individual's attributional bias, explains the *content* of the favoured causal hypothesis generated to explain what is happening. However, something else is needed to explain why that implausible hypothesis is then uncritically adopted and maintained as belief. We think that bias accounts which attempt to explain the adoption of delusional beliefs in terms of the presence of a particular type of individual reasoning bias are inadequate to explain the presence of bizarre delusions which persist despite overwhelming rational counter-argument. Instead, we advocate a deficit model. That is, implausible hypotheses are uncritically adopted as delusional beliefs when there is damage to the normal cognitive system of belief evaluation. In particular, we suggest that normal belief evaluation depends fundamentally upon an ability to suspend automatically prioritized explanatory biases, which reflect, in part, the relative salience of different sources of information: first-person information which we access directly via our senses; second-person information which others tell us about or that we infer from others' actions; and third-person information about the world acquired through learning and past experience. To put it another way in order to clarify the bias versus deficit distinction, prioritizing causal explanations that are based on direct first-person evidence over explanations that are based on indirect sources of information— the latter of which necessarily include subpersonal-level causal explanations— is something which *all* people do; it is not something which only certain people with a particular type of reasoning bias do. Furthermore, there is something else which all people can do, given that everything is operating normally, and that is to access some override safety mechanism which has the job of suspending automatic biases in order to critically evaluate different hypotheses, 're-initialized' as having equal priority whether based on direct or indirect sources of information. Damage to this normal safety-check mechanism (a deficit) is necessary, we think, to explain the presence of delusional beliefs.

In the following section we outline, in more detail, a model of the normal cognitive system of belief generation and belief evaluation which we believe is applicable generally to the explanation of *all* delusions as being caused by damage to one or more components of that normal system.

7. A Cognitive Model of Normal Belief Generation and Evaluation

We propose that delusion formation is best explained in relation to a three-factor model of normal belief generation and belief evaluation which incorporates the following features: (1) there is current information about self and the environment, provided by sensory mechanisms, which requires explanation; (2) universal and individual attributional biases exist which influence the generation of favoured causal explanations; and (3) there are normal belief evaluation processes which suspend the natural favoured status of first-person evidence in order to critically evaluate the plausibility and probability of all hypotheses, given equal priority whether they derive from direct first-person experience or indirect sources of information. The following is a very tentative proposal of how these factors might interact in the normal system of belief formation.[6]

Belief formation begins with current sensory information that is being provided about self and the environment. Some pieces of current sensory information will be promoted as requiring explanation. These seem to be of two types: (1) there is information which we selectively attend to because of heightened personal salience; and (2) there is information which we are automatically oriented towards because it is discordant with our prior experience of how the world should be, whether that discordance be due to perceptual aberrations or due to the occurrence of novel environmental stimuli. It may be that two distinct mechanisms carry out these two respective monitoring functions: (1) a conscious monitoring operation which matches present sensory inputs against sets and expectancies that derive from beliefs of which we can be conscious; and (2) a preconscious monitoring operation which detects mismatches against past regularities of experience. The proposition that two such monitoring mechanisms orient our attention to different sensory information is consistent with Ben-shakhar's (1994) proposal that autonomic responsiveness to significant (personally relevant) stimuli is controlled by a mechanism which differs from the mechanism that directs autonomic orientation to novel nonsignificant changes. The purpose of monitoring is to identify discordant sensory data, novel sensory data and sensory data with heightened personal salience which then requires explanation.

Given the nature of what needs to be explained, hypotheses based on relevant data from different sources are generated: other first-person sensory information; second-person information derived from others; and third-person information derived from our broader web of beliefs, general knowledge (stored in semantic memory) and information from prior experience (stored in episodic memory). Note here the contrast between other first-person sensory information which is available to sufferers of phantom limb experiences and that which is directly available to Capgras patients. Capgras patients only have the single aberrant perception—'he looks right but he doesn't feel right': there is no other directly accessible first-person information available. In contrast, individuals with the phantom-limb experience—'my arm feels like it's there

---

[6]   Note that the early stages of this framework are very similar to Garety and Hemsley's (1994) model of delusion formation.

but I can't see it'—can try and fail to move or touch their arms in order to collect other relevant first-person information.

Based on these various sources of evidence, a prioritized list of possible causal hypotheses is generated. There are at least two different biases which play a role in the generation of an individual's prioritized list of explanations. First, there are individual differences in attributional bias which will influence the particular type of causal hypothesis that an individual will favour. And second there is a universal attributional bias which we all have and that is to favour personal-level causal explanations that satisfy the evidence of our own senses over explanations that are based on second-person and third-person information, which would include subpersonal-level causal explanations.

These prioritized candidates for belief are then submitted to rational evaluation. Rational belief evaluation processes are underpinned by an ability to suspend personalized and individualized priority weightings of generated hypotheses. Re-initializing candidates for belief in this way may involve source-referencing explanations in order to give equal priority to 'what I think is happening', 'what others say is happening' and 'what the doctor says has gone wrong in my brain to cause me to have this experience'. Once hypotheses have been re-initialized as having equal priority, critical evaluation and rationalization processes can proceed. These processes may include assessing how consistent different hypotheses are with our broader web of beliefs, as suggested by Stone and Young (1997), and perhaps some probabilistic assessment of how likely particular hypotheses are—along the lines of 'Has this happened to me before, and if so what caused it then?' or 'When this happens to others what do they think is wrong?'

After the critical evaluation process, a particular hypothesis may be adopted as belief and that belief is then added to our current web of beliefs along with any necessary revision of the other beliefs which we hold. The updated web of beliefs in turn influences how we act and what new expectations we have about incoming sensory information. Alternatively, the result of the rational evaluation process may be to defer selection of any particular hypothesis, on the basis that some other, as yet unspecified, hypothesis might be generated in the future if I were to take the time to collect more information. And note here that difficulty giving equal priority to the possibility that such a future alternative hypothesis might be generated on the basis of as-yet unknown data could lead to less data-gathering and a tendency to jump to conclusions on the basis of immediate first-person evidence. This is entirely consistent with the empirical evidence of a jumping-to-conclusions style of belief formation and a disconfirmatory bias in deluded individuals.

In the case of deluded individuals, normal belief evaluation processes cannot be completed because these individuals have difficulty suspending natural biases in order to give equal priority to all possible hypotheses, regardless of their primary source of information. Consequently, deluded individuals will adopt as belief whichever hypothesis is their natural highest priority explanation—

and that will always be a personal-level causal explanation based on first-person experience, and it will always reflect an individual's particular causal attributional bias.

But it is important to bear in mind here that the naturally favoured causal explanation, generated to explain novel and/or relevant sensory information, will not necessarily be incorrect, even in individuals with a failure of normal belief evaluation. If there is nothing wrong with the neural substrates which provide us with sensory information about the environment (including our own body states) and/or orient our attention towards relevant aspects of the environment, then there is no reason to think that our natural biases will lead us markedly astray. However, they will most certainly lead us astray if a perceptual aberration is present. Hence, we argue that in order to explain bizarre delusions which defy everyday commonsense two components of the normal three-factor model must be damaged: (1) there must be some disruption to the normal operation of sensory and/or attentional mechanisms which provide us with sensory information and/or orient our attention to relevant stimuli within the environment; and (2) there must also be a failure of normal belief evaluation.

In the following section we illustrate how a two-deficit model of delusion formation, incorporating both a perceptual aberration (defining perception very broadly to encompass phenomenological experiences which derive from primary sensory information—sight, hearing, touch, smell, taste—as well as somatic information about body states, and perhaps even emotional states) and a deficit of normal belief evaluation, when mediated by (normal) individual attributional biases, can explain a diversity of bizarre delusions including cases of 'organic' delusions and cases of 'psychotic' delusions.

8. Bizarre Two-Deficit Delusions

8.1 Capgras and Cotard Delusion

Both Capgras delusion and Cotard delusion arise when normal belief evaluation is impaired in individuals who are experiencing the aberrant perception—'he looks right but he doesn't feel right'—which, as argued earlier, arises when an individual loses the sense of affective responsiveness which normally co-occurs with explicit recognition of a familiar face. In the case of Capgras patients, who have an attributional bias to externalize the cause for negative events, the naturally favoured personal-level causal explanation which is then generated and adopted as belief is the bizarre delusion that an impostor has replaced their loved one. In contrast, Cotard patients with an attributional bias to internalize the cause for negative events will generate and adopt as belief the naturally favoured personal-level causal explanation that they are dead (Wright et al., 1993; Young et al., 1993).

8.2 Alien Control Delusions

Schizophrenic delusions of alien control arise when normal belief evaluation fails in individuals who experience a discordant sense of passivity which arises when normal on-line self-monitoring is disrupted, resulting in loss of the sense of self-generation that normally accompanies self-initiated action. Although no studies have investigated the causal attributional styles of patients with delusions of alien control, it seems most likely that this delusion is the naturally favoured personal-level causal explanation of individuals who have an attributional bias to externalize the cause for negative events. In contrast, deluded individuals who experience this perceptual aberration and who have an attributional bias to internalize the cause for negative events might be expected to develop nihilistic delusions of soul-death, for example.

8.3 Auditory Hallucinations and Loss of Boundary Delusions

Frith (1992) has proposed that normal internal monitoring of self-generation is not only required for a sense of ownership of bodily actions (as described above) but is also required for a sense of ownership of inner thoughts. If self-generation in this second sense is lost, then Frith (1992) proposes that affected individuals will experience their inner thoughts with a sense of unintendedness and alien influence. That is, inner thoughts will be experienced as extrapersonal auditory perceptions—as if one is 'hearing voices'. But, in line with what we have argued before, it is possible to have the experience of 'hearing voices' and yet know that for some reason—not directly accessible—the source of those voices is oneself and not some external agency. The experience of 'hearing voices' is not specific to patients with a diagnosis of mental illness. Auditory hallucinations are experienced by individuals with ear disease and can be induced in normal subjects using sleep deprivation, isolation/sensory deprivation and, in some cases, simple suggestion (see Bentall, 1990, and David, 1994, for reviews). And so we think that auditory hallucinations, when these are reported as the voices of real entities (as in patients with schizophrenia), are just another sub-category of delusion—an aberrant perceptual experience being delusionally misinterpreted in the absence of normal belief evaluation.

Individual differences in attributional bias might then manifest in the different motives which patients ascribe to the sources of their voices. For example, some patients, perhaps those with a bias towards internalizing blame for negative events, may believe that the voices are there to punish them for wrongs that they have done; whilst others, perhaps those with a bias towards externalizing blame for negative events, might believe themselves to be innocents being 'picked upon' by malevolent forces.

But then again, attributional biases may play a more fundamental role here. That is, if an individual has lost the sense of self-generation which normally tags inner thoughts as self-sourced, then, if that individual has an externalizing bias for negative events, perhaps it is only thoughts with unpleasant (negative) content which are misattributed to external voices. Voices need not have negative content—there are many non-clinical individuals who hear helpful voices which they interpret positively as spirit guides (Romme and Escher, 1989). However, in the case of schizophrenia, many patients who hear voices are also paranoid and, in such cases, voices are usually experienced as unpleasant, critical and even threatening. Since paranoia is known to be associated with an externalizing bias for negative events, what may be happening in cases of paranoid schizophrenic patients who hear 'negative' voices is that an externalizing bias for negative events interacts with loss of the normal ability to tag self-generated thoughts as one's own, thus causing the misattribution to external voices of thoughts with 'negative', rather than 'positive', content.

Up until now, we have only talked about one type of perceptual aberration being implicated in the presence of auditory hallucinations—that is, loss of the sense of self-generation associated with one's thoughts. However, whereas Frith and colleagues (Frith, 1992; Frith and Done, 1989) interpret auditory hallucinations and other 'loss of boundary' experiences—thought-broadcasting, mind-reading, and thought-insertion—as all being straightforward manifestations of a source-monitoring failure, David (1994) points out that this may only be part of the story. That is, David suggests that two perceptual aberrations, in combination, may be needed to explain the phenomenology of auditory hallucinations—a source-monitoring defect coupled with the loss of subjective privacy normally associated with 'hearing in mind' one's inner thoughts. Recall that earlier we spoke about how loss of a sense of subjective privacy when coupled with different styles of attributional bias might explain why some patients generate different types of 'loss of boundary' delusions. However, David suggests that different 'loss of boundary' experiences might be better understood as reflecting different types of perceptual aberration, in conjunction or in isolation. That is, whereas auditory hallucinations may reflect a source-monitoring defect coupled with the loss of subjective privacy normally associated with 'hearing in mind' one's thoughts, thought-insertion delusions may reflect a source-monitoring defect coupled with an intact sense of 'hearing thoughts' within subjective space. In other words, patients with thought-insertion delusions may 'hear' their thoughts intrapersonally but not as self-instigated. In contrast, there may be other patients who have lost the sense of subjective privacy associated with 'hearing in mind' one's thoughts, and so experience their thoughts extrapersonally, but with an intact sense of self-generation. These patients may then generate delusions of thought-broadcasting.

8.4 Delusions of Reference

Delusions of reference occur when a deluded individual reads personal significance into seemingly trivial comments and activities of others and into completely unrelated and commonplace events. For example, patients with delusions of reference may believe that statements being made by television or radio commentators are specifically directed at themselves or they may

believe that colours and arrangements of everyday objects have been specifically arranged in such a way so as to convey hidden messages to them.
Although there is no empirical basis for assuming that a perceptual aberration
plays a role in the generation of delusions of reference, the phenomenological
self-reports of patients do attest to some perceptual quality being present. For
example, one patient described the experience as a feeling that things and
people 'zoomed in' on them with an overwhelming sense of self-referential
import.

Let's assume, for the sake of argument, that there is some perceptual basis
to delusions of reference and let us now consider how that aberration might
interact with different attributional styles. Delusions of reference often co-
occur with paranoid delusions in patients with schizophrenia. In these cases,
it seems likely that the aberrant perception is interpreted negatively and then
coupled with an attributional bias to externalize blame for negative events.
The result, given a deficit of normal belief evaluation, is that these individuals
will generate and adopt as belief some form of conspiracy theory about being
followed and electronically monitored by agents of forces who are plotting
against them. In contrast, delusions of reference can also be found to co-occur
with grandiose delusions and patients with grandiose delusions are known to
have the same attributional bias as paranoid patients (that is, a tendency to
externalize blame for negative events and internalize blame for positive events).
In these cases then, it seems likely that the same perceptual aberration (to that
experienced by paranoid patients with delusions of reference) is interpreted
positively and then attributed to self, thus generating grandiose delusions about
why that person should be in the spotlight or see significance in events which
others deem commonplace. For example, these individuals might develop
delusions about having psychic powers or about being chosen specially by God
to receive secret communications.

8.5 Hallucinations

Up until now, we have focused on auditory hallucinations, specifically of the
voices commenting type, which are said to arise when normal monitoring of
internal speech fails (Frith, 1992). However, hallucinations can occur in any
modality: auditory, visual, tactile, olfactory, and gustatory. Furthermore, hallucinations in various modalities can co-occur in the same individuals. In such
cases then, it seems more plausible that these hallucinations reflect difficulty
discriminating self-generated imaginary states from externally generated sensory
experiences (Bentall, 1990).

Now consider an individual who has this type of perceptual aberration
(multi-modal hallucinations caused by defective discrimination of imagination
and reality) and a deficit of normal belief evaluation. Such an individual's entire
web of beliefs will quickly get wildly out of kilter: an initial delusion will
prompt imaginings which are then experienced as confirmatory first-person
sensory information for the deluded belief and then further elaborative imagin-

ings will lead to other delusions, and so forth and so forth. It is therefore plausible that one cause of polythematic, or fragmentary, delusions found to occur in cases of schizophrenia is the coupling of a deficit of normal belief evaluation with a single perceptual aberration, which by its very nature (a failure to discriminate self-generated imaginary states from externally generated sensory experiences) has a cascading effect on the individual's entire web of beliefs. However, even here we would argue that if a person is capable of normal belief evaluation, then they will be able to check this disintegration process by taking on board what others are telling them and, thus prompted, test out the plausibility of their wild imaginings in the light of learned general knowledge.

8.6 Non-Hallucinatory Polythematic Delusions

Earlier in the chapter, we noted that any full account of delusions must be able to account for both the diversity of content and the diversity of scope in delusions. In the previous section, we suggested that one cause of widespread polythematic delusions might be the special case of a deficit of normal belief evaluation coupled with multi-modal hallucinations caused by a failure to discriminate reality from imagination. Now we consider other possible causes of non-hallucinatory polythematic delusions.

A possible explanation, which is consistent with what has gone before, is that polythematic delusions may arise when a failure of normal belief evaluation is coupled with a multitude of different perceptual aberrations. This might occur in two ways. First, we have already seen that specific schizophrenic delusions may arise, in part, in response to specific perceptual aberrations— for example, loss of boundary experiences and delusions of reference. Now, given the range of possible perceptual aberrations and the extent of cognitive deficits which have been found in patients with schizophrenia, including, for example, face recognition deficits (Ellis and Young, 1996) and memory deficits (McKenna et al., 1990), it is likely that some cases of polythematic delusions occur when patients are faced with a multitude of different perceptual aberrations which are all jockeying for explanation. However, there is a second possibility. We have already hinted at the idea that anomalous perceptual experiences might arise either because there is dysfunction of one or more sensory mechanisms dedicated to providing certain types of sensory information (e.g. face-recognition information) or because the normal attentional mechanisms which orient us to novel and/or relevant stimuli in the environment are themselves dysfunctional (see Maher and Spitzer, 1993, for a review of abnormal attention and orienting in patients with schizophrenia). If this latter type of perceptual aberration is present, then a multitude of different events which would normally be ignored as mere commonplace might be imbued with an aberrant quality of salience. That idea accords well with schizophrenic patients' self-reports of a heightened sense of significance and meaningfulness accompanying a myriad of everyday events that might otherwise be deemed commonplace or coincidental (Anscombe, 1987). In other words, the idea here is that instead of experiencing a set of perceptual aberrations which each reflect a distinct sensory dysfunction, some schizophrenic individuals may be experiencing the world, in general, aberrantly because of central dysfunction to early attentional/orienting mechanisms which direct us to events in the world requiring explanation.

The above examples have served to illustrate how two deficits in a three-component model of normal belief generation and belief evaluation (in which attributional biases are seen as part of the normal) can explain the diversity of content and the diversity of scope in various 'organic' and 'psychotic' bizarre delusions. Previously, we argued that a single deficit which causes a perceptual aberration, in the absence of a failure of normal belief evaluation, is not sufficient to cause a delusional belief. In these cases, the non-deluded individual is capable of adopting 'as if' accounts of the type espoused by patients with depersonalization disorder: 'it feels as if an alien is controlling my body, but aliens don't really exist, and the doctors tell me that I have a chronic abnormal reaction to stress—so that must be what it is'. In the following section, we consider what happens if there is just a single deficit of normal belief evaluation.

9. The Implications of a Single Deficit of Normal Belief Evaluation

We have already suggested that an individual with a deficit of normal belief evaluation will not necessarily generate naturally favoured personal-level causal explanations which are incorrect. However, even our normal sensory and/or attentional mechanisms are unlikely to operate perfectly all of the time. And so, there may well be times when we think that we see a person's shadow or when events occur with a sense of meaningful contiguity (e.g. someone calls you on the telephone just as you are thinking about that person). In the case of a person who has a deficit of normal belief evaluation, and thus difficulty evaluating the plausibility and probability of generated hypotheses in the light of past experience and general knowledge, such first-person experiences may generate beliefs such as thinking that you have seen a ghost or thinking that you have psychically foreseen the future. But since there is no fixed sensory and/or attentional dysfunction causing continual perceptual aberrations, then these will be relatively isolated events. We therefore think it unlikely that such individuals will generate full-blown delusions which disrupt normal functioning, thus leading to some form of clinical diagnosis. Rather, we think that these individuals will be more likely to present as idiosyncratic non-clinical individuals who are prone to hold unorthodox beliefs.

However, we do acknowledge that there may be some instances when a single deficit of normal belief evaluation can result in delusional beliefs—of an ordinary type. That is, thus far we have focused mainly on bizarre delusions which run counter to the commonsense beliefs of others. However, as mentioned earlier, there is a class of clinically diagnosable delusions which are not bizarre. These 'ordinary' delusions include, for example, delusions of jealousy, the hypochondriacal delusion that you are going to die, or the belief that someone important secretly loves you. Such delusions are diagnosed, usually as cases of delusional disorder, when an individual exhibits delusional thinking—that is, they maintain their beliefs despite the lack of compelling objective evidence—but also when the delusion is about everyday things. That is, in these cases, the content of the delusion is not outside the bounds of commonsense—such things can and do occur. Here we think that what may be happening is that there is a deficit of normal belief evaluation coupled with misperceptions of partial sensory information and misinterpretations of ambiguous cues which are driven by heightened, but not abnormal, attentional and interpretative biases. There is plenty of evidence to suggest that both deluded patients (Bentall and Kaney, 1989; Bentall, Kaney and Bowen-Jones, 1995; Kaney et al., 1992; Leafhead, Young and Szulecka, 1996) and non-deluded individuals with social phobia and anxiety disorders (Matthews and Mackintosh, 1998; McNally, 1998) can be perceptually sensitized to identify certain stimuli and to preferentially elaborate information which conforms to and reinforces their particular expectations and preoccupations. In the case of individuals with a deficit of normal belief evaluation, such misperceptions and misinterpretations of ambiguous, but certainly not bizarre, first-person evidence may lead to the formation of ordinary delusions.

10. Summary and Conclusions

After reviewing the role that perceptual aberrations and attributional biases play in determining the thematic content of different delusions, and reviewing research investigating the presence of abnormal thinking and/or reasoning in deluded individuals, we propose that the formation of delusional beliefs is best explained in terms of damage to one or more components of a three-component system of normal belief generation and belief evaluation. This three-component system includes: (1) attentional/monitoring mechanisms which orient us to current sensory information requiring explanation; (2) universal and individual attributional biases which influence the generation of naturally favoured causal explanations; and (3) belief evaluation processes which are underpinned by an ability to suspend the automatic prioritizing of hypotheses based on immediate first-person experience in order to critically evaluate hypotheses, given equal priority whether based on direct or indirect sources of information.

We have used this model to present a deficit model of delusion formation rather than a bias model. Bias accounts we think inadequate to explain bizarre delusions which defy commonsense and persist despite overwhelming rational counter-argument. More specifically, we propose that damage to the third component of the normal model results in deluded individuals adopting as belief whichever hypothesis is naturally favoured as their highest priority personal-level causal explanation, nuanced by individual attributional biases. This, we think, helps to explain why some deluded individuals can express their bizarre belief with a sense of self-evident incontrovertible certainty, whilst at the same time appearing to be aware on some level (e.g. being confused about why they should think such an odd thing) of the implausibility of that belief.

Bizarre delusions, we argue, require at least two deficits: (1) at least one form of perceptual aberration, whether caused by dysfunction of a sensory mechanism or caused by dysfunction of attentional/orienting mechanisms; and (2) a breakdown of normal belief evaluation. Thus, the existence of deficits which cause one or more perceptual aberrations is not sufficient to explain the formation of delusional beliefs. Furthermore, since naturally favoured causal explanations generated in the absence of a stable perceptual aberration will, most often, be correct, a single deficit of normal belief evaluation will not necessarily lead to full-blown delusions. Such individuals we think more likely to present as non-clinical idiosyncratic individuals who are prone to unorthodox beliefs. However, in cases where an attentional bias, driven by personal preoccupations and expectations, leads to continual misperceptions of partial information and misinterpretations of ambiguous stimuli, then a single deficit of normal belief evaluation may manifest in delusions with ordinary content.

References

Abramson, L.Y., Seligman, M.E.P. and Teasdale, J.D. 1978: Learned helplessness in humans: Critique and reformulation. *Journal of Abnormal Psychology*, 87, 49–74.

Alexander, M.P., Stuss, D.T. and Benson, D.F. 1979: Capgras syndrome: A reduplicative phenomenon. *Neurology*, 29, 334–9.

American Psychiatric Association 1994: *Diagnostic and Statistical Manual of Mental Disorders, Fourth Edition (DSM-IV)*. Washington, DC: American Psychiatric Association.

Angel, R.W. 1976: Efference copy in the control of movement. *Neurology*, 26, 1164–8.

Anscombe, R. 1987: The disorder of consciousness in schizophrenia. *Schizophrenia Bulletin*, 13, 241–60.

Ben-shakhar, G. 1994: The roles of stimulus novelty and significance in determining the electrodermal orienting response: Interactive versus additive approaches. *Psychophysiology*, 31, 402–11.

Benson, D.F., Gardiner, H. and Meadows, J.C. 1976: Reduplicative paramnesia. *Neurology*, 26, 147–51.

Bentall, R.P. 1990: The illusion of reality: A review and integration of psychological research on hallucinations. *Psychological Bulletin*, 107, 82–95.

Bentall, R.P. 1995: Brains, biases, deficits and disorders. *British Journal of Psychiatry*, 167, 153–5.

Bentall, R.P. and Kaney, S. 1989: Content-specific processing and persecutory delusions: an investigation using the emotional Stroop test. *British Journal of Medical Psychology*, 62, 355–64.

Bentall, R.P. and Kaney, S. 1996: Abnormalities of self-representation and persecutory delusions: A test of a cognitive model of paranoia. *Psychological Medicine*, 26, 1231–7.

Bentall, R.P., Kaney, S. and Bowen-Jones, K. 1995: Persecutory delusions and recall of threat-related, depression-related, and neutral words. *Cognitive Therapy and Research*, 19, 445–57.

Bentall, R.P. Kaney, S. and Dewey, M.E. 1991: Paranoia and social reasoning: An attribution theory analysis. *British Journal of Clinical Psychology*, 31, 12–23.

Bentall, R.P. Kinderman, P. and Kaney S. 1994: The self, attributional processes and abnormal beliefs: Towards a model of persecutory delusions. *Behaviour Research and Therapy*, 32, 331–41.

Candido, C.L. and Romney, D.M. 1990: Attributional style in paranoid vs depressed patients. *British Journal of Medical Psychology*, 63, 355–63.

Coltheart, M. 1984: Editorial. *Cognitive Neuropsychology*, 1, 1–8.

Cutting, J. 1985: *The Psychology of Schizophrenia*. Edinburgh: Churchill Livingston.

Damasio, A.R., Tranel, D. and Damasio, H. 1991: Somatic markers and the guidance of behaviour: Theory and preliminary testing. In H.S. Levin, H.M. Eisenberg and A.L. Benson (eds), *Frontal Lobe Function and Dysfunction*. Oxford University Press, 217–29.

David, A.S. 1994: The neuropsychological origin of auditory hallucinations. In A.S. David and J.C. Cutting (eds), *The Neuropsychology of Schizophrenia: Brain Damage, Behaviour and Cognition Series*. Hove, E. Sussex: Lawrence Erlbaum Associates, 269–313.

Davis, K.D., Kiss, Z.H., Luo, L., Tasker, R.R., Lozano, A.M. and Dostrovsky, J.O. 1998: Phantom sensations generated by thalamic microstimulation. *Nature*, 391, 385–7.

Davison, G.C. and Neale, J.M. 1998: *Abnormal Psychology* 7th edn. New York: Wiley.

de Pauw, K.W., Szulecka, T.K. and Poltock, T.L. 1987: Fregoli syndrome after cerebral infarction. *Journal of Nervous and Mental Disease*, 175, 433–8.

Elliott, R. and Sahakian, B.J. 1995: The neuropsychology of schizophrenia: Relations with clinical and neurobiological dimensions. *Psychological Medicine*, 25, 581–94.

Ellis, A.W. and Young, A.W. 1988: *Human Cognitive Neuropsychology*. Hove, E. Sussex: Lawrence Erlbaum Associates.

Ellis, H.D. and Young, A.W. 1990: Accounting for delusional misidentifications. *British Journal of Psychiatry*, 157, 239–48.

Ellis, H.D. and Young, A.W. 1996: Problems of face perception in schizophrenia. In C. Pantelis, H.E. Nelson and T.R.E. Barnes (eds), *Schizophrenia: A Neuropsychological Perspective*. New York: Wiley, 397–416.

Ellis, H.D., Young, A.W., Quayle, A.H. and de Pauw, K.W. 1997a: Reduced autonomic responses to faces in Capgras delusion. *Proceeding of the Royal Society of London: Biological Sciences*, B264, 1085–92.

Ellis, H.D., Young, A.W., Quayle, A.H. and de Pauw, K.W. 1997b: Response from Ellis, Young, Quayle and de Pauw. *Trends in Cognitive Sciences*, 1, 158.

Filley. C.M. and Jarvis, P.E. 1987: Delayed reduplicative paramnesia. *Neurology*, 37, 701–3.

Fleminger, S. and Burns, A. 1993: The delusional misidentification syndromes in patients with and without evidence of organic cerebral disorder: A structured review of case reports. *Biological Psychiatry*, 33, 22–32.

Flor, H., Elbert, T., Muhlnickel, W., Pantev, C., Wienbruch, C. and Taub, E. 1998: Cortical reorganization and phantom phenomena in congenital and traumatic upper-extremity amputees. *Experimental Brain Research*, 119, 205–12.

Freud, S. 1963: *Three Case Histories*. New York: Collier Books/Macmillan Publishing Co.

Frith, C. 1992: *The Cognitive Neuropsychology of Schizophrenia*. Hove, E. Sussex: Lawrence Erlbaum Associates.

Frith, C. and Done, D.J. 1986: Routes to action in reaction time tasks. *Psychological Research*, 48, 169–77.

Frith, C. and Done, D.J. 1989: Experiences of alien control in schizophrenia reflect a disorder in the central monitoring of action. *Psychological Medicine*, 19, 359–63.

Garety, P.A. and Freeman D. 1999: Cognitive approaches to delusions: A critical review of theories and evidence. *British Journal of Clinical Psychology*, 38, 113–54.

Garety, P.A. and Hemsley, D.R. 1994: *Delusions: Investigations into the Psychology of Delusional Reasoning*. Oxford University Press.

Garety, P., Hemsley, D.R. and Wesseley, S. 1991: Reasoning in deluded and schizophrenic and paranoid patients. *Journal of Nervous and Mental Disease*, 179, 194–201.

Graham, S. and Folkes, V.S. 1990: Attribution theory: Applications to achievement, mental health, and interpersonal conflict. Hillsdale, NJ: Lawrence Erlbaum Associates.

Hakim, H., Verma, N.P. and Greiffenstein, M.F. 1988: Pathogenesis of reduplicative paramnesia. *Journal of Neurology, Neurosurgery, and Psychiatry*, 51, 839–41.

Halligan, P.W., Marshall, J.C. and Wade, D.T. 1995: Unilateral somatoparaphrenia after right hemisphere stroke: A case description. *Cortex*, 31, 173–82.

Heider, F. 1944: Social perception and phenomenal causality. *Psychological Review*, 51, 358–74.

Heider, F. 1958: *The Psychology of Interpersonal Relations*. New York: Wiley.

Hewstone, M. 1983: *Attribution Theory: Social and Functional Extensions*. Oxford: Blackwell.

Hewstone, M. 1989: *Causal attribution: From Cognitive Processes to Collective Beliefs*. Oxford: Blackwell.

Huq, S.F., Garety, P. and Hemsley, D.R. 1988: Probabilistic judgements in deluded and non-deluded subjects. *Quarterly Journal of Experimental Psychology*, 40A, 801–12.

Kaney, S. and Bentall, R.P. 1989: Persecutory delusions and attributional style. *British Journal of Medical Psychology*, 62, 191–8.

Kaney, S., Wolfenden, M., Dewey, M.E. and Bentall, R.P. 1992: Persecutory delusions and the recall of threatening and non-threatening propositions. *British Journal of Clinical Psychology*, 31, 85–7.

Kasinin, J.S. 1944: *Language and Thought in Schizophrenia*. Berkeley: University of California Press.

Kemp, R., Chua, S., McKenna, P. and David, A. 1997: Reasoning and delusions. *British Journal of Psychiatry*, 170, 398–405.

Kinderman, P. and Bentall, R.P. 1996a: A new measure of causal locus: The internal, personal, and situational attributions questionnaire. *Personality and Individual Differences*, 20, 261–4.

Kinderman, P. and Bentall, R.P. 1996b: Self-discrepancies and persecutory delusions: Evidence for a model of paranoid ideation. *Journal of Abnormal Psychology*, 105, 106–13.

Kinderman, P. and Bentall, R.P. 1997: Causal attributions in paranoia and depression: Internal, personal, and situational attributions for negative events. *Journal of Abnormal Psychology*, 106, 341–5.

Kinderman, P., Kaney, S., Morley, S. and Bentall, R.P. 1992: Paranoia and the defensive attributional style: Deluded and depressed patients' attributions about their own attributions. *British Journal of Medical Psychology*, 65, 371–83.

Leafhead, K.M., Young, A.W. and Szulecka, T.K. 1996: Delusions demand attention. *Cognitive Neuropsychiatry*, 1, 5–16.

Leudar, I., Thomas, P. and Johnston, M. 1994: Self-monitoring in speech production: Effects of verbal hallucinations and negative symptoms. *Psychological Medicine*, 24, 749–61.

Linney, Y.M., Peters, E.R. and Ayton, P. 1998: Reasoning biases in delusion-prone individuals. *British Journal of Clinical Psychology*, 37, 285–302.

Lyon, H.M., Kaney, S. and Bentall, R.P. 1994: The defensive function of persecutory delusions: evidence from attribution tasks. *British Journal of Psychiatry*, 164, 637–46.

Maher, B.A. 1974: Delusional thinking and perceptual disorder. *Journal of Individual Psychology*, 30, 98–113.

Maher, B.A. 1988: Anomalous experience and delusional thinking: The logic of explanations. In T.F. Oltmanns and B.A. Maher (eds), *Delusional Beliefs*. New York: Wiley, 15–33.

Maher, B.A. 1992: Delusions: Contemporary etiological hypotheses. *Psychiatric Annals*, 22, 260–68.

Maher, B.A. and Ross, J.S. 1984: Delusions. In H.E. Adams and P.B. Sutker (eds), *Comprehensive Handbook of Ppsychopathology*. New York: Plenum Press.

Maher, B.A. and Spitzer, M. 1993: Delusions. In C.G. Costello (ed.) *Symptoms of Schizophrenia*. New York: Wiley.

Matthews, A. and Mackintosh, B. 1998: A cognitive model of selective processing in anxiety. *Cognitive Therapy and Research*, 22, 539–60.

McKenna, P.J., Tamlyn, D., Lund, C.E., Mortimer, A.M., Hammond, S. and Baddeley, A.D. 1990: Amnesic syndrome in schizophrenia. *Psychological Medicine*, 20, 967–72.

McNally, R.J. 1998: Experimental approaches to cognitive abnormality in posttraumatic stress. *Clinical Psychology Review*, 18, 971–82.

Peterson, C., Semmel, A., von Bueyer, C., Abramson, L.Y., Metalsky, G.I. and Seligman, M.E.P. 1982: The attributional style questionnaire. *Cognitive Therapy and Research*, 6, 287–300.

Ramachandran, V.S. and Hirstein, W. 1998: The perception of phantom limbs. The D.O. Hebb lecture. *Brain*, 121, 1603–30.

Roehrenbach, C. and Landis, T. 1995: Dreamjourneys: Living in woven realities, the syndrome of reduplicative paramnesia. In R. Campbell and M.A. Conway, (eds) *Broken Memories: Case Studies in Memory Impairment*. Oxford: Blackwell, 93–100.

Romme, M.A. and Escher, A.D. 1989: Hearing voices. *Schizophrenia Bulletin*, 15, 209–16.

Seligman, M.E.P., Abramson, L.Y., Semmel, A. and von Baeyer, C. 1979: Depressive attributional style. *Journal of Abnormal Psychology*, 88, 242–7.

Sharp, H.M., Fear, C.F. and Healy, D. 1997: Attributional style and delusions: an investigation based on delusional content. *European Psychiatry*, 12, 1–7.

Sims, A. 1988: *Symptoms in the Mind*. London: Baillière Tindall.

Sno, H.N. 1994: A continuum of misidentification symptoms. *Psychopathology*, 27, 144–7.

Stone, T. and Young. A. 1997: Delusions and brain injury: The philosophy and psychology of belief. *Mind and Language*, 12, 327–64.

Sweeney, P.D., Anderson, K. and Bailey, S. 1986: Attributional style in depression: A meta-analytic review. *Journal of Personality and Social Psychology*, 50, 974–91.

Tranel, D., Damasio, H. and Damasio, A.R. 1995: Double dissociation between overt and covert face recognition. *Journal of Cognitive Neuroscience*, 7, 425–32.

Weiner, B. 1988: Attribution theory and attributional therapy: some clinical observations and suggestions. *British Journal of Clinical Psychology*, 27, 93–104.

Weiner, B. 1990: Searching for the roots of applied attribution theory. In S. Graham and V.S. Folkes (eds), *Attribution Theory: Applications to Achievement, Mental Health, and Interpersonal Conflict*. Hillsdale, NJ: Lawrence Erlbaum Associates, 1–16.

Wright, S., Young, A.W. and Hellawell, D.J. 1993: Sequential Cotard and Capgras delusions. *British Journal of Clinical Psychology*, 32, 345–9.

Young, A.W. 1994: Recognition and reality. In E.M.R. Crichley (ed.), *The Neurological Boundaries of Reality*. London: Farrand Press, 83–100.

Young, A.W., Leafhead, K.M. and Szulecka, T.K. 1994: The Capgras and Cotard delusions. *Psychopathology*, 27, 226–31.

Young, A.W., Reid, I., Wright, S. and Hellawell, D.J. 1993: Face-processing impairments and the Capgras delusion. *British Journal of Psychiatry*, 162, 695–8.

Young, A.W., Robertson, I.H., Hellawell, D.J., de Pauw, K.W. and Pentland, B. 1992: Cotard delusion after brain injury. *Psychological Medicine*, 67, 361–70.

List of Contributors

Nora Breen Macquarie Centre for Cognitive Science, Macquarie University, Sydney, NSW 2109, Australia *and* Neuropsychology Unit, Royal Prince Alfred Hospital, Sydney, NSW 2050, Australia.

Diana Caine Neuropsychology Unit, Royal Prince Alfred Hospital, Sydney, NSW 2050, Australia.

Max Coltheart Macquarie Centre for Cognitive Science, Macquarie University, Sydney, NSW 2109, Australia.

Gregory Currie Department of Philosophy, University of Nottingham, University Park, Nottingham NG7 2RD, UK.

Martin Davies Corpus Christi College, Oxford OX1 4JF, UK. *From July 2000* Philosophy Program, Research School of Social Sciences, Australian National University, Canberra, ACT 0200, Australia.

Philip Gerrans Philosophy Program, Research School of Social Sciences, Australian National University, Canberra, ACT 0200, Australia.

Ian Gold Department of Philosophy, Monash University, Clayton, Victoria 3168, Australia.

Julie Hendy CBT Clinical Psychology Centre, 28 Harrow Road, Stanmore, NSW 2048, Australia.

Jakob Hohwy Department of Philosophy, Monash University, Clayton, Victoria 3168, Australia.

Robyn Langdon Macquarie Centre for Cognitive Science, Macquarie University, Sydney, NSW 2109, Australia.

Candida C. Peterson School of Psychology, University of Queensland, Brisbane 4072, Australia.

Michael Siegal Department of Psychology, University of Sheffield, Sheffield S10 2TP, UK.

Corinne Roberts CBT Clinical Psychology Centre, 28 Harrow Road, Stanmore, NSW 2048, Australia.

Andrew W. Young Department of Psychology, University of York, Heslington, York YO10 5DD, UK.

Index